Story Central Plus

CU00736004

Teacher Edition 2 with Teacher Resources

macmillan education

Katie Foufouti

Macmillan Education Limited
4 Crinan Street
London N1 9XW

Companies and representatives throughout the world

Story Central Plus Level 2 Teacher Edition ISBN 978-1-380-06096-9
Story Central Plus Level 2 Teacher Edition with Student eBook, Reader eBook, CLIL eBook, Digital Activity Book, Teacher Resource Center, and Test Generator ISBN 978-1-380-06094-5

Text, design and illustration © Macmillan Education Limited 2021
Written by Katie Foufouti
Student Book Text © Viv Lambert ELT Limited and Mo Choy Design Ltd 2021
The author has asserted her rights to be identified as the author of this work in accordance with the Copyright, Designs and Patents Act 1988.

Story Central is a registered trademark of Macmillan Publishers International Limited

This edition published 2021
First edition entitled "Story Central" published 2015 by Macmillan Education Limited

All rights reserved; no part of this publication may be reproduced, stored in a retrieval system, transmitted in any form, or by any means, electronic, mechanical, photocopying, recording, or otherwise, without the prior written permission of the publishers.

Teacher Edition credits:
Designed by Red Phoenix Design
Page make-up by Mike Brain Graphic Design Limited
Illustrated by Steven Wood (Advocate Art)
Cover design by Wild Apple Design Ltd

Author's acknowledgements
Katie Foufouti would like to thank the Macmillan editorial team for their wonderful support, as well as Marilyn, Dimitri and Ángel.

Student Book credits:
Text © Viv Lambert ELT Limited and Mo Choy Design Ltd 2021
Design and illustration © Macmillan Education Limited 2021
The authors have asserted their rights to be identified as the authors of this work in accordance with the Copyright, Designs and Patents Act 1988.

Designed by Wild Apple Design Ltd
Illustrated by Aardvart pp48, 49; Robin Boyden (Pickled Ink) pp20–21, 23; Paco Cavero (Sylvie Poggio Artist Agency) pp27, 47, 67; Nikki Dyson (advocate Art) pp80–81, 83; Russ Daff (Beehive Illustration) pp15, 18, 68; Pablo Gallego (Beehive Illustration) pp9, 13b,17t, 19, 23b, 33b, 37, 39, 52, 53b, 57, 59, 61, 63b, 65, 69, 79, 83b, 89, 93b, 95; Ayesha Lopez (Advocate Art) pp40–41, 43; Andrew Painter pp50–51, 53; Carl Pearce pp10–11, 13, 17m; Louise Redshaw (Plum Pudding) pp30–31, 32, 33t; Stephen Reed (The July Group) pp70–71, 72, 73; Shahab Shamshirsaz (Sylvie Poggio Artist Agency) pp60–61, 63; Laszlo Veres (Beehive Illustration) pp8, 28, 38, 45b, 88; Steven Wood (Advocate Art) pp4–104 (border design and main character artwork) 4–5, 6–7, 10, 14, 20l, 24, 30l, 34, 40l, 44, 50l, 54, 60l, 64, 70l, 74, 80l, 84, 90l, 94.
Cover design by Wild Apple Design Ltd
Cover artwork by Steven Wood (Advocate Art)
Cover photographs by Paul Bricknell
Picture Research by Sally Cole (Perseverance Works Ltd)

The authors and publishers would like to thank the following for permission to reproduce their photographs:
Alamy/Aflo Foto Agency p49(6), Alamy/Capt Digby p45(ml), Alamy/Imagesource pp3(mb), 88(horse), Alamy/Prisma Bildagentur AG p49(2), Alamy/S.Sangalli p49(5), Alamy/M.Secchi p55(penguin), Alamy/A.Sherratt p49(3), Alamy/D.Watts p87(tr), Alamy/XiXinXing p45(tr); Bananastock p75(c), 75(br); Corbis p95(r), Corbis/Blend Images pp8(t), 8(bl), 65(cl), Corbis/T.Brakefield p55(cheetah), Corbis/Christie's Images p95(tl), Corbis/Cultura p35(cl), Corbis/Dlillc p78(3), Corbis/D.Koebe p8(cl), Corbis/F.Lukasseck p78(5), Corbis/Minden Pictures p78(tl), Corbis/Ocean pp35(l), 75(doctor), 85(ml), Corbis/RelaXimages p88(shopping), Corbis/Sullivan p88(music), Corbis/Sygma p55(Javier), Corbis/Thissen p55(Bolt), Corbis/C.Wessel p49(4); FLPA/

Minden Pictures pp55(kangaroo), 3(cl), 78(4), FLPA/M.Schuyl p85(l); Getty Images/Agefotostock p78(tr), Getty Images/Blend Images pp8(cr), Getty Images/ Michael Bodmann 65(l), Getty Images/E+ pp15, 78(1), Getty Images/Shannon Fagan p65(cr), Getty Images/Imagesource p78(bl), Getty Images/kycstudio p75(hands), Getty Images/Maskot p89(friends), Getty Images/Daniel Smith p49(1), Getty Images Sport p55(swimmer), Getty Images/Jason Todd p88(popcorn), Getty Images/Terry Vine p75(mom), Getty Images/Wild Horse Photography p78(2), Getty Images/Patrick Wittmann p35(cr), Getty Images/UIG p78(grassland); Getty Images RF p78(6); ImageSource p75(chef), 77(l), 77(m); Plainpicture/Cultura pp88(reading), 97(tr), Plainpicture/Maskot p88(game), Plainpicture/Minden Pictures pp79(tc), 79(tr), Plainpicture/Naturepl p78(7), 79(l), 85(tr), Plainpicture/K.Synnatzschke p59; Science Photo Library/Planet Observer p45(mr); Superstock/Agefotostock p85(r), Superstock/Blend Images p75(teacher), Superstock/Corbis pp35(r), 78(br), Corbis/Cultura Ltd p8(br), Superstock/Minden Pictures p85(cr), Superstock/Tetra Images p75(vet); The Bridgeman Art Library/Castle and Sun, 1928 (no 201) (oil on canvas), Klee, Paul (1879-1940) / Private Collection / Giraudon p95(ml), The Bridgeman Art Library/The Massacre of the Innocents, 1593 (oil on panel), Brueghel, Pieter the Younger (c.1564-1638) / Musee Municipal, Lons-le-Saulnier, France / Giraudon p95(mr); Thinkstock/istock pp78(forest), 78(desert).
Commissioned photography by MMStudios pp16, 26, 29, 36, 46, 56, 66, 76, 86, 96.
Prop artwork by Carla Drury

Reader credits:
Text, design and illustration © Macmillan Education Limited 2021
Written by Viv Lambert ELT Limited and Mo Choy Design Limited
The authors have asserted their rights to be identified as the authors of this work in accordance with the Copyright, Designs and Patents Act 1988.

Page design, layout and art editing by Wild Apple Design Ltd
Jack and the Beanstalk illustrated by Carl Pearce; Hilltop School for Young Detectives illustrated by Robin Boyden (Pickled Ink); The Emperor's New Clothes illustrated by Louise Redshaw (Plum Pudding Illustration); A New Pet for Trixie illustrated by Ayesha Lopez (Advocate Art); The Animal Olympics illustrated by Andrew Painter; I'm Late, Late, Late! illustrated by Shahab Shamshirsaz (Sylvie Poggio Artist Agency); The Secret Life of Shelly the Chef illustrated by Stephen Reed (The July Group); The Kangaroo's Pouch
illustrated by Nikki Dyson (Advocate Art); The Town Mouse and the Country Mouse illustrated by Staffan Gnosspelius (Pickled Ink).
Cover design by Wild Apple Design Ltd
Cover artwork; front cover, Carl Pearce, Nikki Dyson (Advocate Art), and Robin Boyden (Pickled Ink): back cover, Stephen Reed (The July Group) and Staffan Gnosspelius (Pickled Ink).

Activity Book credits:
Text, design and illustration © Macmillan Education Limited 2021
Written by Viv Lambert ELT Limited
Additional material written by Tracy Traynor
The author has asserted her right to be identified as the author of this work in accordance with the Copyright, Designs and Patents Act 1988.

Designed by Liz Adcock
Illustrated by Robin Boyden (Pickled Ink) pp16–17; Nikki Dyson (Advocate Art) p65; Staffan Gnosspelius (Pickled Ink) pp72–73; Sarah Horne (Advocate Art) pp7, 10, 14, 22, 26, 30, 37, 47, 55, 58, 62, 63, 66, 74, 76; Andy Keylock (Beehive Illustration) pp4, 5, 10, 12, 14, 18, 20, 26, 28, 30, 35, 36, 38, 39, 41, 42, 45–47, 50, 53, 54, 58, 59, 61, 63, 66, 69, 74, 75, 77, 79, 80, 83, 85, 86, 89, 90, 92, 94; Ayesha Lopez (Advocate Art) pp32–33; Andrew Painter pp40–42; Carl Pearce pp8–9, 12; Louise Redshaw (Plum Pudding Illustration) pp24–25; Stephen Reed (The July Group) pp4, 6, 11, 13, 15, 21, 23, 27, 29, 31, 34, 39, 44, 46, 52, 54, 56, 57, 60, 61, 67, 68, 70, 71, 73, 78, 81, 82, 84, 87, 88, 91–93, 95; Shahab Shamshirsaz (Sylvie Poggio Artist Agency) p49; Steven Wood (Advocate Art) pp3–77, 80.
Cover design by Wild Apple Design Ltd
Cover illustration by Steven Wood (Advocate Art)

These materials may contain links for third party websites. We have no control over, and are not responsible for, the contents of such third party websites. Please use care when accessing them.

Printed and bound in Singapore

2021
80

Contents

Contents

Chapter	Grammar	Vocabulary	Story	CLIL	Song & Phonics
6 **My Day** *page 78*	What do you do in the morning? I brush my teeth. I don't take a shower. What time do you go to bed? I go to bed at 9 o'clock. Do you wake up early? Yes, I do. / No, I don't.	Daily routine activities Times	**I'm Late, Late, Late!**	*Math:* Using Water	*Hush Little Baby* **k** and **ck**
Grammar Booster *page 88*					
7 **Busy Lives** *page 92*	What does she do? She's a doctor. Where does she work? She works in a hospital. He doesn't cook. Does he go to school? Yes, he does. / No, he doesn't.	Professions Verbs that describe professions	**The Secret Life of Shelly the Chef** 	*Social Studies:* People Who Help Me	*Shelly's a Superchef!* **s** and **sh**
Grammar Booster *page 102*					
8 **Habits and Habitats** *page 106*	Fish have fins. They don't have wings. Do they have wings? Yes, they do. / No, they don't. What do they eat? They eat grass.	Animal body parts Geographical features	**The Kangaroo's Pouch**	*Science:* What Is a Habitat?	*Birds Fly in the Sky* **s** and **z**
Grammar Booster *page 116*					
9 **Town and Countryside** *page 120*	What do you like to do on weekends? I like to stay home. I don't like to play tennis. Do you like the town or the countryside? I like the countryside. Why? I like it because there are flowers.	Free time activities Nature	**The Town Mouse and the Country Mouse**	*Art:* Famous Paintings	*I Love the Country* **ou** and **ow**
Grammar Booster *page 130*					
Word List *page 134*					

Competencies

me	act	think	learn	communicate
Activities that encourage children to accept responsibility and reflect on the consequences of lifestyle choices.	Activities that develop societal understanding and identification of children's own circumstances in a wider context.	Activities that develop critical thinking skills to reflect upon, manipulate, process, and interpret information.	Activities that foster learner autonomy, and allow children to demonstrate and put into practice learning strategies.	Activities that promote interpersonal and collaborative skills, develop teamwork, and allow children to express opinions and ideas.

Philosophy

1 Language is power.

Story Central Plus empowers children to communicate effectively and develop their knowledge of the world around them through stories. The course enables children to become critical and active readers, writers, and storytellers through its strong focus on literacy development.

2 An empowered teacher empowers students and changes lives.

Story Central Plus provides teachers with all the support they need to deliver effective and inspiring lessons. Children will respond to the meaningful texts and activities, ensuring that both teachers and children feel a real sense of achievement. Children will develop the skills they need to participate fully in their lives both inside and outside the classroom.

3 The child is not a blank slate.

Children bring their culture, beliefs, and a rich inner world to the classroom. Our materials respect this and recognize that it is key to engaging and interesting children in learning English.

4 Nurturing critical and creative thinking helps children become well-rounded and innovative adults.

Story Central Plus actively encourages creative, divergent, and playful thinking, and consistently supports the acquisition of academic knowledge.

Methodology

Literacy

Reading and writing skills are developed throughout the course. Each chapter is based around a story. An extract from the story is introduced in Student Book Lesson 3, allowing opportunities to develop reading skills and encouraging children to think creatively as they analyze the language in a meaningful context, and predict story developments. The full story is given in the beautifully illustrated Reader. Use of the Reader is fully integrated and the story links together the chapter theme and target language, providing language-rich input and enabling holistic learning. Activities engage children's interest and imagination as they are encouraged to read for pleasure. After children have read the story, their writing skills are developed through personal responses and creative writing. A love of literature is further fostered by the Oral Storytelling Videos.

Critical Literacy

Story Central Plus takes children beyond understanding texts. The material and activities help them analyze and respond, as they develop the skills of questioning and interpreting the information they encounter. Children are encouraged to discuss the story's meaning and how the values expressed relate to their lives and the world around them. Children are supported in expressing their opinions through presentations, role play, and extended writing. These essential skills will empower them to use language effectively later in life.

Critical and Creative Thinking

Critical and creative thinking are actively encouraged. Children are given every opportunity to figure things out for themselves and share their ideas. Vocabulary is presented in context, requiring them to use textual and visual clues to process and deduce meaning. Prediction, reflection, and drawing conclusions all play an important part in developing an imaginative and reflective response.

Story Central is a cool club where kids hang out with their friends and read great books. They also share ideas and stories, plan events, do homework, and drink milkshakes! In Story Central you can explore, discover, learn, research, and interact. It's the sort of place where kids really want to be!

Children will love getting to know the fun characters who hang out in Story Central. They appear in Lesson 3 and Lesson 6 in every chapter.

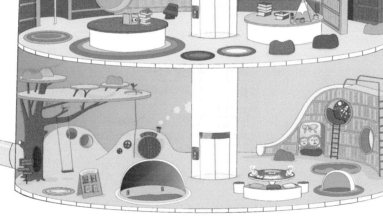

Level 2 Characters

Libby is a 19-year-old engineering student who runs Story Central in her spare time because she loves books and reading.

Ellie is a 6-year-old girl who attends the local school. She is intelligent, outgoing, and loves reading.

Tom is Ellie's next-door neighbor. Tom enjoys books about superheroes, and he is always ready to join in the fun at Story Central.

Biblio is a small, useful robot who helps out in Story Central. Biblio is always doing something funny in Story Central!

Component Overview

For the Student

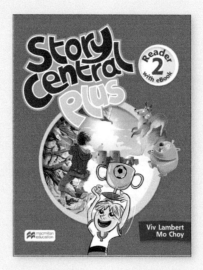

Student Book
Consists of 9 thematic chapters, featuring a story extract, literacy development, competency coverage, CLIL content, and project work. Focuses on developing critical thinking, creativity, communication, and collaboration. NEW! Grammar Booster section per chapter presents and provides further grammar practice of the target grammar.

Reader
Consists of 9 stories of different genres and styles. Focuses on promoting critical literacy and reading skills through developing a love of reading.

Activity Book
Consists of follow-on lessons for every Student Book lesson. Focuses on consolidating key language and skills, and developing creative use of language in writing. NEW! Exam Booster section per chapter provides Cambridge YLE practice activities.

eBooks
The Student Book has an access code which provides access to eBooks for the Student Book, Reader, and CLIL Book. The eBooks have embedded audio, video, and a set of tools to interact with the pages to provide flexibility for remote learning and give children more ways to read and learn.

The Inks Vocabulary Practice App
The Inks Apps provide a fun way for students to practice the vocabulary words they've learned for better retention. They're free and available to download from the App Store and Google Play.

Digital Activity Book
These books provide children an interactive way to practice. Children's answers are sent automatically to the gradebook so teachers and caregivers can monitor progress.

For the Teacher

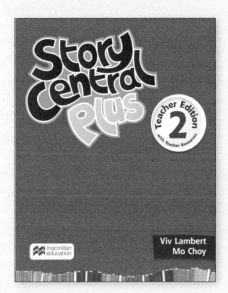

Teacher Edition
Consists of teaching notes for each lesson of the Student Book, Reader, and Activity Book and suggestions on when and how to use digital components. Focuses on providing clear and concise support for lesson planning and teaching.

Teacher Resource Center
Consists of the class audio, and additional resources and ideas to extend lessons and learning, and give further practice of key language. Focuses on giving teachers flexibility and the means to deliver dynamic and varied lessons.

Test Generator
Pre-written tests for each chapter, mid-year, and end-of-year are available to download from the Teacher Resource Center. In addition, the Test Generator allows teachers to customize and create new tests from a bank of activities.

Teacher Presentation Kit
the Student eBook, Digital Activity Book, Reader eBook and CLIL eBook.

Student eBook
This eBook provides a digital version of the Student Book with integrated audio, video and answer keys.

Digital Activity Book
This eBook provides an interactive version of the Activity Book that is linked to a gradebook.

Oral Storytelling Videos
bring the stories to life with mesmerising narration set in *Story Central Plus*. These are available for Chapters 1, 3, 5, 7, and 9.

Music Videos
will get children dancing! They can copy the actions modeled on screen for the songs from Chapters 2, 4, 6, and 8.

American Sign Language Vocabulary Videos
present all of the target vocab from Lessons 1 and 5 with a clear audio model and the ASL sign to promote inclusion and accessibility in the classroom and beyond.

Reader eBook
This eBook provides a digital version of the Reader with embedded audio and Storytelling Videos.

CLIL eBook
This eBook provides a digital version of the CLIL Book with embedded audio.

Teaching with *Story Central Plus*

Lesson 1 Vocabulary

High-impact openers introduce the chapter theme to create interest, and engage children.

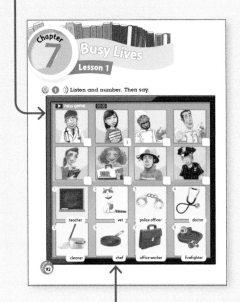

Fun activities **consolidate new language** and provide opportunities for extra practice.

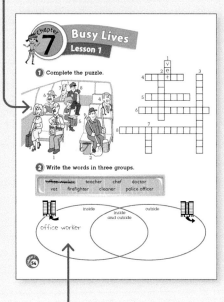

Vocabulary is introduced through visual clues to develop **critical thinking skills**, encouraging children to deduce meaning.

Categorization activities **empower children** by giving them **choices** about how they learn.

American Sign Language Vocabulary Videos provide clear audio models of the new words supported by the ASL sign to reinforce learning (available in the Student eBook).

Lesson 2 Grammar

Grammar is presented clearly and accessibly, recycling Lesson 1 vocabulary.

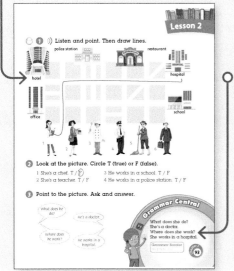

Grammar Central highlights new grammar structures, providing a useful reference for activities.

Further grammar practice in the Activity Book consolidates language.

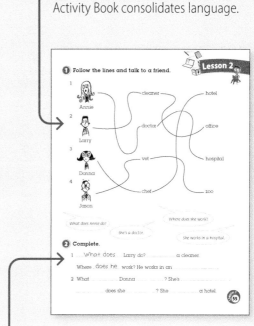

Writing activities provide well-supported and progressive development of writing skills.

NEW! Grammar Booster sections in the Student Book at the end of each chapter provide four pages of extra support. They include detailed grammar boxes and scaffolded practice for lessons 2 and 6, a review page that combines the grammar points in both lessons and a challenge page. These pages offer support for different language proficiency levels in the classroom. They can be assigned to individual children or the entire class.

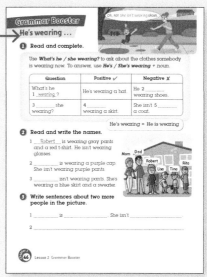

Supplementary **grammar worksheets** can be downloaded from the Teacher Resource Center to further consolidate learning in class or as homework.

Lesson 3 Reading: Story Extract

The children predict what the story is about before reading, to develop their **visual literacy**.

A **functional dialogue** featuring the Story Central characters teaches useful language for the classroom.

Comprehension questions about the story extract check understanding.

Comprehension questions develop reading skills and strategies.

The **story extract** (beginning, middle, or end) engages children but leaves plenty to the imagination.

A **prediction activity** asks children to use their **imagination** to figure out what will happen in the story.

Reader

Children read the whole story in their Reader.

A wide variety of story genres and narrative styles gives a **rich literary experience**.

Beautiful illustrations motivate children to **read for pleasure** and develop **a lifelong love of reading**.

Extensive language input allows **holistic language learning**, with the focus on **overall understanding**.

Lesson 4 Reading Comprehension and Critical Literacy

After reading the story in the Reader, children answer comprehension questions which help develop **reading strategies**.

The **I Can Read!** feature focuses awareness on text conventions.

Graphic organizer activities develop **study skills**.

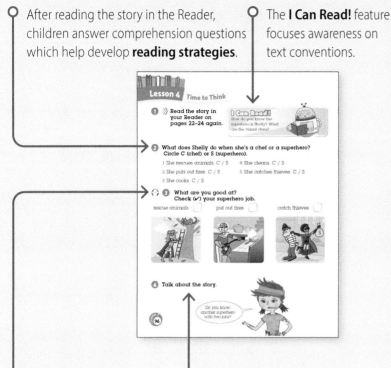

Critical literacy activities encourage children to analyze the text, reflecting on the main issues and relating them to their own lives.

Personalization questions prompt children to make links between the story and other texts, providing opportunities for discussion and self-expression.

Children practice the Student Book **I Can Read!** text conventions.

Children express their own **opinions** about the story.

In the **Oral Storytelling Videos** professional storytellers act out and bring to life the Reader stories for Chapters 1, 3, 5, 7, and 9 (available in the Student eBook and Reader eBook).

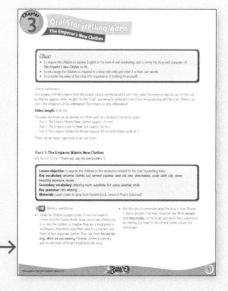

Teaching notes and worksheets for the Oral Storytelling Videos provide activities ideas for before, during, and after watching (downloadable from the Teacher Resource Center). A **Literacy Handbook** gives support and ideas for developing literacy skills with young learners.

Lesson 5 Vocabulary, Song, and Phonics

Vocabulary is introduced through textual and visual clues to develop **critical thinking skills** (deduction of meaning).

Catchy **songs** present new vocabulary in a fun, memorable, and motivating context.

Word work activities consolidate vocabulary and help develop strategies for memorizing vocabulary.

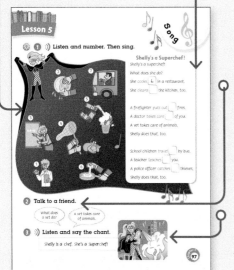

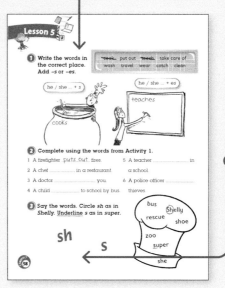

Speaking activities give practice in a meaningful context to develop fluency.

Children practice **phonics** in a fun chant.

Children identify and practice the sounds from the Student Book **phonics** feature.

Supplementary **phonics worksheets** can be downloaded from the Teacher Resource Center to further consolidate learning in class or as homework.

Music Videos for Chapters 2, 4, 6 and 8 encourage children to move to the music and the actions consolidate the learning of the target vocabulary (available in the Student eBook).

American Sign Language Vocabulary Videos provide clear audio models of the new words supported by the ASL sign to reinforce learning (available in the Student eBook).

The lively clan of The Inks on the **Student's App** provide children with motivating and challenging games to practice the chapter vocabulary from Lesson 1 and Lesson 5 outside the classroom. *The Inks* Apps are free and available on the App Store and Google Play.

Lesson 6 Grammar and Reading

The Story Central characters present new **grammar** in a lively, meaningful context which recycles the vocabulary from the chapter.

Grammar Central highlights new grammar structures and provides a useful reference.

Children are given the opportunity for controlled **written practice** of the new structures.

Supplementary **grammar worksheets** can be downloaded from the Teacher Resource Center to further consolidate learning in class or as homework.

Grammar practice activities give staggered support.

A **guided writing** activity consolidates grammar and progressively develops writing skills.

NEW! Grammar Booster sections in the Student Book at the end of each chapter provide four pages of extra support. They include detailed grammar boxes and scaffolded practice for lessons 2 and 6, a review page that combines the grammar points in both lessons and a challenge page. These pages offer support for different language proficiency levels in the classroom. They can be assigned to individual children or the entire class.

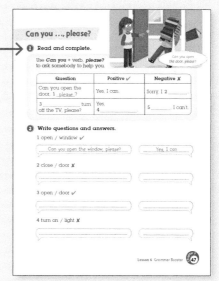

Lesson 7 CLIL

The **CLIL** focus gives the opportunity to find out about other curricular areas (such as science, math, social science) through English.

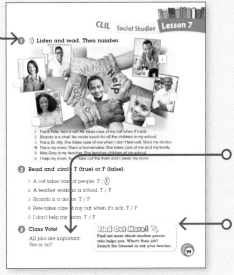

Children are encouraged to express their own opinions in a **Class Vote!**

The **Find Out More!** feature motivates children to be **independent learners**.

Children use their **Find Out More!** research to complete a mini-project extending the CLIL topic.

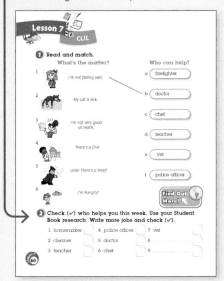

Lesson 8 Project

Children do a **craft activity** that relates to the chapter theme and Reader story.

Photographs provide clear, step-by-step instructions.

The craft item is then used in a collaborative **performance activity** as children act out the Reader story together.

Each CLIL lesson has an optional **graphic organizer** template to help children organize their findings. Printable **Project templates** are also supplied for Lesson 8 (downloadable from the Teacher Resource Center).

An interactive speaking task—a **fun game, puzzle,** or **quiz** for children to complete in pairs—rounds off the chapter.

The **CLIL eBook** expands the CLIL topics from the Student Book with **additional real-world content and practice activities**.

Review

The Review lesson provides **further practice and consolidation** of language from the chapter.

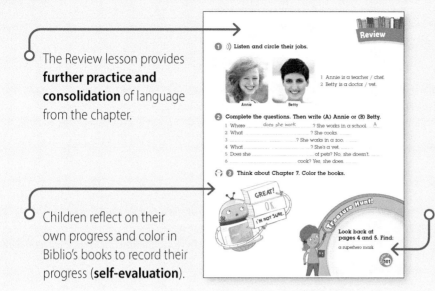

Children reflect on their own progress and color in Biblio's books to record their progress (**self-evaluation**).

A fun **Treasure Hunt!** activity takes children back to the Welcome section (pp. 4–5) to find an item from that chapter.

NEW! **Exam Booster sections** in the Activity Book (pp. 78–104) provides **Cambridge English Young Learners Exams**-style activities practicing the language from each chapter. These help prepare for the Reading and Writing, Listening and Speaking papers of the Cambridge English Exam.

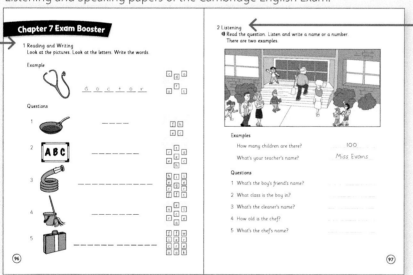

Class audio for the listening activities are in the Teacher Resource Center.

The Teacher Resource Center provides a wealth of assessment support including pre-written chapter, mid-year, and end-of-year tests. **CEYLT** (**Cambridge YLE**)-style speaking prompts and tips are also available.

Festival worksheets and teaching notes to be used during the year bring the whole outside into the classroom and help to foster an understanding of different cultures.

Teacher Edition Overview

Chapter Overview

An **Overview** at the start of every chapter provides a quick reference point to show what is covered.
The **Competency Focus** shows where competencies are developed throughout the chapter.
The **Digital Overview** shows the variety of digital resources available for the chapter.

Student Book and Activity Book Lessons

Each lesson opens with the lesson objectives, key language, and any materials required.

A **Warmer** activity introduces children to the lesson topic, activating prior knowledge, and getting the children energized!

Reduced pages for the **Student Book** and the **Activity Book** give easy reference to the components being used.

The **Competency Focus** shows how competencies are developed in the lesson.

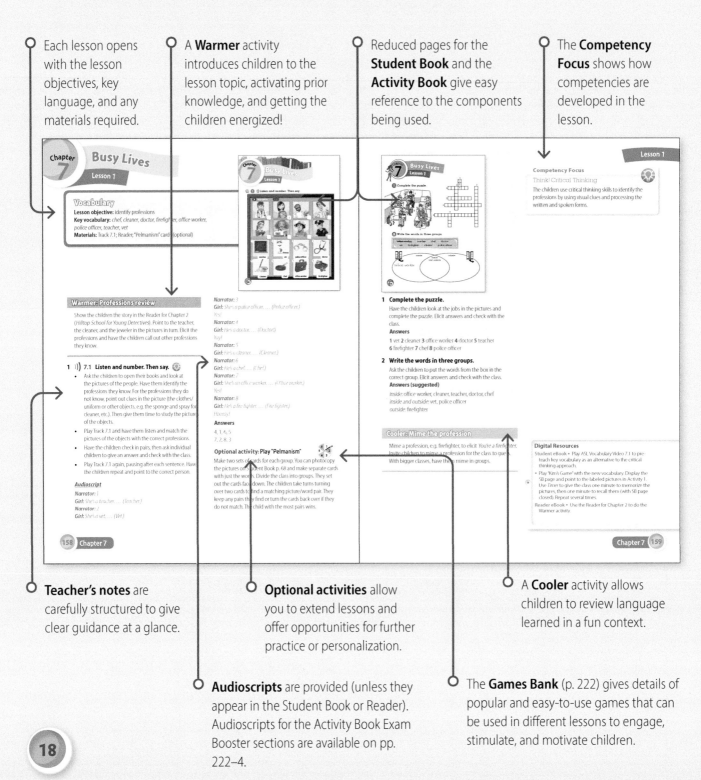

Teacher's notes are carefully structured to give clear guidance at a glance.

Optional activities allow you to extend lessons and offer opportunities for further practice or personalization.

A **Cooler** activity allows children to review language learned in a fun context.

Audioscripts are provided (unless they appear in the Student Book or Reader). Audioscripts for the Activity Book Exam Booster sections are available on pp. 222–4.

The **Games Bank** (p. 222) gives details of popular and easy-to-use games that can be used in different lessons to engage, stimulate, and motivate children.

Reader

The **Reader** lesson contains a range of additional activities that you can use as you please. You can get children to read the Reader story at home or in class.

Story Time helps you get the most out of the Reader component, helping teachers become more effective storytellers in the classroom.

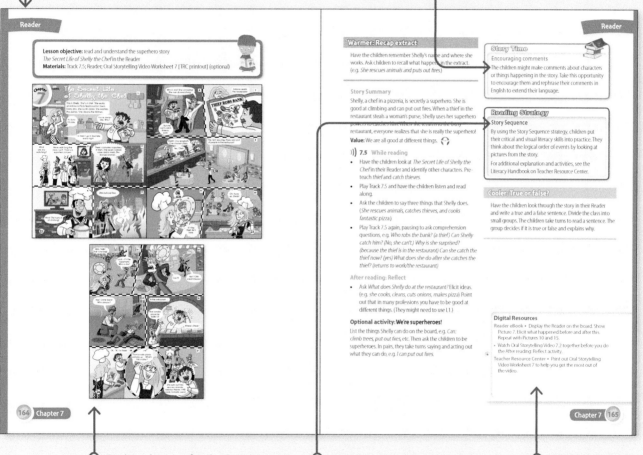

Reduced pages for the Reader give easy reference to the component being used.

Reading Strategy helps you develop children's literacy, with further explanation and activities in the **Literacy Handbook** on the Teacher Resource Center.

Teaching notes suggest how and when to use the **digital components**.

Story Central

Lesson objectives: remember *Story Central* and sing a song
Key language: *come in, choose a book, close the door, come again, listen to a story, play a game, read a poem, sit on a chair/the floor, take a look, walk around, watch a show*
Materials: Track 0.2

Warmer: I'm the teacher now!

Agree actions for the key language in the song, e.g. *close the door, sit on a chair*, etc. The children do these when you give the instruction. Then say *It's your turn to be the teacher.* Children take turns saying actions for the class to do. With big classes, children can do this in groups.

1))) 0.2 Listen and sing.

- Give the children time to study the picture and find the main characters: Tom, Biblio, Ellie, and Libby.

- Ask *How many books can you see?* (16) Ask *Who's drawing?* (two boys) Ask *What are they drawing?* (*a dog and a cat*) Continue like this to elicit more objects in the picture, e.g. *tree, table, chairs*, etc.
  (You might need to use L1.)

- Play Track 0.2 and have the children listen and read along. Then read out each command for the children to do the action.

- Play Track 0.2 again. The children sing along and mime.

Optional activity: Welcome!

Point to the photo of the man in the computer game. Call on children to say a sentence, e.g. *He has a beard. He has short hair.* The children continue in pairs for the other people in the photos. Monitor and make sure they use *He/She has … correctly.*

Write the following dialog on the board and demonstrate with a child.

A: *Hello.*

B: *Hi.*

A: *What's your name?*

B: *My name's …*

A: *How old are you?*

B: *I'm …*

A: *Nice to meet you.*

B: *Nice to meet you too.*

Shake hands to explain *Nice to meet you.* Have the children mingle and practice the dialog in pairs. Encourage them to shake hands when they say *Nice to meet you (too).*

1 Complete. Then ask and answer for the author.

Have the children complete the questions using the words supplied. They then ask and answer in pairs, with one child pretending to be the author.

Answers

1 name **2** favorite **3** pets **4** like **5** Can **6** When's **7** please

2 What are your favorite stories? Write the titles.

The children write their favorite stories. Have them compare their answers in groups.

Answers

Children's own answers.

Cooler: Yes or no?

Ask the children to look at the picture. Say yes/no sentences, e.g. *The children can read books here. (yes) There are six girls. (No—there are seven girls.)*, etc.

Digital Resources

Student eBook, Digital Activity Book • All SB and AB pages can be shown on the board. Use them for "heads-up" teaching and reference throughout the lesson. For "heads-up" teaching activities, ask the children to close their book so that you have their full attention.

• You can access the tool in the tool bar along the top of the screen, e.g. *Timer, Highlighter.* The audio, answer keys and videos (in the SB) can be accessed by buttons next to the corresponding activities.

Welcome Back, Everyone

Lesson objectives: revise vocabulary and grammar from *Story Central Plus* 1
Key vocabulary: animals, food, hobbies, months, sports
Key grammar: *What's your name? My name's . . .*, *Do you have any pets? Yes, I do.*
I have (two cats). Can you skate? No, I can't, but I can dance!
Materials: Track 0.3; Activity 2 questions on strips of paper (optional)

Warmer: Welcome back!

Model a dialogue with a child: A: *Hello, (name)!* B: *Hi, (name)!*
A: *Welcome back!* B: *Thanks.* Have the children mingle, shake
hands, and greet each other in the same way.

1 Write the number of the correct book.

* Have the children look at the picture. Pre-teach *authors*
  and *Top 5*.

* Read out the story titles for the children to point to.
  Explain that they are going to read these stories in *Story
  Central* 2. Elicit which they prefer.

* Have the children find and write the number of each
  book described. Elicit answers.

Answers

a story about sports: 1
a story about a mouse: 3
a story in a school: 2

2))) 0.3 Listen and match.

* The children match the questions to the answers.

* Play Track 0.3 for the children to listen and check.

* Play Track 0.3 again, pausing for the children to repeat.
  They then ask and answer in pairs.

Answers

1 c 2 a 3 g 4 b 5 f 6 d 7 e

3 Write about you.

* The children complete the text about themselves.
  Monitor and help as necessary.

* The children compare in pairs. Then ask children to read
  their text to the class.

Optional activity: Ask a friend

Write the questions from Activity 2 on strips of paper (one
set for each group). Divide the class into groups. Read the
questions on the strips to elicit answers from the class. Hand
out the strips face down. The children take turns reading a
question and answering. Monitor and help as necessary.

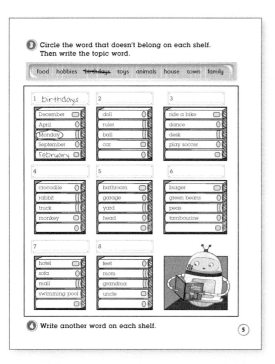

3 Circle the word that doesn't belong on each shelf. Then write the topic word.

The children find and circle the odd word in each category, then label the categories using the words supplied.

Answers

1 birthdays: Monday **2** toys: ruler **3** hobbies: desk
4 animals: truck **5** house: head **6** food: tambourine
7 town: sofa **8** family: feet

4 Write another word on each shelf.

Have the children write one more word for each category. Elicit ideas.

Answers

Children's own answers.

Cooler: Categories

Write on the board *Animals, Food, Sports, Hobbies, Months* for the children to copy the headings on a piece of paper. Elicit an example for each category. Give groups four minutes to write as many words as they can. The group with the most words wins.

Digital Resources

Digital Activity Book • Encourage the children to imagine a new friend and think up details about them using the prompts in SB Activity 3. Have children use *Pen* to write in a detail each.

Chapter 1

Tall or Short?
Overview

The children will:

- use critical thinking skills to describe physical appearance.
- ask and answer questions about people's appearance.
- read, understand, and act out a story.
- identify and use opposites.
- find out how to grow a beanstalk.
- make a beanstalk.

Key Vocabulary

- **Appearance:** beard, blond, curly, glasses, long, mustache, straight, short
- **Opposites:** asleep/awake, dark/light, night/day, old/young, rich/poor, up/down

Key Grammar

- What does she look like?
- She's (tall). She has (long hair and glasses).
- Is she (old) or (young)? Does she have (blond hair) or (brown hair)?
- Who is it? It's (Ellie).

Reading Skills

- **Story:** *Jack and the Beanstalk*
- **Genre:** fairy tale

Literacy Development

- predict story content from title and pictures
- notice who is speaking in the story
- predict what characters will do

Functional Language

- This is / These are for you.
- Thank you. That's nice.

Phonics

- The children practice pronunciation of hard *g* sound as in *g*olden and *g*oose.

CLIL: Science — How to grow a beanstalk

- The children find out how to grow and look after a beanstalk.

Competency Focus

The children will:

use critical thinking skills to describe people's appearance. (Lesson 1)

predict the content of a story. (Lesson 3)

identify opposites by relating them to a song. (Lesson 5)

apply new grammar to previously learned vocabulary. (Lesson 2)

use opposites to ask about people's appearance. (Lesson 6)

work in pairs to act out a dialogue. (Lesson 3)

work in groups to act out the story. (Lesson 8)

hypothesize about the main characters' action. (Lesson 4)

evaluate their own progress in the chapter. (Review)

find out about how plants grow and what they need. (Lesson 7)

Digital Overview

Teacher Presentation

Student eBook and Digital Activity Book

- ASL Vocabulary Video 1.1: Appearance
- ASL Vocabulary Video 1.3: Opposites
- Oral Storytelling Video 1.2: *Jack and the Beanstalk*
- Interactive versions of AB activities
- Integrated audio and answer key for all activities

Teacher resources for planning, lesson delivery, and homework

Teacher Resource Center

- Class Planner Chapter 1
- Worksheets to print out (including notes and answers):
  - Grammar Worksheet 1A: What does she look like? She's …
  - Grammar Worksheet 1B: Is she old or young?
  - Oral Storytelling Video Worksheet 1: *Jack and the Beanstalk*
  - Phonics Worksheet 1
  - CLIL Graphic Organizer 1
  - Test Chapter 1
- Test Generator
- Literacy Handbook

Watch the Oral Storytelling Video

Children's resources for consolidation and practice at home

Student eBook

- ASL Vocabulary Video 1.1: Appearance
- ASL Vocabulary Video 1.3: Opposites

Student eBook and Reader eBook

- Oral Storytelling Video 1.2: *Jack and the Beanstalk*

The Inks **Student's App**

Vocabulary games: Appearance and opposites

Tall or Short?

Lesson 1

Vocabulary

Lesson objective: describe people's appearance

Key vocabulary: *beard, blond hair, curly hair, glasses, long hair, mustache, short hair, straight hair*

Materials: Track 1.1; pictures from magazines (Warmer)

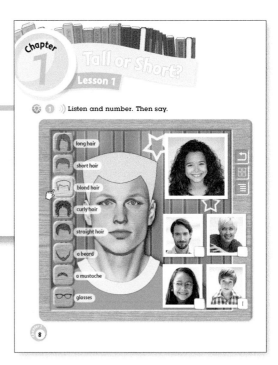

Warmer: Look at my hair!

Put up around the room magazine pictures of long/short/straight/curly/blond/black/brown hair. Have the children mingle and find a picture of someone who has the same style of hair as they do.

1))) **1.1 Listen and number. Then say.**

- Have the children look at the pictures. Ask *How many boys/girls/men/women can you see?* Elicit answers and point out that they all have different hair.

- Give them time to look at the pictures down the side of the screen and draw lines matching each feature to the corresponding person.

- Play Track 1.1 and ask the children to listen and number the photos in the order they hear them. Play Track 1.1 again for the children to say the words and check their answers. Ask children to give their answers and check with the class.

- Have the children take turns in pairs. They call out a feature on the screen (e.g. *beard*) for their friend to say the picture number (e.g. *four*) Note that for some features (e.g. *short hair, straight hair*) there is more than one option. Monitor and make sure they pronounce *curly, beard,* and *mustache* correctly.

Audioscript

Woman: *Look at this game! It's great!*

Girl: *Look at the girl. She has long hair … She has curly hair.*

Boy: *Ha, ha! She has long curly hair.*

Narrator: *1*

Woman: *Now there's a boy. What color is his hair?*

Boy: *He has straight brown hair.*

Narrator: *2*

Woman: *Look at this woman. She has short hair. It's blond.*

Boy: *Yes. She has short blond hair.*

Narrator: *3*

Woman: *This girl has long straight hair. And, um, she has glasses.*

Narrator: *4*

Boy: *And now there's a man. Look! He has a beard and a mustache!*

Answers

man 4, woman 2, girl 3, boy 1

Optional activity: Describe them!

Point to the photo of the man in the computer game. Elicit a description, e.g. *He has a beard. He has short hair.* The children continue in pairs for the other people in the photos. Monitor and make sure they use *He/She has …* correctly.

1 Look and circle.

Ask the children to look at the picture and circle the correct words.

Answers

1 short hair **2** curly hair **3** black hair **4** mustache **5** hat

2 Write the words from Activity 1 in two groups for you.

Have the children complete the two columns with the words from the previous activity. Call on children to read their answers to the class.

Answers

Children's own answers.

Cooler: Listen and draw

Ask the children to secretly draw the face of a man. Tell them to draw and color his hair, and to add other features (glasses, mustache, beard). In pairs or small groups, they take turns describing the man for the others to draw. Then have them compare their drawings to check the details.

Competency Focus

Think! Critical Thinking

The children use critical thinking skills to identify people's physical appearance by using visual clues and processing the written and spoken forms.

Digital Resources

Student eBook, Digital Activity Book • All SB and AB pages can be shown on the board. Use them for "heads-up" teaching and reference throughout the lesson.

• TIP All audio is accessible within the SB/AB pages: press on the audio buttons on the pages.

Digital Activity Book • Use the AB page to give feedback on activities, using the built-in interactive activity or answer key, as appropriate.

Student eBook • Use ASL Vocabulary Video 1.1 to pre-teach key vocabulary as an alternative to the critical thinking approach.

Grammar

Lesson objectives: ask and answer about what people look like

Key grammar: *What does she look like? She's (tall). She has (long hair and glasses).*

Materials: Track 1.2; Grammar Worksheet 1A [TRC printout] (optional)

Warmer: Chant

Chant with the class: *Long hair, short hair! Curly hair, straight hair! Beard, mustache, and glasses!* Gesture as you chant, e.g. draw a twirl in the air for *curly*, point to your upper lip for *mustache*, etc.

1)) 1.2 Listen and number.

- Have the children look at the picture. Ask questions, e.g. *Who's the man? (a teacher/Mr. Wilson)*

- Explain that they are going to listen and find each person in the picture, then write the picture number by the name. Play Track 1.2 twice. Have the children number the names, then listen again to check.

- Invite children to say an answer and a description, e.g. *Number 1 is Patrick. He has brown hair.*

Audioscript

Boy: *Look, Mom! This is my school picture! Can you see Patrick?*

Narrator: *1*

Mom: *What does Patrick look like?*

Boy: *He's tall. He has brown hair. He has blue eyes and glasses.*

Narrator: *2*

Mom: *Oh, yes. And your friend Sara? What does she look like?*

Boy: *She's short. She has red hair. Look.*

Mom: *Oh, yes! She has curly red hair.*

Narrator: *3*

Boy: *And this is George. He has short blond hair and glasses.*

Narrator: *4*

Mom: *What does Sophie look like?*

Boy: *Oh, she's small. She has long blond hair. This is Sophie.*

Mom: *It's a great picture!*

Answers

Patrick 1, Sara 2, George 3, Sophie 4

Grammar Central

What does she look like? …

Ask the children to look at the question and sentences. Explain that we use *look like* to talk about people's appearance. Point out the difference between this and *What does she like?* (preference).

For extra practice, try the **Grammar Booster** section in the Student Book (p. 18).

Answers p. 18

Activity 1: **1** look like **2** He's **3** has **4** What does **5** She's **6** has

Activity 2: **1** look, She's, has **2** does she look like, She's short, She has **3** does he look like, He's, has

2 Look at the teacher. Read and circle.

- The children use the picture of the teacher in Activity 1 to complete the sentences, circling the correct option each time. Elicit answers.

- Have the children work in pairs. They point to a boy or girl in the picture and ask *What does he/she look like?* Their friend says one or two sentences in response.

Answers

1 he **2** tall **3** short **4** curly **5** beard

3 Play a guessing game.

- Brainstorm words to describe appearance, e.g. *blond hair, glasses,* etc.

- Have one child choose a friend without naming him/ her. Ask *What does he/she look like?* The child describes their friend for the class to guess.

- Have the children work in pairs. Monitor and help as necessary.

Optional activity: My best friend

Have the children draw their best friend in their notebook and write a few sentences to describe them. Then have them present their best friend to the class.

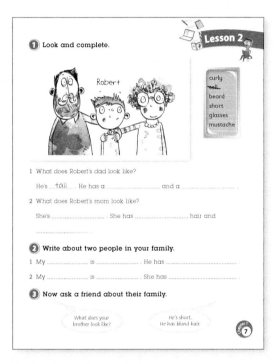

Cooler: True or False?

Say true/false sentences about the people in Student Book Activity 1, e.g. *George has glasses.* (*true*) Have the children agree or disagree, correcting you as necessary. Divide the class into small groups. Children take turns prompting.

Competency Focus

Learn

By identifying people's appearance in a different context with new grammatical structures, the children demonstrate their understanding of previously acquired vocabulary from Lesson 1.

1 Look and complete.

The children use the picture to complete the answers with the words supplied. Elicit answers.

Answers

1 tall, beard, mustache **2** short, curly, glasses

2 Write about two people in your family.

The children write about two people in their family.

Answers

Children's own answers.

3 Now ask a friend about their family.

Choose two children to read the example aloud. In pairs, the children talk about their family using their sentences from Activity 2.

Digital Resources

Student eBook • Focus on one person at a time. Say sentences for the children to respond *true* or *false*, e.g. *He has long hair and glasses.* Ask *What do they look like?* to elicit descriptions.

Teacher Resource Center • Print out Grammar Worksheet 1A for extra practice after SB Activity 2.

Reading: Story Extract

Lesson objectives: offer and accept things; use the title and pictures to predict story content;
read the extract from *Jack and the Beanstalk* (start)
Functional language: *This is/These are for you. Thank you. That's nice.*
Secondary language: *beans, beanstalk, buy, money*
Materials: Tracks 1.3 and 1.4

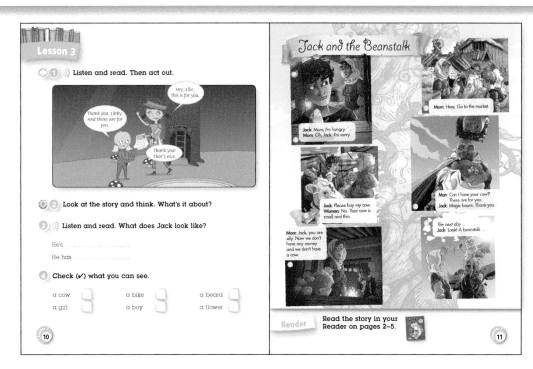

Warmer: Describe your teacher

Ask *What does your teacher look like?* Choose a child to say an example, e.g. *Our teacher has short hair.* Have the children say more sentences about you in pairs. Then invite children to share with the class.

Functional language

1))) 1.3 Listen and read. Then act out.

- Have the children look at the picture and elicit that Libby and Ellie are exchanging things. (You might need L1.)
- Play Track 1.3 and ask them to listen and read. Ask *What does Libby give to Ellie?* (*a worksheet*) *What does Ellie give to Libby?* (*flowers*)
- Point out that we use *This is for you.* for one thing and *These are for you.* for more than one.
- Play Track 1.3 again. Then have the children act out the dialogue in pairs.

Before reading

2 Look at the story and think. What's it about?

- Have the children look at the title and the pictures. Ask *What's it about?* Elicit answers in L1. (*a boy called Jack and a beanstalk*)
- Ask questions to help them think about the story, e.g. *What happens with the beanstalk?*

3))) 1.4 Listen and read. What does Jack look like?

- Play Track 1.4 and have the children listen and read along.
- Ask them to point to Jack in the pictures. Ask *What does he look like?* Elicit a sentence to describe him.
- Have the children complete and then compare their answers in pairs. Then check as a class.

Answers

He's thin/small/short.
He has short/brown/curly hair/blue eyes.

4 Check (✔) what you can see.

- Choose a child to read the list of words.
- Have the children look at the pictures and check the items they can see on the list.
- Ask *What does Jack sell?* (*a cow*) *Who buys it?* (*the man with the beard*) *How does he pay?* (*with magic beans*) *Is Jack's mom happy?* (*no*)

Answers

a cow, a boy, a beard

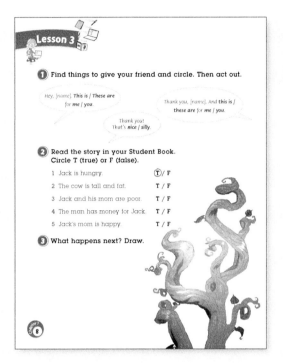

1 Find things to give your friend and circle. Then act out.

Give the children time to choose an object to give their friend. Then have them circle the correct words and act out their dialogues. Ask pairs to act out for the class.

Answers

This is / These are, you; this is / these are, you; nice

2 Read the story in your Student Book. Circle T (true) or F (false).

Have the children read the sentences and circle T (true) or F (false). Elicit answers and check with the class.

Answers

1 T 2 F 3 T 4 F 5 F

3 What happens next? Draw.

Ask the children what they think happens next and have them draw a picture. Invite children to show their picture to the class.

Read statements from the story extract to elicit who said each one, e.g. *Go to the market.* (*Mom*)

Competency Focus

Collaborate and Communicate

The children work together, putting into practice new functional language by acting out a realistic dialogue.

Think! Critical Thinking

By looking at the story artwork, the children use prediction skills to help them engage with the story.

Digital Resources

Student eBook, Digital Activity Book • Show the features available for each activity. Choose the audio/answer key button; the materials will appear in a pop-up window.

- TIP Hover over each icon in the tool bar to reveal the function of each button.

Lesson objective: read and understand the fairy tale
Jack and the Beanstalk in the Reader
Materials: Track 1.5; Reader; Oral Storytelling Video Worksheet 1 [TRC printout] (optional)

Warmer: Character review

Write on the board *Jack, Jack's mom, man with beard*. Divide the class into small groups to remember what they can about the story characters. (They may need L1.) Set a time limit. Then invite children to share with the class.

Story Summary

Jack and his mom are poor and hungry. Jack uses magic beans to grow a beanstalk. A scary giant and his kind wife live at the top of the beanstalk in a castle. They have a goose that lays golden eggs. Jack steals the goose and escapes. He cuts down the beanstalk and kills the giant. Jack and his mom are rich and happy.

Value: Work together.

))) **1.5 While reading**

- Ask the children to look at *Jack and the Beanstalk* in their Reader. Give them time to study the pictures carefully.

- If necessary, pre-teach *giant, kind, gold,* and *goose* using the pictures in the story.

- Play Track 1.5 and have the children listen and read along. Ask general comprehension questions, e.g. *Are Jack and his mother safe at the end of the story? Are they happy? Why?*

- Play Track 1.5 again, pausing and asking: after picture 8 *What does Jack see when he climbs the beanstalk?* (*a big castle*); after picture 14 *Who lives in the castle?* (*the giant and his wife*) *Are they rich?* (*yes*); after picture 18 *Why does Jack go back?* (*to get the gold*) *What does he take from the giant?* (*a goose that lays golden eggs*) (You might need to use L1.)

After reading: Reflect

- Ask the children if they would climb the beanstalk again to go back to the castle like Jack did. Would they be afraid to look for the gold? Would the giant catch them? (They may need L1.)

Optional activity: **Finish the sentence!**

Prompt with a sentence from the story, e.g. *Please buy my ...* Have the children scan the story and say the last word. (*cow*) Then have them work in small groups. They take turns reading out a sentence and stopping before the last word.

Story Time

Tips for storytelling

Encourage the children to focus on the tone of the characters' voices to identify emotions and get involved with the story. Choose sentences from the story and drill them with the correct tone of voice. For example, *Jack, you are silly.* (picture 5, angry/annoyed tone); *Help! Oh, good, he's asleep.* (picture 11, panicked, then relieved tone), etc.

Reading Strategy

Summarizing

Summarizing is a very useful strategy for readers of all ages in every context. It helps them focus on the most important points of a story and look for the underlying message. It activates their critical reading skills and improves their memory.

For additional explanation and activities, see the Literacy Handbook on Teacher Resource Center.

Cooler: Do you have the gold?

Have the children stand up in a circle. Have one child be "Jack" in the middle. Move in circles and chant *Jack, do you have the gold?* Stop and have Jack point to a classmate and say *He/She has the gold!* It is then that child's turn to be Jack.

Digital Resources

Reader eBook • Display the Reader story on the board. Review the story extract. Then elicit predictions on what will happen before the children read the rest of the story.

• Watch Oral Storytelling Video 1.2 together before you do the After reading: Reflect activity.

Teacher Resource Center • Print out Oral Storytelling Video Worksheet 1 to help you get the most out of the video.

Reading Comprehension and Critical Literacy

Lesson objectives: understand usage of colons (:) after the speakers in the story; predict what characters will do when they are rich

Materials: Track 1.5; Reader; Oral Storytelling Video Worksheet 1 [TRC printout] (optional)

Lesson 4 Time to Think

1.))) Read the story in your Reader on pages 2–5 again.

   I Can Read!
   Look at picture 7.
   Who says I can climb it?
   How do you know?

2. Check (✔) the correct words.
   The giant is...
   tall ☐   beautiful ☐   ugly ☐   kind ☐

3. 🎧 What do you think Jack and his mom buy with the gold? Draw.

   [ ]

4. Talk about the story.

   Do you know a story like this in your language?

   12

Note: Please ensure that your class has read the Reader story before you do this lesson.

Warmer: Disappearing text

Write a short text from the story on the board, e.g. *That's my goose. Come back.* Then delete words one by one. Every time you erase a word, have the children say the whole text. Continue until the children can say the whole text without visual prompts.

1))) 1.5 Read the story in your Reader.

- Have the children read the story. (Alternatively, play Track 1.5 and have them read along.) Ask them to remember how Jack and the giant are different. (*beautiful/ugly, poor/rich*, etc.)

I Can Read!

Ask the children to look at the story and notice the speaker name at the start of each line. Explain that we add a colon (:) after the speaker's name.

Have the children count how many times Jack speaks. (*18—1 is a thought bubble*) Ask children to choose their favorite line by Jack and read it aloud.

Answer

Jack. **Jack:** before the text.

2 Check (✔) the correct words.

- Have the children check the correct adjectives for the giant, using the story if necessary.
- Elicit answers. Ask *Who is kind to Jack?* (*the giant's wife*) *How?* (*She protects Jack./She gives Jack food.*) (You might need to use L1.)

Answers

tall, ugly

3 What do you think Jack and his mom buy with the gold? Draw. 🎧

- Ask *Why are Jack and his mom rich now?* (*golden eggs*)
- Have a child read the question. Brainstorm ideas. (You might need to use L1.)
- The children draw one or more objects in their book. Invite children to the front to present their drawings.

4 Talk about the story.

- Ask the children *Did you like the story? Why?/Why not?*
- Have a child read Libby's question. Ask the children if there is a version of *Jack and the Beanstalk* in their own language and elicit differences. Ask them which version of the story they prefer.

Optional activity: Jack's list

Have the children place their book open at p. 12. Invite them to walk around and look at each other's drawings. Then ask them to brainstorm as a class all the things that Jack buys. Vote for the best object.

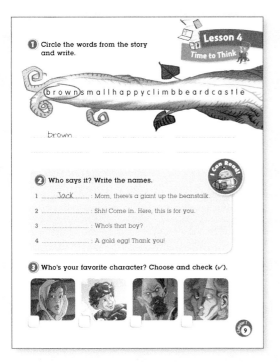

① Circle the words from the story and write.

brownsmallhappyclimbbeardcastle

brown

② Who says it? Write the names.

1 ....Jack...... : Mom, there's a giant up the beanstalk.
2 .... : Shh! Come in. Here, this is for you.
3 .... : Who's that boy?
4 .... : A gold egg! Thank you!

③ Who's your favorite character? Choose and check (✔).

Competency Focus

Me: Critical Literacy

The children use critical literacy skills to reflect on the story and hypothesize about the characters' next action.

1 Circle the words from the story and write.

Have the children circle the words in the wordsnake and write them on the lines. Then elicit a sentence for each word.

Answers

brown, small, happy, climb, beard, castle

2 Who says it? Write the names.

The children practice the **I Can Read!** feature by reading the sentences and writing the name of the character.

Answers

1 Jack **2** Giant's wife **3** Giant **4** Mom

3 Who's your favorite character? Choose and check (✔).

Ask the children to choose their favorite character. Elicit answers with reasons.

Answers

Children's own answers.

Cooler: I have a golden egg

Say *You have a golden egg*. Ask the children to write or draw three gifts they would buy. Explain they will give these to a family member, a friend, people in the world, etc. Ask some children to present their drawings.

Digital Resources

Reader eBook • Display the Reader on the board. Say key items for the children to circle using *Pen*, e.g. the characters, important things like beans/gold eggs/goose.

• If you haven't already, watch Oral Storytelling Video 1.2, pausing to elicit what happens next.

Teacher Resource Center • If you haven't already, print out Oral Storytelling Video Worksheet 1 to do the support activities.

Vocabulary, Song, and Phonics

Lesson objectives: use opposites; practice the hard *g* sound with a chant

Key vocabulary: *up/down, day/night, dark/light, asleep/awake, rich/poor*

Secondary language: *giant, goose, quick*

Materials: Tracks 1.6 and 1.7; pictures for Key vocabulary (Warmer) ; Phonics Worksheet 1 [TRC printout] (optional)

Warmer: Opposites

Pre-teach the vocabulary using mimes and/or pictures. Chant the opposite pairs together. Have the children mime as they chant.

1)) 1.6 Listen and write the letter for the opposite. Then sing.

- Have the children look at the pictures and say the characters they can see. (*Jack, giant, goose, Jack's mom*) Point to the words around the song and check understanding by asking, e.g. *Who's rich/poor?*, etc.

- Play Track 1.6 and have the children listen and match. Elicit answers.

- Call out words for the class to say the opposite. Write the pairs of words on the board.

- Play Track 1.6 again and have the children sing and mime some of the words, e.g. *climb up/down*, etc.

Answers

1 d **2** c **3** b **4** e **5** a

2 Play an opposites game.

- Demonstrate the game with one child. Say *It's night.* Encourage the child to say *No, it isn't. It's day.* Do another example, e.g. *He's rich.* to elicit *No, he isn't. He's poor.*

- Divide the class into pairs and have them play the opposites game. Monitor and help with structures if necessary.

3)) 1.7 Listen and say the chant.

- Ask *What can you see in the picture?* (*the goose and a golden egg*)

- Play Track 1.7 and have the children listen to the chant. Then play Track 1.7 again, pausing for them to repeat the sentences.

- Practice the chant a few times with the class.

Optional activity: More opposites

Ask the children to write the pairs of opposites from Activity 1 in their notebook. Have them think of more opposites, e.g. *big/small, open/close, ugly/beautiful, tall/short, white/black.* Invite children to write a pair of words on the board for the others to copy.

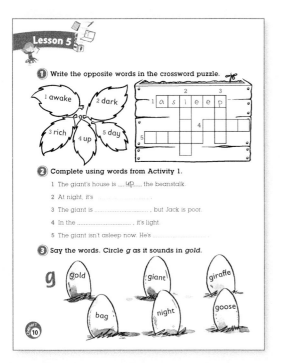

Cooler: g chant

Write more words with the *g* sounds on the board: *go/bag/ tiger/grandpa/frog/dog/legs; orange/giraffe/giant/magic*. In pairs, the children say the words. Ask children to circle on the board the words with the *g* sound as in *goose*. Correct if necessary. When they finish, chorally drill the words.

Competency Focus

Think! Critical Thinking

The children use critical thinking skills to match the opposites by processing the written and spoken forms.

1 Write the opposite words in the crossword puzzle.

Have the children complete the crossword by writing in the opposites. Elicit answers and check with the class.
Answers

1 asleep **2** light **3** poor **4** down **5** night

2 Complete using words from Activity 1.

Ask the children to complete the sentences with words from Activity 1. Have the children check their answers in pairs. Then invite individuals to read a sentence for the class.
Answers

1 up **2** dark **3** rich **4** day **5** awake

3 Say the words. Circle *g* as it sounds in *gold*.

Have the class say *gold*. Then ask them to circle the words with the *g* sound. Elicit answers and check with the class.
Answers

Circled: **g** in **g**old, ba**g**, **g**oose

Digital Resources

Student eBook • Use ASL Vocabulary Video 1.3 to pre-teach key vocabulary. Play the video, pausing for the children to repeat the word and copy the sign.

• When you play the audio for the song, point to the SB page to help the children follow the song lyrics.

Teacher Resource Center • For phonics practice, print out Phonics Worksheet 1.

Grammar and Reading

Lesson objective: ask questions to identify people
Key grammar: *Is she* (old) *or* (young)? *Does she have* (blond hair) *or* (brown hair)? *Who is it? It's* (Ellie).
Secondary language: *card, long, old, short, young*
Materials: Track 1.8; Grammar Worksheet 1B [TRC printout] (optional)

Warmer: Call the opposite!

Ask the children to think of four opposites, e.g. *in/out, up/down*, etc. In pairs, the children take turns saying a word and its opposite.

1))) 1.8 Listen and read.

- Have the children look at the pictures. Ask *Who can you see?* (Tom, Biblio, and Ellie) Point to the ID card and explain what it is.

- Play Track 1.8 and ask them to listen and read along. Ask *Why can't they read the name on the card?* (The card got wet.) *Whose card is it?* (Ellie's) *Why does she have a mustache?* (Tom drew it with a pen.) (They may need L1.)

- Play Track 1.8 again, pausing for them to repeat. Pay attention to the contractions *can't, it's, doesn't.*

2 Complete the questions about the picture.

- Have the children read and complete the questions. Elicit answers and check with the class.

- Remind the children that we put adjectives before nouns, e.g. *brown hair.*

- Have the children practice the questions and answers in pairs to consolidate question forms and pronunciation.

Answers

1 Is he **2** short **3** Does, or **4** is, Tom

Grammar Central

Is she old or young? …

Ask the children to read out the first two questions and the answers in the text in Activity 1. Write the questions on the board. Explain that we do not use *do/does* to ask questions with the verb *to be*, but we do use *do/does* to ask questions with other verbs, e.g. *have.* Point out the position of *she* in the two questions (after the verb *to be*; between *do/does* and other verbs). Then have the children read the third question and its answer. Highlight the structure: *Who* + the verb *to be.*

For extra practice, try the **Grammar Booster** section in the Student Book (p. 19–21).

Answers p. 19

Activity 1: **1** Is **2** Is **3** Does **4** have **5** Who **6** It's

Activity 2: **1** Is he **2** or **3** Does he have **4** Is he **5** Who, King Jade

p. 20

Activity 1: **1** Who **2** It's **3** does he **4** He's **5** Does he have **6** he has

Activity 2: **1** c **2** d **3** a **4** b **5** e

p. 21

Activity 1: H **2** A **3** F **4** E **5** K **6** G

Activity 2: Children's own answers.

Optional activity: Who is it? It's …

Ask the children to write down a friend's name secretly. Brainstorm words to describe a person, e.g. *tall, young,* etc. Invite a child to the front. The other children take turns asking a question to guess the name. Continue with different children.

Cooler: Is he old or young?

Write on the board *old/young, blue/brown eyes, short hair/ long hair, straight hair/curly hair, glasses/mustache.* Have the children draw a man, secretly choosing one of each item. Then, in pairs, have them take turns asking questions (e.g. *Is he old or young?*) and answering (e.g. *He's young.*) Then they show their pictures.

Competency Focus
Learn
The children demonstrate their understanding of the new grammatical patterns by reading the text and completing the activity.

1 Circle the correct word.

Have the children circle the correct words for the pictures. Elicit answers and check with the class.
Answers

1 young **2** tall **3** long hair **4** mustache

2 Complete for the pictures in Activity 1. Then ask and answer.

Have the children complete the questions for each picture. Then they ask and answer in pairs. Invite pairs to demonstrate for the class.
Answers

1 Is she **2** Is he **3** Does she have **4** Does he have

3 Draw a picture of you and complete the identity card.

Ask the children to draw a picture of themselves in the box. Then they complete the information for themselves. Have them swap and read a friend's card.

Digital Resources

Student eBook • Show the Grammar Central box. The children use *Highlighter* to select questions in Activity 1 text.

Teacher Resource Center • For extra grammar practice, print out Grammar Worksheet 1B.

CLIL: Science—How to grow a beanstalk

Lesson objective: find out how to grow and look after a beanstalk
Materials: Track 1.9; CLIL Graphic Organizer 1 [TRC printout] (optional); beans, plastic cups, cotton balls (optional)

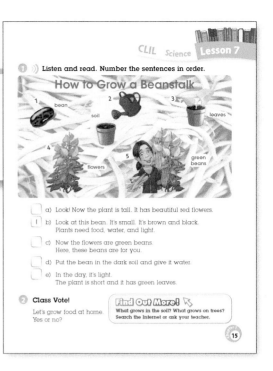

Warmer: Sing the song

Have the children sit in a circle. Say the chant: *I'm a flower. I'm a flower. When it rains, we have a shower. Water helps us grow. Hello! Hello!* While saying the chant, slowly rise up from the floor and finish standing, waving your hands, and swaying. Repeat a few times.

1))) 1.9 Listen and read. Number the sentences in order.

- Have the children say what they can see in the pictures. Point out that they show how a beanstalk grows. Pre-teach *soil, water the plant, leaves*.

- Play Track 1.9 twice. The children listen and read. Have them number the sentences in order.

- Elicit answers and check with the class.

Answers

a 4 **b** 1 **c** 5 **d** 2 **e** 3

2 Class Vote!

- Organize your class vote. Ask *Do you grow food at home? What food do you grow? Is it easy?* (They might need to use L1.)

- Then ask *Is it a good idea to grow things at home?* Give them a minute to think. Then write *Yes* and *No* on the board. Have the children raise their hand for each answer. Count the votes and write the totals on the board. Elicit the result of the vote.

Find Out More!

Ask the children *Do carrots grow in the soil or on a tree?* (*in the soil*) Repeat with apples and elicit that they grow on trees. Then ask them to find out more about where fruit and vegetables grow. Suggest appropriate resources, e.g. Internet, library books, etc., or provide the information yourself. The children will need to complete this research before doing the follow-up activity in the Activity Book. (It can be set as homework if you are planning to move on to the Activity Book in the next lesson.)

Optional activity: Grow your own beanstalk

Organize a class project. Supply real beans, plastic cups, and cotton balls. The children put the bean in the cup and cover it with cotton. With a few drops of water each day, a little plant will grow within a week. Encourage the children to take the plant home and keep a diary, adding drawings, or taking pictures to show the different stages of its development. Then have them bring their diary and plant in to show the class.

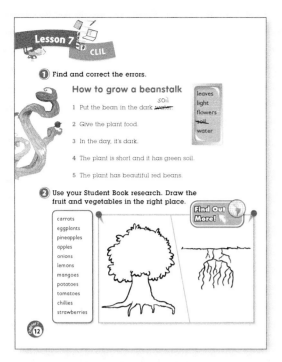

Competency Focus

Act

The children carry out research to find out more about what grows in the soil and what grows on trees. This helps them expand their learning and relate it to their world, both inside and ouside the classroom.

1 Find and correct the errors.

Have the children correct an error in each sentence using the words supplied. Elicit answers and check with the class.

Answers

1 ~~water~~ soil 2 ~~food~~ water 3 ~~dark~~ light 4 ~~soil~~ leaves
5 ~~beans~~ flowers

2 Use your Student Book research. Draw the fruit and vegetables in the right place.

Ask the children what kinds of fruit and vegetables grow in the soil and what kinds grow on trees. Then have them look at the list and draw pictures on the tree or in the soil. Elicit answers and check with the class.

Answers

Tree: apples, lemons, mangoes

Above ground: eggplants, pineapples, tomatoes, chillies, strawberries

Below ground: carrots, onions, potatoes

Cooler: We like plants, trees, flowers

Write on the board *plants, trees, flowers*. Help the children brainstorm why they are important, e.g. *They grow vegetables and fruits./They are pretty./They smell nice.*, etc. (You might need to use L1.) Ask the children to draw pictures to represent their ideas.

Digital Resources

Student eBook • Display the SB page on the board to do Activity 1 point 1 as an alternative "heads-up" introduction to the topic. This helps the children engage. Choose the audio button to play the recording. The children can read the text in their SB.

• TIP Store ideas in *Add personal note* during the lesson.

Teacher Resource Center • Print out CLIL Graphic Organizer 1 for the children to use in collating their Find Out More! research.

CLIL eBook • The children can use the CLIL eBook to expand their knowledge of the lesson topic.

Project

Lesson objectives: review language from Chapter 1; complete a craft project—making a beanstalk; act out the story from the Reader

Materials: Reader; small sheets of paper, sticky tape, watercolor paints and paintbrushes, small strips of colored paper (optional)

Warmer: What is it?

Draw a beanstalk slowly on the board. Invite the children to say what it is and spell it. Write *beanstalk* on the board. Elicit what they know about beans and beanstalks. (They may need L1.)

Prepare

1 Make a beanstalk.

- Have the children look at the completed beanstalk. Tell them they are going to make their own beanstalk.
- Hold up the materials to show the class. Point to the pictures and explain the stages. (You might need to use L1.)
- Demonstrate how to make a beanstalk, stage by stage.
- Divide the class into pairs or groups if it is necessary to share materials. Give out the materials.
- As the children make their beanstalks, monitor and give help as necessary.

Alternative craft activity

A simpler option would be to have the children work together to make a single beanstalk. In pairs or small groups, they draw a branch on one piece of paper. They then put their drawings together to make a big class beanstalk.

Showcase

2 Tell the story. Use your beanstalk.

- Stick a beanstalk on the board. Choose four children to help you act out part of the story (pictures 6–15). As they act out the scenes, invite "Jack" to mime climbing up and down the beanstalk.
- Divide the class into groups to act out the story (ideally pictures 6–22). Allocate a role to each child and give them time to practice acting out the story using their Reader. Monitor and give help with pronunciation, intonation, and gestures.
- Call out groups to the front of the class to perform.

Optional activity: Message beanstalk

Display the beanstalk(s) in class. Distribute strips of colored paper and ask the children to think of and write a short message, e.g. *Be happy! Let's be friends!*, etc. Invite them to stick their messages on the beanstalk.

1 Play "Who Is It?"

Ask the children to color the people's hair, using a wide range of appropriate colors. Then read the words in the box. Demonstrate the game with a child. Have them choose a person in the pictures. Ask questions until you guess the person. Have the children play in pairs.

Cooler: Play "Simon Says"

Have the children play the game with actions from the lesson, e.g. *go up the beanstalk, climb down, cut down, get the goose, eat your breakfast,* etc. (see Games Bank p. 222).

Competency Focus

Collaborate and Communicate

By acting out the story, the children consolidate their understanding in a fun and engaging way. They also demonstrate their ability to work with friends and use interpersonal skills.

Digital Resources

Student eBook • For the craft activity, display the SB page on the board. Show the Prepare photos, stage by stage, as you talk the class through the process.

Digital Activity Book • For the "Who Is It?" game in AB Activity 1, use *Timer*. Set a time limit for each person to be guessed.

Language Review

Lesson objective: review language from Chapter 1
Materials: Tracks 1.10 and AB 1.1

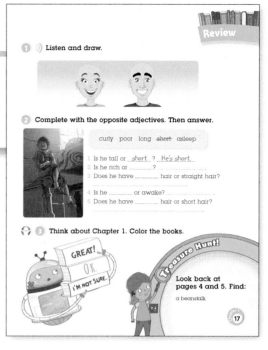

Warmer: Play "Ready, Set, Draw!"

Have the children play the game with words from Lessons 1 and 5 (see Games Bank p. 222).

1))) 1.10 Listen and draw.

- Ask the children to look at the picture. Ask *What's wrong?* (*They don't have hair.*, etc.) Explain there are more things missing.

- Play Track 1.10 twice and have the children draw the missing features. Then have them compare their answers in pairs before you check as a class. Ask questions to check answers, e.g. *Does Mom have brown eyes?* (*no—blue*) *Who has a beard?* (*Dad*)

Audioscript

Narrator: What does your mom look like?
Girl: She has straight blond hair. She has blue eyes. She has glasses.
Narrator: What does your dad look like?
Girl: He has curly black hair. He has brown eyes. He has a beard.

Answers

First face: straight blond hair, blue eyes, and glasses.

Second face: curly black hair, brown eyes, and a beard.

2 Complete with the opposite adjectives. Then answer.

- Point to Jack and ask *Who's this?* Have a child read the adjectives in the box and the example. Point out that the questions and answers are about Jack.

- Give them time to complete the questions and answers, then compare in pairs. Elicit responses.

Answers

1 short, He's short.

2 poor, He's poor.

3 curly, He has curly hair.

4 asleep, He's awake.

5 long, He has short hair.

3 Think about Chapter 1. Color the books.

- Have the children look back at Chapter 1. Elicit their favorite parts. The children then color the book which represents how they feel about their own progress (self-evaluation).

Treasure Hunt!

Ask the children to look at Student Book pp. 4–5 and find a beanstalk. Have them raise their hand when they find it.

Cooler: Tap the opposite!

Invite children to write opposites on the board, but have them spread the words out (e.g "in" is on the left side of the board and "out" is in the center or on the right). Divide the class into two groups. Call out a word and have a child from each group tap the opposite word on the board.

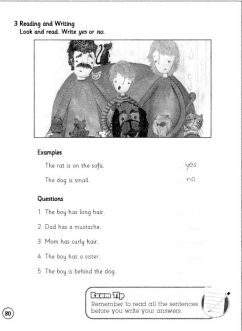

the sister's long hair is blond/yellow, and the curly hair of the girl speaking is black.

3 Reading and Writing. Look and read. Write yes or no.

Have the children read the sentences and use the picture to respond yes or no to each one. Check answers.

Answers

1 no **2** yes **3** no **4** no **5** yes

Competency Focus

Me: Self-evaluation

The children reflect on the chapter and express their opinions about their own progress. This encourages them to evaluate and make decisions about how they learn and what they need to revisit.

Digital Resources

Teacher Resource Center • Print out Test Chapter 1 to use at the end of this lesson. The Test Generator also allows you to create customized tests.

• For the Exam Booster activities on the AB page, choose the audio button on the page to access the recordings.

Student's App • Encourage the children to play the games on their smartphone/tablet as a fun way to review the chapter vocabulary. (*The Inks* Apps are free and available on the App Store and Google Play.)

1 Reading and Writing. Look and read. Write *yes* or *no*.

Have the children read the sentences and use the picture to respond *yes* or *no* to each one. Check answers.

Answers

1 yes **2** no **3** yes **4** yes **5** no

2))) AB 1.1 Listening. Listen and color. There is one example.

Children listen and color the hair/mustache according to the recording. Play Track AB 1.1 twice, then elicit and check.

Answers (Audioscript on p. 222)

Picture colored as follows: the brother's hair is blond/ yellow, the dad's mustache is gray and his hair is brown,

Chapter 2
Our School
Overview

The children will:

- use critical thinking skills to identify school items.
- ask and answer questions about who objects belong to.
- read, understand, and act out a story.
- talk about school subjects.
- practice numbers up to 100 and measure height and hand spans.
- make a cup.

Key Vocabulary

School items: cap, jacket, lunch box, sneakers, sweater, water bottle

School subjects: art, computer studies, English, geography, history, math, P.E., recess, science, Spanish

Key Grammar

- Whose (pen) is this? Whose (glasses) are these?
- It's their (ball). They're our (glasses).
- It's (Libby)'s pencil. It's (Tom)'s notebook.

Reading Skills

Story: *Hilltop School for Young Detectives*
Genre: modern detective story

Literacy Development

- predict story content from title and pictures
- notice the information on the back cover of books
- analyze clues to solve a mystery

Functional Language

- How do you spell ("mystery")?

Phonics

The children practice pronunciation of *sp* as in *Sp*anish and *sc* as in *sc*hool.

CLIL: Math—Numbers to 100; Measuring our bodies

The children practice numbers 1–100. They measure their body and hands to find out their height and hand spans.

Competency Focus

The children will:

use critical thinking skills to identify school items. (Lesson 1)	apply new grammar to previously learned vocabulary. (Lesson 2)	work in pairs to act out a dialogue. (Lesson 3)	solve a mystery, giving their own opinions. (Lesson 4)	measure their height and hand spans. (Lesson 7)
predict the content of a story. (Lesson 3)	ask and answer about who objects belong to. (Lesson 6)	work in groups to act out the story. (Lesson 8)	evaluate their own progress in the chapter. (Review)	
identify school subjects. (Lesson 5)				

Digital Overview

Teacher Presentation

Student eBook and Digital Activity Book

- ASL Vocabulary Video 2.1: School items
- ASL Vocabulary Video 2.4: School subjects
- Music Video 2.2 (2.3): *The School for Young Detectives*
- Interactive versions of AB activities
- Integrated audio and answer key for all activities

Teacher resources for planning, lesson delivery, and homework

Teacher Resource Center

- Class Planner Chapter 2
- Worksheets to print out (including notes and answers):
  - Grammar Worksheet 2A: Whose … is this/are these? It's …
  - Grammar Worksheet 2B: It's …'s pencil.
  - Phonics Worksheet 2
  - CLIL Graphic Organizer 2
  - Festival Worksheet: Teacher's Day
  - Test Chapter 2
- Test Generator
- Literacy Handbook

Watch the Music Video

Children's resources for consolidation and practice at home

Student eBook

- ASL Vocabulary Video 2.1: School items
- ASL Vocabulary Video 2.4: School subjects
- Music Video 2.2 (2.3): *The School for Young Detectives*

The Inks Student's App

Vocabulary games: School items and school subjects

Vocabulary

Lesson objective: identify school objects
Key vocabulary: *cap, jacket, lunch box, sneakers, sweater, water bottle*
Materials: Track 2.1; cardboard box (Cooler)

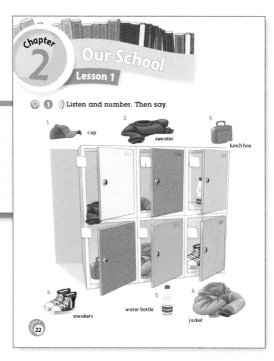

Warmer: What's in your bag?

Call out classroom objects for the children to hold up, e.g. *pen, pencil,* etc. In pairs, the children tell each other three objects they have in their school bag, one of which is not true. They guess which object is not there. Then have them show the two objects they do have.

1))) 2.1 Listen and number. Then say.

- Have the children look at the picture. Pre-teach *locker.* Ask *How many lockers can you see? What colors are they?* Elicit answers, then ask about the objects: *Which of these things do you have with you today?*

- Play Track 2.1 and have them number the lockers in the order they hear them. Play Track 2.1 again and ask them to repeat. Have them compare answers in pairs before you check as a class.

- In pairs, the children practice pointing to a locker and saying *This locker is (blue). (There's a water bottle) in this locker.* Monitor and make sure they use *there's/ there are* correctly.

Audioscript

Narrator: Look at the lockers. They are yellow, red, blue, brown, green and pink.
Narrator: 1
Boy 1: This is my locker. It's red.
Narrator: What's in your locker?
Boy 1: My cap. Look!
Narrator: 2 What color is your locker?
Girl 1: It's yellow. My sweater is in my locker.
Narrator: 3
Boy 2: My lunch box is in my locker. My locker is brown.
Narrator: 4
Girl 2: Look! My locker is pink. These are my sneakers.
Narrator: 5
Girl 3: This is my locker. It's blue. Look! There's my water bottle.
Narrator: 6
Girl 4: My jacket is in my locker. My jacket and locker are green!

Answers

Top row left to right: 2, 1, 5
Bottom row left to right: 3, 6, 4

Optional activity: Where's the cap?

Ask a child *Where's the cap?* Tell them to say the answer without looking in the book. (*It's in the red locker.*) The children play the memory game in groups, taking turns asking a question.

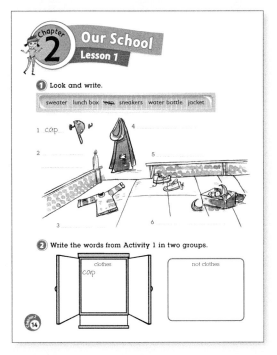

Competency Focus

Think! Critical Thinking

The children use critical thinking skills to identify school objects by using visual clues and processing the written and spoken forms.

1 Look and write.

Have the children label the items in the picture with the words supplied. Elicit answers and check with the class.

Answers

1 cap **2** water bottle **3** sweater **4** jacket **5** sneakers
6 lunch box

2 Write the words from Activity 1 in two groups.

Ask the children to write the Activity 1 words in the correct groups. Elicit answers and check with the class.

Answers

clothes: cap, sweater, sneakers, jacket
not clothes: lunch box, water bottle

Cooler: In the locker ...

Secretly, put objects in a box. Say *This is my locker.* Show the contents to a few children. Then invite the rest of the class to guess the contents by asking *Is there (a water bottle) in the locker?* The children who have looked answer appropriately, e.g. *Yes, there is.*, etc.

Digital Resources

Student eBook • Use *Add personal note* to write yourself a reminder to assemble items for the "locker" box in the Cooler activity.

• Play ASL Vocabulary Video 2.1 to pre-teach key vocabulary as an alternative to the critical thinking approach.

• Call out the SB Activity 1 items in random order. Children use *Pen* to circle each one in the appropriate locker.

Grammar

Lesson objectives: ask and answer about who objects belong to
Key grammar: *Whose (pen) is this? Whose (glasses) are these? It's their (ball). They're our (glasses).*
Materials: Track 2.2; Grammar Worksheet 2A [TRC printout] (optional); children's own school objects, a cardboard box

Warmer: What's missing?

Place objects on your desk, e.g. a ball, a pen, etc. Have the children look, then cover their eyes. Remove one or two objects and ask them to look again. Have them call out or write down what is missing. Check with the class.

1))) 2.2 Follow the lines. Then listen and say.

- Have the children look at the picture. Ask *What can you see?* to elicit *soccer ball, jackets*, etc.

- Play Track 2.2 and have the children listen and follow the lines. Ask *Whose (ball/sweater) is this? Whose glasses are these?* Have them answer by pointing to the picture.

- In pairs, the children take turns to say, e.g. *It's (their ball). They're (her glasses).*, pointing to the objects and people in the picture.

Audioscript

Narrator: 1
Teacher: Whose lunch box is this?
Girl: It's my lunch box.
Narrator: 2
Teacher: Whose ball is this?
Girl: It's their ball.
Narrator: 3
Teacher: Whose bag is this?
Girl: It's her bag.
Narrator: 4
Teacher: Whose jackets are these?

Boy 1 & Boy 2: They're our jackets.
Narrator: 5
Teacher: Whose glasses are these?
All kids: They're your glasses!
Teacher: Oh, yes! Thank you!

Grammar Central

Whose pen is this? …

Have children read the question and sentences aloud. Explain that we use *whose* to ask who something belongs to. Remind them that we use *this* for one object and *these* for two objects or more. Write *my, his/her, our, their* on the board. Elicit examples with real objects around the class.

For extra practice, try the **Grammar Booster** section in the Student Book (p. 32).

Answers p. 32

Activity 1: **1** your **2** her **3** their **4** Whose **5** my **6** are **7** They're
Activity 2: **1** is this, his **2** are these, their **3** is this, my **4** Whose, our

2 Look at the picture. Read and circle.

- Read the example. Ask who *her* refers to. (*the teacher*)

- Have the children read the sentences and circle the correct words.

- Check answers, eliciting who the words refer to.

Answers

1 her **2** her **3** her **4** their

3 Ask and answer.

- Take a pen from one of the children and ask that child *Whose pen is this?* to elicit *It's my pen.* Then ask a second child, who answers *It's his/her pen.*

- The children practice the questions and answers in groups using real objects. To practice *our/their*, divide the class into groups.

Optional activity: their/they're and his/he's

Write *their, they're, his, he's* on the board. Point out that *their* and *they're* sound the same. Have the children write a sentence for each word. Monitor and help. Then have them compare sentences in pairs and say which word has been used.

1 Read and color.

Have the children read the text underneath each picture carefully and use the information to color the picture. Elicit answers and check with the class.

Answers

Colored as follows:

The Reds: red and white jackets; green water bottles
The Blues: blue and yellow jackets; pink water bottles

2 Complete with *our, their,* or *whose.*

Ask the children to look at the pictures and the initials carefully. Using the pictures as prompts, they then complete the questions and answers. Elicit answers.

Answers

Question: Whose **1** our **2** their
Question: Whose **3** their **4** our

Cooler: Whose pen is this?

Invite children to put a pen, pencil, or eraser in a box. Shake the box and choose an object. Ask the class *Whose (pen) is this?* Have children point and say *It's his/her pen.* Pair children up to elicit sentences with *their* and repeat.

Competency Focus

Learn

By identifying people's objects in a different context with new grammatical structures, the children demonstrate their understanding of previously acquired vocabulary from Lesson 1.

Digital Resources

Student eBook • Show the SB Grammar Central box. Use *Highlighter* to focus on key grammar structures.

Teacher Resource Center • For extra grammar practice, print out Grammar Worksheet 2A.

Reading: Story Extract

Lesson objectives: ask how to spell something; use the title and pictures to predict story content; read the extract from *Hilltop School for Young Detectives* (middle)

Functional language: *How do you spell ("mystery")?*

Secondary language: *clue, detective, footprint, mystery*

Materials: Tracks 2.3 and 2.4

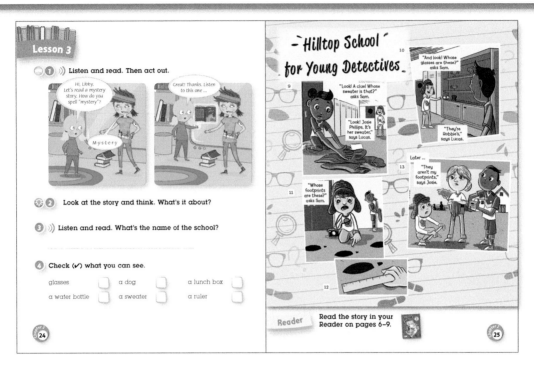

Warmer: Alphabet revision

Divide the class into two groups. Invite a child from each group to the board. Call out a letter (e.g. *g*) for them to write on the board. The first group to write it correctly wins a point. Repeat with different letters.

Functional language

1)) **2.3 Listen and read. Then act out.**

- Have the children look at the picture of Ellie and Libby. Ask *What's the title of the book?* (*The Castle*)
- Play Track 2.3 and ask the children to listen and read. If necessary, explain *mystery*.
- Divide the class into pairs and have them act out the dialogue. Brainstorm more types of stories on the board, e.g. *funny, scary, detective*, etc. The children repeat the dialogue with a different friend, replacing *mystery* with another word.

Before reading

2 Look at the story and think. What's it about?

- Have the children look at the pictures and identify items they recognize, e.g. *sweater, glasses, ruler*.
- Ask a child to read the title. Ask *What's it about?* (*solving mysteries*) (They might need to use L1.)
- Pre-teach *footprints*. Ask what Sam is doing with the ruler. (*measuring the footprint*) Have the children say what the clues are in the pictures.

3)) **2.4 Listen and read. What's the name of the school?**

- Play Track 2.4 and have the children listen and read along. Point to the characters to elicit their names. (*Sam, Lucas, Josie*)
- Have the children write the answer to the question. The class spell it for a child to write on the board.

Answer

Hilltop School

4 Check (✔) what you can see.

- Choose a child to read the list of words. Have the children look at the pictures and check the objects they can see.

- Check with the class. For each object ticked, ask a *Whose …?* question, e.g. *Whose glasses are they?*

Answers

glasses, a sweater

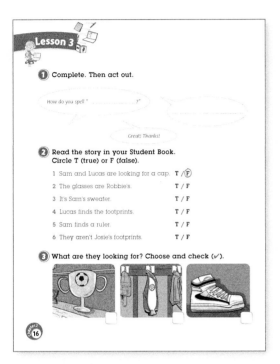

1 Complete. Then act out.

Have the children complete the dialogue and act it out with a friend. Ask pairs to act out for the class.

2 Read the story in your Student Book. Circle T (true) or F (false).

Have the children circle true or false for each sentence. Elicit answers and check with the class.

Answers

1 F 2 T 3 F 4 F 5 F 6 T

3 What are they looking for? Choose and check (✔).

Have the children predict what they are looking for by checking one of the pictures. Elicit ideas.

Answers

Children's own answers.

Explain the extract is from the middle of the Reader story. Ask the children to predict what happened before and after. Elicit ideas from the class. Then elicit ideas as to what mystery the children are trying to solve. (They might need to use L1.)

Competency Focus

Collaborate and Communicate

The children work together, putting into practice new functional language by acting out a realistic dialogue.

Think! Critical Thinking

By looking at the story artwork, the children use prediction skills to help them engage with the story.

Digital Resources

Student eBook • The SB Warmer can be done using *Pen*.

- TIP Choose the audio buttons on the SB page to access recordings for listening activities.

Digital Activity Book • To give feedback on AB Activity 2, have children do the interactive digital activity.

Lesson objective: read and understand the modern detective story *Hilltop School for Young Detectives* in the Reader
Materials: Track 2.5; Reader

Warmer: Unscramble the words

Write on the board scrambled versions of the young detectives' names (*Sam* and *Lucas*). Have the children unscramble the names in pairs. Elicit answers and check with the class. Ask *Who are the detectives in the story?* (*Sam, Lucas*) Elicit again the children's ideas about what the mystery is.

Story Summary

Hilltop School wins a soccer cup. Everyone admires the cup until one day it goes missing. Two children decide to investigate who stole the cup and follow the clues. They discover that the Principal, Mrs. Parker, took the cup to the jewelry store to get it engraved.

Value: Don't take things that don't belong to you.

))) **2.5 While reading**

- Have the children study the pictures in the Reader.
- Ask them to look at the first page and identify the teachers. (*Mr. Brown, Mrs. Parker*) Focus on the children in the first four pictures and ask *Are they happy or sad?* (*happy because they won a cup*)
- Ask *Where's the cup?* (*We don't know.*) *Who has the cup?* Elicit possible solutions to the mystery. (They might need to use L1.)
- Now play Track 2.5 and have the children listen and read along with the story. Ask them to say who took the cup and why. (*Mrs. Parker took the cup to get it engraved/ Hilltop's name on it.*) Did they guess correctly? (You might need to use L1.)

After reading: Reflect

- Have the children make a list on the board of all the suspects (*Josie, Robbie, Perkins, Mrs. Parker*) and all the clues (*Josie's sweater, Robbie's glasses, the footprints*). Ask *Are Sam and Lucas good detectives. Why?/ Why not?* Elicit what the children would have done differently. (They might need to use L1.)
- Have the children look at the last picture. Ask *Why are Lucas and Sam sorry?* (*because they thought Mrs. Parker stole the cup*)

Story Time

Comprehension check

When you are reading the story in class, let the children listen to and read the story once without interruption. Then read the story again, pausing to ask questions to check comprehension and to elicit opinions with reasons.

Reading Strategy

Inference

Making inferences is essential in understanding the plot and what role each character plays. It is particularly useful when trying to solve a mystery. It requires readers to use their own knowledge and apply critical and visual literacy skills.

For additional explanation and activities, see the Literacy Handbook on Teacher Resource Center.

Optional activity: Comic strip

Divide the class into pairs. Have each child draw a picture of a character in a comic book with a large empty speech bubble. They swap and complete their friend's picture. Have the children show and tell the class about their pictures.

Cooler: Whose footprints are these?

Write short dialogues from the story, e.g. *Whose footprints are these? They aren't my footprints!* Read the questions in a suspicious tone and the answers in an innocent tone. The children repeat. Then they practice in pairs.

Digital Resources

Reader eBook • For the Warmer, point to the young detectives and elicit their names.

- Show two pictures from the story at a time as you play the audio. Elicit predictions on what happens next and who took the cup.
- Have children use *Pen* to circle all the clues the young detectives find. Elicit what each clue is and who left it.

Reading Comprehension and Critical Literacy

Lesson objectives: recognize blurbs on the back cover of books; analyze clues to solve a mystery

Materials: Track 2.5; Reader; storybooks (four–five popular books in English and L1)

Note: Please ensure that your class has read the Reader story before you do this lesson.

Warmer: Characters

Write the story characters on the board without the vowels, e.g. *L_c_s.* The children write the names. Elicit answers and who each character is (in L1).

1))) 2.5 Read the story in your Reader.

- Have the children read the story. (Alternatively, play Track 2.5 and have them read along.) Ask *Where is the cup now?* (*in the school*)

I Can Read!

Show the children a storybook back cover. Have a child read the text or read it yourself. Explain that this is called a *blurb.* Ask *What's it for?* (They might need to use L1.)

Answer

Information about or introduction to the story.

2 Number. Whose things are these?

- Have the children look at the pictures and say what they can see. (*sweater, footprint, glasses*)
- They match the characters to the clues, writing the correct number by each picture. Elicit answers.

Answers

sweater 3, footprint 1, glasses 2

3 Who did you think took the cup? Circle. Then write their words.

- Ask the children to say the names of the characters in the picture.
- Encourage them to think about when they were reading the story, before they reached the end. Have them circle the character they thought took the cup. (You might need to use L1.)
- Then ask them to find the character's words in the story and copy them next to the picture. Monitor and help.
- Check answers. Encourage children to explain why they chose that character. (They might need to use L1.)

Answers

Children's own answer.
Mrs. Parker: "Look at their beautiful cup."
Josie: "I'm the winner!"
Robbie: "This cup is beautiful./I don't have any cups."
Perkins: "Hm. Nice cup."

4 Talk about the story.

- Ask the children if they thought this was a good mystery story.
- Have a child read Libby's question. Encourage the children to share stories about detectives and explain the plot briefly. (They might need to use L1.)

Optional activity: Which book is it?

Show the front covers and titles of other books. You can use a mixture of English and L1 books. Ask the children to copy the titles. Then invite children to read the blurbs to the class. The class match them to the titles. Elicit answers and check with the class.

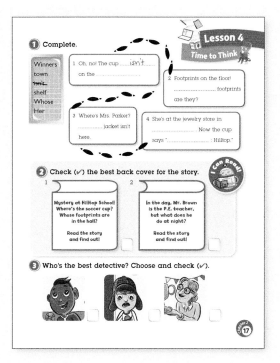

Read out statements from the story. The class repeats and calls out the name of the character who said it. Correct pronunciation and intonation if necessary.

Competency Focus

Me: Critical Literacy

The children use critical literacy skills to reflect on the story and think about clues that help them solve a mystery, giving their own opinions.

1 Complete.

Have the children complete the text from the story with the words supplied. Elicit answers and check with the class.

Answers

1 isn't, shelf 2 Whose 3 Her 4 town, Winners

2 Check (✔) the best back cover for the story.

The children practice the **I Can Read!** feature by reading the back covers and checking the best one for the story. Check answers.

Answer

1

3 Who's the best detective? Choose and check (✔).

Ask the children to decide who the best detective is. Elicit answers and reasons from the class.

Answer

Children's own answer.

Digital Resources

Reader eBook • Show the pictures from the story. Use this for a guided retelling of the story.

Student eBook, Digital Activity Book • TIP You can move the answer key pop-up window around the screen to have the activity and the answers side by side.

Vocabulary, Song, and Phonics

Lesson objectives: talk about school subjects; practice the clusters *sp* and *sc* with a chant

Key vocabulary: *art, computer studies, English, geography, history, math, P.E., recess, science, Spanish*

Secondary language: *clues, mysteries, solving, young*

Materials: Tracks 2.6 and 2.7; pictures for Key vocabulary (Warmer) ; Phonics Worksheet 2 [TRC printout] (optional)

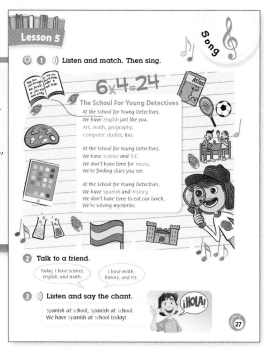

Warmer: A weekly timetable

Review the days of the week by saying them in order and stopping for the class to supply the next one. Pre-teach the new vocabulary using pictures you have brought in or in the Student Book, or do drawings on the board. Then show part of each picture to elicit the school subject.

1))) 2.6 Listen and match. Then sing.

- Ask the children to look and say what they can see in the pictures.(e.g. *a flag, numbers, a castle*)
- Play Track 2.6 and ask them to listen and point to the pictures as they hear the school subjects/recess.
- Give the children time to match the words to the pictures. Have them compare in pairs.
- Check as a class and point out that English, Spanish, and P.E. have capital letters. Explain that P.E. stands for Physical Education.
- Play Track 2.6 again and ask children to sing along and point to the correct picture when they hear a school subject/recess.

Answers

English—book, art—paints, math—equation, geography—atlas, computer studies—tablet screen, science—test tubes, P.E.—racket and soccer ball, recess—children outside, Spanish—flag, history—castle

2 Talk to a friend.

- Ask the children to take out their timetables or write the school subjects they have today in their notebook.
- Have two children read the example. In pairs, they practice with their real timetables.

3))) 2.7 Listen and say the chant.

- Ask the children to identify what language the boy in the picture is speaking. (*Spanish*)
- Play Track 2.7 and have the children listen to the chant.
- Play Track 2.7 again, pausing for them to repeat.
- Practice the chant a few times with the class. Focus on the pronunciation of *sp* and *sc*.

Optional activity: My dream timetable

Have the children draw a timetable. Then have them complete it with their favorite subjects. Monitor and help as necessary. In pairs, they talk about their weekly timetable, e.g. *On Friday, we have … ,* etc. Ask children to talk about their timetable.

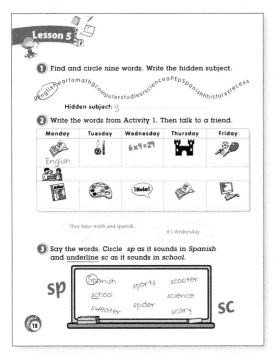

Cooler: Tongue twisters

Write the tongue twisters on the board and invite children to read them aloud. Have them practice in pairs and then as a class.

A spider in Spain looks at the stars in space.
We ski and skip at school.

Competency Focus

Think! Critical Thinking

By matching the words to the pictures, the children use critical thinking skills to identify school subjects and assimilate the written and spoken forms.

1 Find and circle nine words. Write the hidden subject.

Have the children find and circle the words in the wordsnake, then write the hidden subject using the letters they did not circle.

Answers

English, art, math, computer studies, science, P.E., Spanish, history, recess
Hidden subject: geography

2 Write the words from Activity 1. Then talk to a friend.

Have the children label the pictures using the Activity 1 words. In pairs, they take turns saying the subjects on a particular day to elicit the day.

Answers

Monday: English, geography
Tuesday: science, art
Wednesday: math, Spanish
Thursday: history, English
Friday: P.E., computer studies
All days: recess

3 Say the words. Circle *sp* as it sounds in *Spanish* and underline *sc* as it sounds in *school*.

Have the children circle *sp* and underline *sc* in the words. Elicit answers and check with the class.

Answers

Circled: **sp** in **Sp**anish, **sp**orts, **sp**ider
Underlined: **sc** in **sc**hool, **sc**ooter, **sc**ary

Digital Resources

Student eBook • Play ASL Vocabulary Video 2.4 to pre-teach key vocabulary, pausing for the children to repeat the word and copy the sign.

• Play Music Video 2.2 (2.3). Encourage the class to dance and sing along. Linking movements with words makes them more memorable. The lyrics appear on screen for support.

Teacher Resource Center • For phonics practice, print out Phonics Worksheet 2.

Grammar and Reading

Lesson objectives: ask and answer who objects belong to
Key grammar: *It's (Libby)'s pencil. It's (Tom)'s notebook.*
Secondary language: *arm, mess, Ouch!, trip*
Materials: Tracks 2.6 and 2.8; a selection of school objects and a tray (optional); Grammar Worksheet 2B [TRC printout] (optional)

Warmer: Stand up song

))) **2.6**

Divide the class into four groups. Allocate two items of key vocabulary from Lesson 5 to each group (e.g. *P.E., recess,* etc.). Play Track 2.6. The class sing along, with each group standing up and sitting down again quickly when they hear one of their words.

1))) 2.8 Listen and read.

- Ask the children to close their books. Write *school trip* on the board. Explain that Libby is taking Ellie and Tom on a school trip. Invite the class to guess where. (They might need to use L1.)

- Then ask them to open their books and find out. (*museum*) Play Track 2.8 and have them listen and read along.

- Have them look at picture 2 and read out the checklist. Ask *What do the children need for the trip?* (*a notebook and pencil, a lunch box and a water bottle, a jacket*) Invite them to explain what they need the notebook and pencil for. (*to write down new things they learn*)

Grammar Central

It's Libby's pencil. ...

Have the children read the sentences. Explain that we put a name/person with *'s* before an object to say that it's his/hers/theirs. Give an example with a child's name and write it on the board. Say the sentences and have them repeat, pronouncing the *'s* clearly.

For extra practice, try the **Grammar Booster** section in the Student Book (p. 33–35).

Answers p. 33

Activity 1: **1** It's **2** They're **3** 's **4** 's

Activity 2: **1** It's Mariam's. **2** It's Connor's **3** They're Jane's **4** It's Jimmy's

p. 34

Activity 1: **1** b **2** e **3** a **4** d **5** e

Activity 2: **1** They're Emma's sneakers. **2** It's Emma's cap. **3** Whose sweater is this? **4** They're Matt's glasses. **5** Whose book is this?

p. 35

Activity 1: **1** my **2** my **3** our **4** my **5** your **6** 's

Activity 2: **1** It's Terry's bag. **2** Whose, It's Marie's violin. **3** are these, They're David's sneakers. **4** Whose glasses are these? They're Agatha's glasses. **5** Whose doll is this? It's Emily's doll.

2 Look at the story again. Answer.

- Ask the children to look at pictures 3, 4, and 5 and say what Libby is holding. (*a lunch box, a jacket, an arm*)

- Have the children read the example question and answer. Give them time to write the answers for the other two questions.

- Have them compare answers in pairs before you check as a class.

Answers

1 It's Tom's lunch box. **2** It's Ellie's jacket. **3** It's Biblio's arm.

Optional activity: Play "Kim's Game"

Put a selection of school objects on a tray. Give the class 30 seconds to study them. Take the tray away or cover it. The children say the objects. Repeat several times.

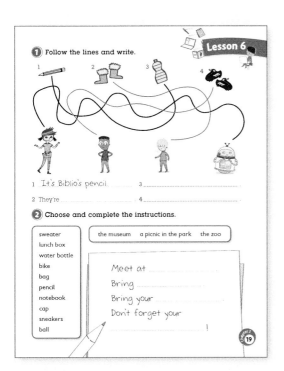

2 Choose and complete the instructions.

Have the children complete their invitation using some of the words in the boxes. Then have them read their invitations in pairs or small groups.

Answers

Children's own answers.

Cooler: School subjects survey

Ask *Is history your favorite subject?* (*Yes, it is./No, it isn't.*) Ask the children to write two more questions about different subjects. Then have them ask their friends and write *yes/no* or ☺/☹ next to each question. They then share their findings. (e.g. *Math is/isn't (Anna)'s favorite subject.*)

Competency Focus

Learn

The children demonstrate their understanding of the new grammatical patterns by looking at the story and completing the activity.

1 Follow the lines and write.

Ask the children to follow the lines from the objects to the characters and write sentences. Elicit answers and check with the class.

Answers

1 It's Biblio's pencil. **2** They're Ellie's boots.
3 It's Libby's water bottle. **4** They're Tom's sneakers.

Digital Resources

Student eBook • Display the SB page on the board. Read through the Story Central story one picture at a time,. Ask questions to check comprehension as you go.

- To give feedback on SB Activity 2, ask children to write in the answers using *Pen*, then use the answer key to confirm.

Teacher Resource Center • For extra grammar practice, print out Grammar Worksheet 2B.

CLIL: Math—Numbers to 100; Measuring our bodies

Lesson objectives: practice numbers up to 100; measure height and hand spans; use meters and centimeters

Materials: Tracks 2.9 and 2.10; CLIL Graphic Organizer 2 [TRC printout] (optional); numbers 1–20 on papers, sticky tape (Warmer); tape measure/height wall chart, ruler(s)

CLIL Math **Lesson 7**

1)) **Listen and read. Then match.**

Let's Measure Our Bodies!
There are one hundred centimeters in a meter. Can you count to 100?

ten   eighty   twenty   forty   seventy

0 10 20 30 40 50 60 70 80 90 100

thirty   fifty   one hundred   sixty   ninety

2)) **Listen and write the numbers.**

twenty-three	23	fifty-one		eighty-nine	
thirty-five		sixty-eight		ninety-six	
forty-seven		seventy-two	

3 **Now measure your hand and your body.**

My Hand
How big is your hand?
My hand is .... centimeters.

My Body
How tall are you?
I am 1 meter and .... centimeters.

4 **Class Vote!**
Measuring is fun. Yes or no?

Find Out More!
How tall is the tallest man? How big are his hands and feet? Search the Internet or ask your teacher.

29

Warmer: Numbers 1–20 revision

Write the numbers 1–20 on separate pieces of paper and hide them around the classroom before the lesson. When the children come in, ask them to look for the numbers and stick them on the board in order. Drill the numbers in order.

1)) 2.9 Listen and read. Then match.

- Ask the children to look at the picture. Pre-teach *meter* and *centimeter*.

- Play Track 2.9 and have the children listen and point to the numbers as they hear them. Then have them match the numbers with the words. Elicit answers.

- In pairs, they take turns pointing to and saying a number.

2)) 2.10 Listen and write the numbers.

- Play Track 2.10. The children listen and write the numbers. Elicit answers.

Answers

23, 35, 47, 51, 68, 72, 89, 96

Optional activity: Number line

Invite eight children to the front of the class and give each one of the eight answers to remember (*51, 89,* etc.). Have them tell each other their numbers and position themselves in a line from the lowest number to the highest. (*23, 35, 47, 51, 68, 72, 89, 96*) Repeat with different children and numbering.

3 Now measure your hand and your body.

- Show the tape measure and/or height chart and pre-teach *measure*. Demonstrate measuring a child's height. Have a child measure your height in preparation for Activity Book Activity 3.

- Draw the outline of your hand on a piece of paper. Then draw a line using a ruler from top of the middle finger to the wrist. Say how long your hand is, e.g. *My hand is (15) centimeters.*

- Give each child a piece of paper. Have the children draw/measure their hands and complete the sentence. Ask them to write their names on the sheets and collect them for later use.

- Measure the children's height. Ask them to complete Activity 3.

Answers

Children's own answers.

4 Class Vote!

- Organize your class vote. Ask children if they think measuring is fun. Give them a minute to think. Then write *Yes* and *No* on the board. Have the children raise their hand for each answer. Count the votes and write the totals on the board. Elicit the result of the vote.

Find Out More!

Ask the children to find out who the tallest man is and how big his hands and feet are. Suggest appropriate resources, e.g. Internet, library books, etc., or provide the information yourself. The children will need to complete this research before doing the follow-up activity in the Activity Book. (It can be set as homework if you are planning to move on to the Activity Book in the next lesson.)

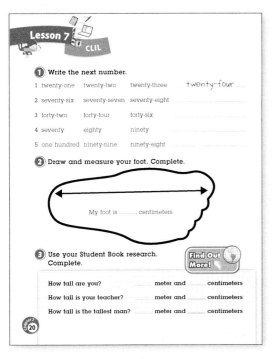

1 Write the next number.

Have the children write the next number in each sequence. Elicit answers and check with the class.

Answers

1 twenty-four **2** seventy-nine **3** forty-eight **4** one hundred **5** ninety-seven

2 Draw and measure your foot. Complete.

Ask the children to measure their foot using a ruler. Then have them complete the sentence. Ask children to read their answer. Find out who has the smallest/biggest foot in the class.

Answer

Children's own answers.

3 Use your Student Book research. Complete.

Ask the children to answer the first two questions. Use a tape measure in class to help them find the answers. Then have them share what they found out for the last question.

Answers

Children's own answers.

Cooler: 13 or 30?

Divide the board in two and give each section a heading: –*teen* and –*ty*. Call out numbers between 13 and 19, and from the set 20, 30, 40, etc., in random order for children to write on the board. Then invite children to point to a number for the class to say.

Competency Focus

Act

The children carry out research to find out about the tallest man in the world. This helps them expand their learning and relate it to their world, both inside and outside the classroom.

Digital Resources

Student eBook • Use *Pen* to practice numbers. Call out random numbers between 1 and 100 for children to write. Ask children to say numbers as prompts.

• TIP You can set a time limit using *Timer* to make any activity more competitive and fun. Use it here for SB Activity 2.

Teacher Resource Center • Print out CLIL Graphic Organizer 2 for the children to use in collating their Find Out More! research.

CLIL eBook • The children can use the CLIL eBook to expand their knowledge of the lesson topic.

Project

Lesson objectives: review language from Chapter 2; complete a craft project—making a cup; act out the story from the Reader

Materials: Reader; scissors, glue, paintbrush, yellow paint, yellow paper, a big and a small plastic cup, streamers; props for acting, e.g. ruler, drawing of footprint, sweater, glasses

Warmer: Story recap

Ask the children to look at the story in their Reader and find the two words written on the school cup. Ask *Who won the cup? (Hilltop School) Why did they win the cup? (for soccer)*

Prepare

1 Make a cup.

- Have the children look at the completed cups. Tell them they are going to make their own cup.
- Hold up the materials to show the class. Point to the pictures and explain the stages. (You might need to use L1.)
- Demonstrate how to make a cup, stage by stage.
- Divide the class into pairs or groups if it is necessary to share materials. Give out the materials.
- As the children make their cups, monitor and give help as necessary.

Alternative craft activity

A simpler option would be to have the children draw a cup on cardboard paper, decorate it, and cut it out. They can hold the cup from the handles the same way.

Showcase

2 Tell the story. Use your cups.

- Divide the class into groups. Ask the children to look at the story again. Allocate parts of the story to groups, assigning children two or three shorter roles (e.g. a child can act out the role of Mr. Brown, Perkins, and the jeweler).
- Give them time to practice the story. Walk around, monitor, and give help with pronunciation and intonation.
- Encourage them to use other props, e.g. a ruler, a pair of glasses, a sweater, etc.
- Call out groups to the front of the class to perform.

Optional activity: Class quiz

Divide the class into small groups. Ask them a question about the story. They have one chance to answer it. If they are wrong, it is the next group's turn. If they are correct, they lift the cup and say *We're the winners!*

1 Play "It's My Pen."

Help the children prepare their cards, following the instructions. Then have them play in groups. They shuffle and distribute their cards in their group so every child has a card from each person in their group—four in total. Demonstrate the game. Then have the children play, taking turns to show a card and start the dialogue.

Cooler: Whose cup is this?

Ask the children to hold up their cups. Walk around the classroom pointing to cups and asking *Whose cup is this?* (*It's (Carmen)'s cup.*)

Competency Focus
Collaborate and Communicate

By acting out the story, the children consolidate their understanding in a fun and engaging way. They also demonstrate their ability to work with friends and use interpersonal skills.

Digital Resources

Student eBook • TIP Show the Prepare photos, stage by stage, as you talk the class through the activity process.

Language Review

Lesson objective: review language from Chapter 2
Materials: Tracks 2.11, AB 2.1 and AB 2.2, 3 x3 Bingo grids (Warmer—optional)

Warmer: Play "Bingo!"

Play the game with numbers 20–40,
then 40–70, then 80–100 (see Games Bank p. 222).

1 Look and circle T (true) or F (false).

- Ask the children to look at the picture. Have them call out the people. Draw their attention to the different objects (sweater, sneakers, caps, etc.) by asking *Who's wearing sneakers?* (*Robert*)
- Give them time to read the sentences and refer to the picture before choosing true or false.
- Elicit answers and check with the class. Ask children to correct the false sentences.

Answers

1 F 2 T 3 T 4 F 5 F

2 2.11 Listen and write.

- Ask a child to read the days in the timetable and the school subjects. Brainstorm the rest of the school subjects.
- Play Track 2.11 and have the children listen and complete the timetable.
- Play Track 2.11 again for the children to check their answers.
- Have the children compare answers in pairs. Then check as a class.

Audioscript

On Monday, we have Spanish and art, then recess. On Tuesday, we don't have geography. We have history and computer studies, then lunch. On Wednesday, we have P.E. and math, then English. We don't have science.

Answers

Monday: art
Tuesday: history
Wednesday: English

3 Think about Chapter 2. Color the books.

- Have the children look back at Chapter 2. Elicit their favorite parts. The children then color the book which represents how they feel about their own progress (self-evaluation).

Treasure Hunt!

Ask the children to look at Student Book pp. 4–5 and find Tom's lunch box. Have the children raise their hand when they find it.

Cooler: I can't see it!

Have children come to the front of the class and close their eyes. Place an object that belongs to another child in their hands. Have them say what they think the object is and then say who they think it belongs to. (e.g. *It's a book. It's Jane's book.*) Then have the class say if they are correct or not. The children continue in small groups or pairs.

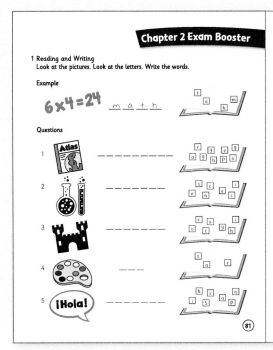

1 Reading and Writing. Look at the pictures. Look at the letters. Write the words.

Have the children write the words. Check answers.

Answers

1 geography **2** science **3** history **4** art **5** Spanish

2))) AB 2.1 Listening. Read the question. Listen and write a name or a number. There are two examples.

Play Track AB 2.1. Children write a name or number. .

Answers (Audioscript on p. 222)

1 Dan's **2** seven **3** Wilson **4** Old **5** 150

3))) AB 2.2 Listening. Read the question. Listen and write a name or a number. There are two examples.

Give the children time to read the questions. They then listen and write a name or number for each one. Play Track AB 2.2 twice, then check answers.

Answers (Audioscript on p. 222)

1 Pat **2** Tony **3** 65 **4** Newton **5** 11

Competency Focus

Me: Self-evaluation

The children reflect on the chapter and express their opinions about their own progress. This encourages them to evaluate and make decisions about how they learn and what they need to revisit.

Digital Resources

Teacher Resource Center • Print out Test Chapter 2 to use at the end of this lesson. The Test Generator also allows you to create customized tests.

• Print out Festival Worksheet: Teacher's Day to expand the children's knowledge of US culture.

chapter 3

What's the Weather Like?
Overview

The children will:

- use critical thinking skills to identify clothes.
- ask and answer questions about what people are wearing.
- read, understand, and act out a story.
- talk about the weather.
- ask and answer requests in a polite way.
- find out about seasons and weather around the world.
- make a crown.

Key Vocabulary

Clothes: boots, dress, jeans, pants, shirt, shoes, shorts, skirt, T-shirt
Weather: cloudy, cold, cool, hot, raining, snowing, sunny, wet, windy

Key Grammar

- What's she wearing? She's wearing (a coat). She isn't wearing (shorts).
- Can you (open the window), please? Yes, I can. / Sorry, I can't.

Reading Skills

Story: *The Emperor's New Clothes*
Genre: fairy tale

Literacy Development

- predict story content from title and pictures
- notice when new lines start in a story
- analyze characters' behavior, personality, and feelings

Functional Language

- What's the weather like?
- It's cold and windy.

Phonics

The children practice pronunciation of *w* as in *wet* and *v* sound as in *very*.

CLIL: Geography—World weather and seasons

The children find out about the weather and seasons in other countries.

Competency Focus

The children will:

use critical thinking skills to identify clothes. (Lesson 1)

predict the content of a story. (Lesson 3)

ask about and describe the weather. (Lesson 5)

apply new grammar to previously learned vocabulary. (Lesson 2)

make requests and respond politely. (Lesson 6)

work in pairs to act out a dialogue. (Lesson 3)

work in groups to act out the story. (Lesson 8)

personalize their response to the story by thinking of their own behavior and decisions, and the consequences. (Lesson 4)

evaluate their own progress in the chapter. (Review)

find out more about weather in a country of their choice. (Lesson 7)

Digital Overview

Teacher Presentation

Student eBook and Digital Activity Book

- ASL Vocabulary Video 3.1: Clothes
- ASL Vocabulary Video 3.3: Weather
- Oral Storytelling Video 3.2: *The Emperor's New Clothes*
- Interactive versions of AB activities
- Integrated audio and answer key for all activities

Teacher resources for planning, lesson delivery, and homework

Teacher Resource Center

- Class Planner Chapter 3
- Worksheets to print out (including notes and answers):
    - Grammar Worksheet 3A: What's she wearing? She's wearing ...
    - Grammar Worksheet 3B: Can you ..., please? Yes/Sorry, ...
    - Oral Storytelling Video Worksheet 3: *The Emperor's New Clothes*
    - Phonics Worksheet 3
    - CLIL Graphic Organizer 3
    - Project Template 3
    - Festival Worksheet: Christmas
    - Test Chapter 3
- Test Generator
- Speaking Assessment: Cambridge English Young Learners Exams

Watch the Oral Storytelling Video

- Literacy Handbook

Student resources for consolidation and practice at home

Student e-Book

- ASL Vocabulary Video 3.1: Clothes
- ASL Vocabulary Video 3.3: Weather

Student eBook and Reader eBook

- Oral Storytelling Video 3.2: *The Emperor's New Clothes*

***The Inks* Student's App**

Vocabulary games: Clothes and weather

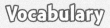

Chapter 3

What's the Weather Like?

Lesson 1

Vocabulary

Lesson objective: identify clothes
Key vocabulary: *boots, dress, jeans, pants, shirt, shoes, shorts, skirt, T-shirt*
Materials: Track 3.1

Warmer: Guess the clothing

Draw a T-shirt slowly on the board and ask *What is it?* Repeat with other items of clothing. Allow the children to guess in L1. Choose children to find a friend in class wearing one of the items.

1))) 3.1 Listen and number. Then say.

- Have the children open their books and say what they can see in the picture. Give them time to study the clothes.

- Play Track 3.1 and have them listen and number the characters in order depending on the clothes they are wearing. Then play Track 3.1 again, pausing for the children to repeat. Tell them to compare answers.

- Describe them in short sentences, e.g. *They're yellow. We wear them on our feet.*, and do a mime (e.g. putting on your boots). Ask the children to indicate the correct picture and help them say the word. (*boots*)

- Ask the children to think of a name for each character in the game and have them say what clothes each character has, e.g. *Anna has a pink skirt.* Monitor and ensure that they use the article *a* with the singular but not the plural words.

Audioscript

Girl: Look at this game! It's fun. Do you like this girl's clothes?
Girl on computer: I have a dress and shoes.
Narrator: 1
Girl: Look at this girl. She has a sweater, a skirt, and boots.
Narrator: 2
Girl: This boy has pants and a shirt.
Narrator: 3
Girl: This girl has a jacket, jeans, and shoes.
Narrator: 4
Girl: And this boy has a T-shirt, shorts, and a cap.

Answers

2, 1, 4, 3

Optional activity: Do you remember my clothes?

Have the children draw themselves wearing four clothing items. In pairs, they look at each other's pictures, then cover their pictures and take turns saying sentences, e.g. *I have shoes.* Their friend responds *Yes, you have shoes. / No, you don't have boots.*

Competency Focus

Think! Critical Thinking

The children use critical thinking skills to identify clothes by using visual clues and processing the written and spoken forms.

1 Find and circle. Write.

Have the children find and circle the clothes words in the wordsearch. Then they label the pictures. Check answers.

Answers

Horizontal: T-shirt, boots, jeans, skirt, pants
Vertical: dress, shorts, shirt, shoes

1 dress **2** T-shirt **3** boots **4** skirt **5** shirt **6** pants **7** jeans **8** shoes **9** shorts

2 Write the words from Activity 1 in three groups.

Have the children write the words in the correct group. Elicit answers and check with the class.

Answers

top of body: T-shirt, shirt
bottom of body: pants, jeans, skirt, boots, shorts, shoes
both: dress

Cooler: Play "Spelling Bee"

Play the game with words from the lesson (see Games Bank p. 222).

Digital Resources

Student eBook • Play ASL Vocabulary Video 3.1 to pre-teach key vocabulary as an alternative to the critical thinking approach.

• Say the items of clothing in SB Activity 1. Children use *Pen* to circle them on the people in the pictures.

Digital Activity Book • TIP The interactive activities in the AB can be done again and again, giving different children the chance to participate.

• Use *Add personal note* to keep the team scores in the Cooler game.

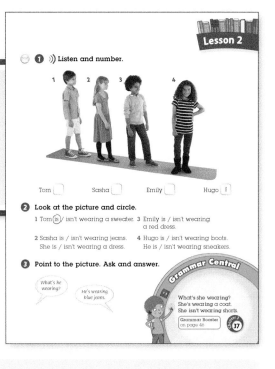

Grammar

Lesson objectives: ask and answer questions about what people are wearing

Key grammar: *What's she wearing? She's wearing (a coat). She isn't wearing (shorts).*

Materials: Track 3.2; Grammar Worksheet 3A [TRC printout] (optional)

Warmer: Our clothes

Invite a child to the front and say false sentences about their clothes, e.g. *(Pablo) has shorts. (He) doesn't have boots.* The class disagree explaining why, e.g. *No, he has jeans. No, he has sneakers.* Repeat with different children.

1))) 3.2 Listen and number.

- Tell the children to look at the picture. Point and ask *What's he/she wearing?* Elicit answers.

- Play Track 3.2 and have them listen and number the names. Play Track 3.2 again for them to check.

- Elicit answers by asking, e.g. *Who's Tom? (number 3)*

Audioscript

Mom: Look at Tom. What's he wearing?
Boy: Tom is wearing jeans and a sweater. He's wearing blue shoes.
Mom: What's Sasha wearing?
Boy: Sasha isn't wearing jeans. She's wearing a pink dress. She's wearing gray shoes.
Mom: Now, Emily. What's she wearing?
Boy: Emily is wearing red jeans and she's wearing black boots.
Mom: Here's Hugo. What's he wearing?
Boy: He isn't wearing pants. He's wearing yellow shorts and a blue shirt. He's wearing blue sneakers.

Answers

Tom 3, Sasha 2, Emily 4, Hugo 1

Grammar Central

What's she wearing? …

Have children read the question and sentences aloud. Explain that we use *What's he/she wearing?* and *He/She is/isn't wearing …* to ask and answer about clothes people are wearing right now. Divide the class into pairs and have them talk about other pairs.

For extra practice, try the **Grammar Booster** section in the Student Book (p. 46).

Answers p. 46

Activity 1: **1** wearing **2** isn't **3** What's **4** She's **5** wearing

Activity 2: **1** Robert **2** Lisa **3** Rita

Activity 3: Children's own answers.

2 Look at the picture and circle.

- Have a child read the example. Ask *What's Tom wearing? (He's wearing jeans/a sweater/shoes.)*

- Then have them look and circle *is/isn't* accordingly.

- Ask them to compare answers with a friend before you check as a class.

Answers

1 is **2** isn't, is **3** isn't **4** isn't, is

3 Point to the picture. Ask and answer.

- Choose two children to read the model question and answer. Invite a different pair to talk about another child in Activity 1.

- Divide your class into pairs. Have them take turns pointing and asking, and answering about the children's clothes. Monitor the response, making sure they say the color before the clothing object.

Optional activity: Our clothes!

Divide the class into small groups. Have them take turns asking about children in the class, e.g. *What's (Juan) wearing?* The children in the group give an answer each, e.g. *(He)'s wearing (green pants). (He) isn't wearing (a white T-shirt).*

Ask the children to look at the picture in Activity 1 for 30 seconds, then have them close their books. Ask questions, e.g. *What's (Sasha) wearing? (She's wearing a pink dress.)* or say sentences, e.g. *Sasha isn't wearing (a brown dress). (No, she's wearing a pink dress.)*

Competency Focus

Learn

By identifying people's clothes in a different context with new grammatical structures, the children demonstrate their understanding of previously acquired vocabulary from Lesson 1.

1 Read and match.

Ask the children to read the text and match the names to the people. Elicit answers and check with the class.

Answers

Max b, Annie e, Peter a, Sally d, Jane c

2 Look at the picture and complete with *is wearing* or *isn't wearing*.

Have the children look at the pictures and complete the sentences. Ask children to read a sentence for the class.

Answers

1 is wearing **2** is wearing **3** isn't wearing **4** isn't wearing **5** is wearing

Digital Resources

Digital Activity Book • Have the children do the AB interactive digital activities or set them for homework.

Teacher Resource Center • For extra grammar practice, print out Grammar Worksheet 3A.

Reading: Story Extract

Lesson objectives: talk about the weather; use the title and pictures to predict story content; read the extract from *The Emperor's New Clothes* (start)

Functional language: *What's the weather like? It's cold and windy.*

Secondary language: *dressmakers, emperor, servant, silly, suit*

Materials: Tracks 3.3 and 3.4

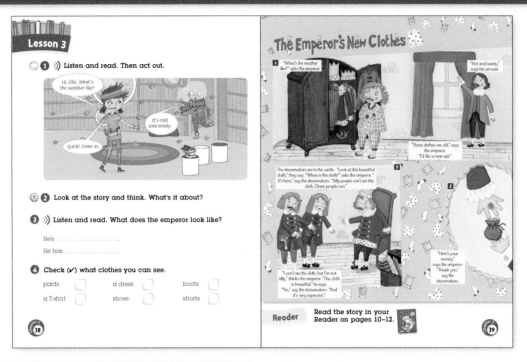

Warmer: Who is it?

Describe a child in the class saying, e.g. *She isn't wearing a black T-shirt. She's wearing a yellow T-shirt. Who is it?* Invite the children to say who it is. Encourage individuals to describe a different child for the class to guess.

Functional language

1))) 3.3 Listen and read. Then act out.

- Ask the children to look at the picture and point to a coat, a scarf, jeans, boots (Ellie), and sneakers (Libby). Then ask about the colors of the clothes, e.g. *What color coat is Ellie wearing?* (brown)

- Play Track 3.3. The children listen and read. Say *It's hot and windy, right?* to elicit *No! It's cold and windy!*

- Play Track 3.3 again, pausing for the children to repeat and mime. Choose two children to act out the dialogue. Then divide your class into pairs to act out.

Before reading

2 Look at the story and think. What's it about?

- Point to and read the title of the story. Elicit that an emperor is like a king.

- Have the children look at the pictures. Point to the dressmakers and ask *Who are they?* Point to the money and ask *Why do they get money?* (*They make clothes.*) Ask *What's the story about?* (*new clothes for the emperor*)

3))) 3.4 Listen and read. What does the emperor look like?

- Play Track 3.4 and have the children listen and read along.

- Ask *What does the emperor look like?* Elicit ideas, e.g. *He's short. He has a moustache.* Have the children complete the sentences about the emperor, then compare with a friend. Elicit answers.

- Play Track 3.4 again, pausing after the first picture and asking *Why does the emperor want new clothes?* (*His clothes are old.*) Pause again after the second picture and ask *What is the dressmaker holding?* (*nothing*) *What does the emperor buy?* (*nothing*) (You might need to use L1.)

Answers

He's short/big. He has gray hair/curly hair/a mustache.

4 Check (✔) what clothes you can see.

- Choose a child to read the list of words. Have the children look at the pictures and check the clothes they can see.

- Elicit answers and check with the class.

Answers

pants, shoes, boots

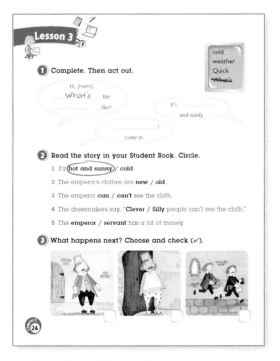

1 Complete. Then act out.

Have the children complete the dialogue. Then have them practice it in pairs. Ask pairs to act out for the class.

Answers

What's, weather; cold; Quick

2 Read the story in your Student Book. Circle.

Have the children look at the story extract again and complete the sentences by circling the correct words. Elicit answers and check with the class.

Answers

1 hot and sunny **2** old **3** can't **4** Silly **5** emperor

3 What happens next? Choose and check (✔).

Ask the children to guess what happens next in the story, choosing one of the three picture options. Have them compare their answer in pairs. Elicit answers and ideas from the class.

Answers

Children's own answers.

Cooler: I'm a dressmaker!

Have the children pretend to be dressmakers. Working in pairs, they write a description of the beautiful new clothes they can make the emperor. Elicit ideas.

Competency Focus

Collaborate and Communicate

The children work together, putting into practice new functional language by acting out a realistic dialogue.

Think! Critical Thinking

By looking at the story artwork, the children use prediction skills to help them engage with the story.

Digital Resources

Student eBook, Digital Activity Book • Do not be afraid to turn off the screen! Children benefit from variety and sometimes you will want to work just with books or without prompts. Use the digital material in the way that suits you best.

Digital Activity Book • Show each of the AB Activity 3 pictures. Elicit a simple description of what happens next using the picture.

Lesson objective: read and understand the fairy tale
The Emperor's New Clothes in the Reader
Materials: Track 3.5; Reader; Oral Storytelling Video Worksheet 3 [TRC] (optional)

Warmer: Story review

Have the children look at the story pictures in the Reader and describe what the characters are wearing. Ask *Do people wear clothes like these today?*

Story Summary

Dressmakers tell the emperor that silly people cannot see the beautiful suits they make. The emperor says he can see the suit so that he appears clever. He puts on the "suit" and everyone pretends to see it but one young boy tells the truth. There is no suit—the emperor is in his underwear! The emperor is very embarrassed.

Value: It's important to think critically.

))) 3.5 While reading

- Ask the children to look at *The Emperor's New Clothes* in their Reader. Give them time to study the pictures carefully.

- Ask *How many times do the dressmakers get money?* (*three*)

- Play Track 3.5 and have the children listen and read along.

- Check comprehension of the story by asking *What does the emperor think he's wearing when he goes out?* (*new pants and a jacket*) *Is his new suit real?* (*no*) *Why don't the people and the servant tell the emperor the truth?* (*They're silly or afraid to be honest.*) (L1 will be necessary.)

- Play Track 3.5 again, pausing to have the children repeat the characters' lines, copying their tone of voice. Encourage them to mime, too, e.g. *Here's your money. I'm a little cold, but I like it.*, etc.

After reading: Reflect

- Ask *Who did the right thing in the story? The emperor? The dressmakers? The people? The boy? Why?* Elicit ideas.

Optional activity: Oops! I made a mistake.

Read the story aloud and have the children follow in their Reader. Tell them you might make mistakes. Ask them to raise their hand when this happens. As you read, change words, e.g. *Arms? 85 centimeters.* Elicit corrections.

Avoid explaining words

Children enjoy reading stories and looking at pictures. Help them focus on meaning and general comprehension rather than teaching isolated vocabulary—it might take the magic of the story away.

Reading Strategy

Anticipation Guide

Anticipating what will happen helps children engage with the story and the characters by using their own knowledge to predict the plot. It also prepares them to analyze the story and answer "while reading" and "after reading" comprehension questions.

For additional explanation and activities, see the Literacy Handbook on Teacher Resource Center.

Cooler: I'm a dressmaker

Invite three pairs of children to the front. In each pair, one is the dressmaker and the other is the emperor. The dressmakers measure the emperor's arm, leg, and body. They say, e.g. *Arms?* The class responds, e.g. *80 centimeters!*

Digital Resources

Reader eBook • Show Reader Picture 8. Ask *What's happening to the emperor?* to elicit a description and story predictions in L1.

• Watch Oral Storytelling Video 3.2 together before you do the After reading: Reflect activity.

Teacher Resource Center • Print out Oral Storytelling Video Worksheet 3 to help you get the most out of the video.

Reading Comprehension and Critical Literacy

Lesson objectives: notice when new lines start in a story; analyze characters' behavior, personality, and feelings

Materials: Track 3.6; Reader; Oral Storytelling Video Worksheet 3 [TRC printout] (optional)

Lesson 4 Time to Think

I Can Read!
When do we start a new line in the story?

1))) Read the story in your Reader on pages 10-12 again.

2 Who is clever? Who is silly? Write *clever* or *silly*.

3 Check (✔) what you learned from the story.
- Think for yourself.
- Wear new clothes.
- Emperors are clever.

4 Talk about the story.

Do you know another story about clothes?

40

Note: Please ensure that your class has read the Reader story before you do this lesson.

Warmer: Clap or stand!

Ask the children to look at the story pictures. Point to pictures and say a few true/false sentences e.g. *There's a dress in the picture.* If it is true the children clap. If it is false, have them stand up and correct it.

1))) 3.6 Read the story in your Reader.

- Have the children read the story. (Alternatively, play Track 3.6 and have them read along.) Ask *Why are the people laughing in the end?* (*The emperor isn't wearing a suit.*) *Why is the emperor's face red?* (*He's angry and embarrassed.*) (You will need L1.)

I Can Read!

Ask the children to look at the story and notice when new lines start. Elicit that a new line starts when a different character speaks. Have the children close their books. Write a few lines from the story on the board as continuous text. Ask them to tell you where new lines should start.

Answer

When a different character speaks.

2 Who is clever? Who is silly? Write *clever* or *silly*.

- Explain *clever* and *silly* again if necessary.

- Have the children look at the pictures and say who the story characters are. (*people, emperor, dressmakers*) Have the children write *clever* or *silly* under each picture.

- Check answers and encourage them to find more clever and silly people. (*clever: the boy, silly: the servants*)

Answers

people—silly (then clever), emperor—silly, dressmakers—clever

3 Check (✔) what you learned from the story.

- Have the children say how some characters in the story were silly. (*They believed what the dressmakers said.*)

- Ask them to check the message of the story. Elicit the answers. Ask why this is important. (*Some people tell lies and play tricks on us.*) (You might need to use L1.)

Answer

Think for yourself.

4 Talk about the story.

- Ask the children if they liked the story and why/why not.

- Have a child read Libby's question. Invite children to share other stories about clothes. It could be a story they read in a book or a personal story.

Optional activity: My favorite character

Ask the children to choose and draw their favorite character in the story. Have them write a short sentence explaining why they like the character, e.g. *I like (the boy) because (he is clever)*. Walk around, checking and admiring their work.

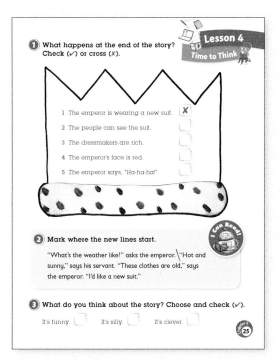

Cooler: I like the story!

Ask the children to choose their favorite picture from the story. Have them compare answers in small groups. Ask them to underline their favorite word and sentence. Have them compare answers again. Then invite children to show their favorite picture, word, and sentence.

Competency Focus

Me: Critical Literacy

The children use critical literacy skills to reflect on the story and think about what it meant to them.

1 What happens at the end of the story? Check (✔) or cross (✗).

Ask the children to say how the story ends. Then have them read the sentences and write a check or a cross in each box. Elicit answers and check with the class.

Answers

1 ✗ 2 ✗ 3 ✔ 4 ✔ 5 ✗

2 Mark where the new lines start.

The children practice the **I Can Read!** feature. Have them say when a new line starts. Then ask them to draw one more line in the text. Elicit answers.

Answers

Line after "servant."

3 What do you think about the story? Choose and check (✔).

Tell the children to choose one of the three opinions. Ask children to say which they chose and why.

Answers

Children's own answers.

Digital Resources

Digital Activity Book • Use the AB page to give feedback on activities, using the built-in interactive activity or the answer key, as appropriate.

Student eBook, Reader eBook • If you haven't already, show Oral Storytelling Video 3.2.

Student eBook, Digital Activity Book • TIP Give the children the opportunity to be your assistant! Ask a child to be responsible for choosing the relevant buttons.

Teacher Resource Center • If you haven't already, print out Oral Storytelling Video Worksheet 3 to do the support activities.

Vocabulary, Song, and Phonics

Lesson objectives: describe the weather, practice the sounds *v* and *w* with a chant

Key vocabulary: *cloudy, cold, cool, hot, raining, snowing, sunny, wet, windy*

Secondary language: *What's the weather like today? Is it (sunny)?*

Materials: Tracks 3.7 and 3.8; pictures for Key vocabulary (Warmer) ; Phonics Worksheet 3 [TRC printout] (optional)

Warmer: Favorite weather

Pre-teach the new vocabulary using pictures and mimes. Have a class vote on the favorite type of weather: say each weather word and have the children raise their hand. Keep a tally. Then ask *What's the weather like today?* to elicit today's weather.

1)) 3.7 Listen and number. Then sing.

- Have the children look at the picture and ask *What's the emperor doing?* (*looking at the weather*) *What's he wearing?* (*pajamas, slippers, and his crown*)
- Agree on mimes for the weather words, e.g. draw a big circle with your arms for *sunny*, wave an imaginary fan for *hot*, hold an imaginary umbrella for *raining*, etc. Say the words for the children to mime and repeat.
- Play Track 3.7 and have the children listen. Then they match the words to the pictures. Elicit answers.
- Play Track 3.7 again and have the class sing along and mime.

Answers

1 snowing 2 cold 3 sunny 4 hot 5 raining/wet 6 cool
7 wet/raining 8 cloudy 9 windy

2 Talk to a friend.

- Choose two children to read the example question and answer.
- Then divide your class into pairs. Have them take turns asking the question and pointing to a picture in Activity 1, and answering. Monitor and help if necessary.

3)) 3.8 Listen and say the chant.

- Ask *What's the weather like in the picture?* (*windy and wet*)
- Play Track 3.8 and have the children listen to the chant. Then play Track 3.8 again, pausing for them to repeat.
- Practice the chant a few times with the class. Focus on the pronunciation of *w* and *v*. Show them the position of the lips for *w* and how the upper teeth rest on the lower lip for *v*. Practice saying more words with *w* (*weather, where, what*) and *v* (*every, clever, expensive*).

Optional activity: Mime the weather

Invite a child to the front and show them a weather word. Ask *What's the weather like today?* Have the child mime the word for the class to say, e.g. *It's raining.* Repeat with different children and words.

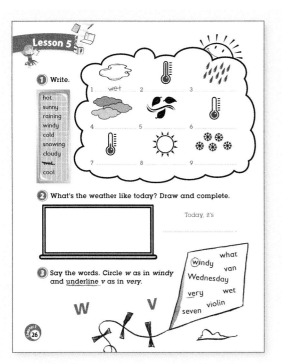

Cooler: Chant competition

Divide the class into three groups. Have each group say the chant in Activity 3 loudly and clearly as in a competition. Then challenge them to say the chant as a class, as fast but as clearly as possible.

Competency Focus

Think! Critical Thinking

By matching the words to the pictures, the children use critical thinking skills to identify the weather and assimilate the written and spoken forms.

1 Write.

Have the children label the pictures with the words supplied. Elicit answers and check with the class.

Answers

1 wet **2** hot **3** raining **4** cloudy **5** windy **6** cold **7** cool **8** sunny **9** snowing

2 What's the weather like today? Draw and complete.

Ask the children to describe the weather. Then have them draw a picture and complete the sentence.

Answers

Children's own answers.

3 Say the words. Circle *w* as in *windy* and underline *v* as in *very*.

Ask the children to circle *w* and underline *v* in the words. Have them say the words as a class.

Answers

Circled: **w** *in* **w**indy, **w**hat, **W**ednesday, **w**et
Underlined: **v** *in* **v**an, **v**ery, se**v**en, **v**iolin

Digital Resources

Student eBook • Play ASL Vocabulary Video 3.3 to pre-teach key vocabulary, pausing for the children to repeat the word and copy the sign.

Student's App • Encourage the children to play the games on their smartphone/tablet. Ask them to record their scores to compare in the next lesson. (*The Inks* Apps are free and available on the App Store and Google Play.)

Teacher Resource Center • For phonics practice, print out Phonics Worksheet 3.

Grammar and Reading

Lesson objectives: ask and answer requests in a polite way

Key grammar: *Can you open (the window), please?*
Yes, I can. / Sorry, I can't.

Secondary language: *I'm too short; machines, notice, shelf, turn off*

Materials: Track 3.9; Grammar Worksheet 3B [TRC printout] (optional); strips of paper with requests written on them (optional)

Warmer: Can you ..., please?

Say *Can you ..., please?* requests for the class to follow. Ask them to open their book to page ..., close their book, raise a pencil, etc., ending each request with *please*. Have them say *Yes, I can.* when they do the action.

1))) 3.9 Listen and read.

- Ask the children to look at the pictures and ask *What are they doing?* (tidying up) Ask *Do you tidy up the classroom?*

- Play Track 3.9 and ask them to listen and read along. Ask *Who closes the window?* (Biblio) *Who turns off the lights?* (Ellie) *Who opens the door?* (Ellie) *Who turns off Biblio?* (Ellie) *Why does she do that?* (because he's a machine too) Explain that it is important to save energy. (You might need to use L1.)

- Put the children in pairs and have them act out the last picture. The children who are Biblio say *Goodnight, Ellie. Zzzzz ...*

Grammar Central

Can you open the window, please? ...

Have the children look at the question and answers. Explain that we use *Can you ..., please?* to ask people politely to do things. To respond politely, we use *Yes, I can.* or *Sorry, I can't.* Then divide your class into small groups and have them think of more requests using *Can you ..., please?* Encourage them to share with the class and invite individuals to respond politely.

For extra practice, try the **Grammar Booster** section in the Student Book (p. 47–49).

Answers p. 47

Activity 1: **1** please **2** can't **3** Can you **4** I can **5** Sorry

Activity 2 : **1** Can you open the door, please? **2** Yes, I can. 2 Can you close the door please? Sorry, I can't. **3** Can you open the door, please? Yes, I can. **4** Can you turn on the light, please? Sorry, I can't.

p. 48

Activity 1: **1** Sorry, I can't. **2** put **3** Sorry, I can't. **4** wearing **5** She's wearing **6** can

Activity 2: **1** b **2** c **3** a **4** c

p. 49

Activity 1: He doesn't have long hair. He has short hair. **2** She isn't wearing a red skirt. She's wearing a purple skirt. **3** He isn't wearing blue shorts. He's wearing blue jeans. **4** She doesn"t have blond hair. She has brown hair. **5** He isn"t wearing gray pants. He"s wearing green pants.

2 Complete the blanks.

- Have the children look at Activity 1 to complete the sentences. Elicit answers.
- Remind them to be polite when asking someone to do something. They should always say *please* and *thank you*.
- Divide the class into pairs. Have them practice saying the questions and sentences. Ensure their pronunciation and intonation are correct.

Answers

1 please **2** I can/sure **3** Can **4** can't

Optional activity: Guess the request!

Write *Can you ..., please?* requests on slips of paper, e.g. turn the lights on/off, etc. Give a request to a child to do the action. The rest of the class says what the request is. Repeat with different children.

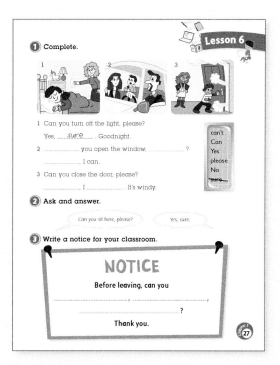

1 Complete.

Ask the children to look at the pictures and complete the dialogues with the words supplied. Invite pairs to read out a dialogue for the class.

Answers

1 sure **2** Can, please, Yes **3** No, can't

2 Ask and answer.

Have the children work in pairs. They take turns asking their friend to do things and replying. Invite pairs to demonstrate for the class.

3 Write a notice for your classroom.

Tell the children to complete the notice with three requests. Elicit ideas from the class.

Answers

Children's own answers.

Cooler: Play "Whisper it!"

Have the children play the game with requests from the lesson (see Games Bank p. 222).

Ask children to bring in pictures of their country for Activity Book Activity 1 in the next lesson.

Competency Focus

Learn

The children demonstrate their understanding of the new grammatical patterns by reading the text and completing the activity.

Digital Resources

Student eBook • Display the SB page. Ask the children to predict what the story is about.

- Show the Grammar Central box. Have children use *Highlighter* to identify in the SB Activity 1 text examples of requests with *Can you ...?*, then positive and negative responses.

Teacher Resource Center • For extra grammar practice, print out Grammar Worksheet 3B.

CLIL: Geography—World weather and seasons

Lesson objective: find out about the weather and seasons in other countries

Materials: Track 3.10; CLIL Graphic Organizer 3 [TRC printout] (optional); map of the world (optional), large sheets of paper for posters (optional); pictures of the children's country (AB Activity 1)

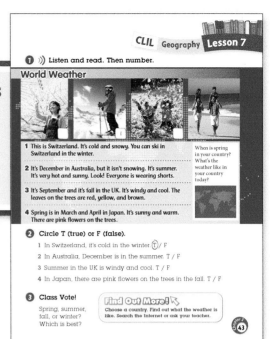

Warmer: Months

Divide the class into pairs and have them write the months in their notebook. Encourage them to help each other with spelling. Invite children to write a month on the board.

1))) 3.10 Listen and read. Then number.

- Circle the spring months on the board and write *spring*. Explain that spring is a season. Ask *How many seasons are there?* (*four*) Circle the rest of the months on the board by season and add *summer*, *fall*, and *winter* accordingly.

- Have the children look at the photos and describe the weather, e.g. *It's cold. It's snowy.* Play Track 3.10 and have the children listen, read, and number the pictures. Elicit answers and check with the class.

- Play Track 3.10 again and tell the children to raise their hand when they hear a season. Pause and elicit the season.

- Invite children to say which country they like best and why.

- Divide the class into pairs and ask them to read and answer the two questions. Elicit answers and check with the class.

Answers

Order left to right: 4, 1, 3, 2

2 Circle T (true) or F (false).

- Ask the children to read the sentences silently and refer to the texts in Activity 1 to choose true or false. Monitor and help if necessary.

- Elicit answers and check with the class. Ask children to correct the false sentences.

Answers

1 T **2** T **3** F **4** F

3 Class Vote!

Organize your class vote. Ask the children which season they think is the best. Give them a minute to think. Then write *spring, summer, fall, winter* on the board. Have the children raise their hand for each answer. Count the votes and write the totals on the board. Elicit the result of the vote.

Find Out More!

Write a list of countries on the board and elicit where they are. (Use the map or the Internet to show.) Ask the children to choose a country and find out what the weather is like in each season. Suggest appropriate resources, e.g. Internet, library books, etc., or provide the information yourself. The children will need to complete this research before doing the follow-up activity in the Activity Book. (It could be set as homework.)

Optional activity: Country poster

Divide the class into four groups. Allocate each group a different season for their poster about a country of their choice. Have each group brainstorm words and ask them to find out about typical foods and holidays during their season. Distribute large sheets of paper to each group. Encourage them to create posters using pictures, drawings, and writing.

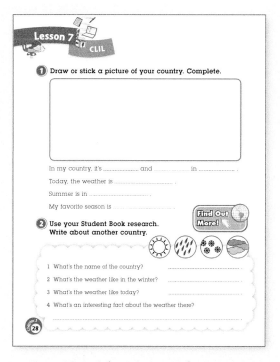

1 Draw or stick a picture of your country. Complete.

Have the children draw or stick their picture. Then have them complete the text with information about their own country. Have them show and tell in pairs.

Answers

Children's own answers.

2 Use your Student Book research. Write about another country.

Ask the children what they know or found out about other countries. Divide the class into groups so they can share their information. Then have them answer the questions.

Answers

Children's own answers.

Cooler: Our country

Have the children say or write the sentences again in Activity 2, but change the facts to make them true for their country. Elicit answers from the class.

Competency Focus

Act

The children carry out research to find out more about weather in another country. This helps them expand their learning and relate it to their world, both inside and outside the classroom.

Digital Resources

Student eBook, Digital Activity Book • When using the board for "heads-up" teaching, give the children as much opportunity as possible to participate. Make sure you ask plenty of questions.

Student eBook • TIP You can use *Add personal note* to log the results of the class vote.

Teacher Resource Center • Print out CLIL Graphic Organizer 3 for the children to use in collating their Find Out More! research.

CLIL eBook • The children can use the CLIL eBook to expand their knowledge of the lesson topic.

Project

Lesson objectives: review language from Chapter 3; complete a craft project—making a crown; act out the story from the Reader

Materials: Reader; Project Template 3 [TRC printout]; scissors, glue, buttons, colored paper, foil, cotton, wool, beads

Warmer: Crown

Draw a crown on the board. Invite the children to say what it is and spell the word. Ask them to look through the Reader story (*The Emperor's New Clothes*) and count the crowns in the main pictures. Elicit the answer. (*eleven*)

Prepare

1 Make a crown.

- Have the children look at the completed crowns. Ask *Which do you like best?* Tell them they are going to make their own crown.

- Hold up the materials to show the class. Point to the pictures and explain the stages. (You might need to use L1.)

- Demonstrate how to make a crown, stage by stage.

- Divide the class into pairs or groups if it is necessary to share materials. Give out the materials.

- As the children make their crowns, monitor and give help as necessary.

Alternative craft activity

A simpler option would be to have the children draw a crown on a piece of paper and decorate it with materials.

Showcase

2 Tell the story. Use your crowns.

- Divide the class into groups of five (emperor, servant, two dressmakers, and narrator).

- Ask the children to look at the story. Give them time to practice, reading from their books. Monitor and help with pronunciation.

- Call out groups to the front of the class to perform the story. The emperor in each group should wear their crown. The rest of the class can play the part of the watching crowd during these performances.

Optional activity: Move your crown

Ask the children to hold their crown. Make requests and say *Can you put your crown on your head, please? Can you put it under the table, please?*, etc. Encourage them to say *Yes, I can.*

1 Look and circle six more differences.

Ask the children to look at the two pictures and circle the differences.

Answers

The differences are as follows:

	Picture A	**Picture B**
Sky:	sunny	cloudy
Boy walking:	has a bike	doesn't have a bike
Boy with soccer ball:	wearing shorts	wearing pants
Girl running:	wearing shoes	isn't wearing shoes
Boy jumping:	wearing a T-shirt	wearing a shirt
Girl kicking:	wearing sneakers	wearing boots
Girl skating:	wearing a dress	wearing a skirt and T-shirt

2 Now point to the pictures and talk to a friend.

Read out the example with the class. Have the children talk about the differences in pairs.

Cooler: Find the crown!

Ask the children to wear their crowns. Describe a child and say, e.g. *He's wearing a crown with red and blue.* Invite the class to look around and find who you have described, e.g. *It's José!* Continue with different children and crowns.

Competency Focus

Collaborate and Communicate

By acting out the story, the children consolidate their understanding in a fun and engaging way. They also demonstrate their ability to work with friends and use interpersonal skills.

Digital Resources

Student eBook • Show the Prepare photos, stage by stage, as you talk the class through the activity process.

• Play ASL Vocabulary Videos 1.1–3.3 to review vocabulary from previous chapters. Have the children vote to select a topic to review.

Digital Activity Book • Use *Timer* to give the class a time limit of one minute to complete AB Activity 1.

Teacher Resource Center • Print out Project Template 3 to use for the SB craft activity.

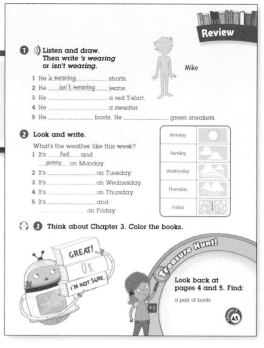

Language Review

Lesson objective: review language from Chapter 3
Materials: Tracks 3.11, AB 3.1, AB 3.2 and AB 3.3; quiz questions (optional)

Warmer: Stand up and point

Call out words for clothes, e.g. *Shoes!* Have the class stand up if they are wearing the specific clothing object and point to it. If they are not wearing it, have them remain seated and point to a friend who is wearing it.

1))) 3.11 Listen and draw. Then write 's *wearing* or *isn't wearing.*

- Ask the children to open their books and look at the picture. Explain that they have to listen and draw Mike's clothes on him. Have them prepare their colored pencils.

- Play Track 3.11 twice and have the children draw the clothes. Draw a stickman (Mike) on the board. Check answers by inviting children to add an item of clothing.

- Ask a child to read the example sentences. Have the children look at Mike and complete the sentences. Elicit answers.

Audioscript

Narrator: What's Mike wearing?
Girl: Mike is wearing shorts and a red T-shirt. He's wearing green sneakers.

Answers

1 is wearing **2** isn't wearing **3** 's wearing **4** isn't wearing **5** isn't wearing, 's wearing

2 Look and write.

- Ask the children to look at the pictures next to each day. Ask *What's the weather like on Monday?*

- Have the children complete the sentences.

Answers

1 hot, sunny **2** cloudy **3** windy **4** rainy/raining
5 cold, snowy/snowing

3 Think about Chapter 3. Color the books.

- Have the children look back at Chapter 3. Elicit their favorite parts. The children then color the book which represents how they feel about their own progress (self-evaluation).

Treasure Hunt!

Ask the children to look at Student Book pp. 4–5 and find a pair of boots.

Cooler: Picture dictation

Have the children draw a picture of a girl and boy. In pairs, they describe their drawing for their friend to draw. They compare their versions.

Competency Focus

Me: Self-evaluation

The children reflect on the chapter and express their opinions about their own progress.

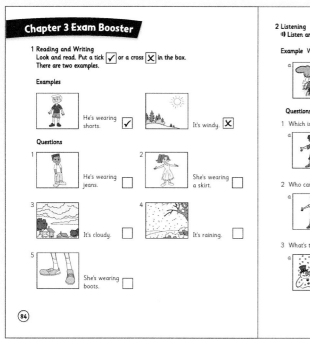

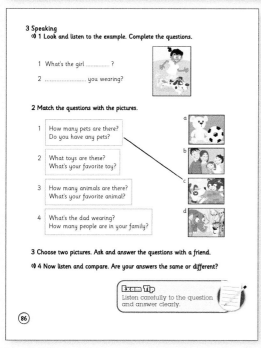

Ask the children to listen and write the missing words.

Answers (Audioscript on p. 223)

1 wearing **2** What are

3.2 Speaking. Match the questions with the speakers.

Children match the questions and pictures.

Answers

1 C **2** A **3** D **4** B

3.3 Speaking. Choose two pictures. Ask and answer the questions with a friend.

Children ask and answer the questions.

3.4))) AB 3.3 Speaking. Now listen and compare. Are your answers the same or different?

Ask the children to listen and compare their answers.

(Audioscript on p. 223)

1 Reading and Writing. Look and read. Put a tick (✔) or a cross (✗) in the box. There are two examples.

Children respond with ✔ or ✗.

Answers

1 ✔ **2** ✗ **3** ✔ **4** ✗ **5** ✗

2))) AB 3.1 Listening. Listen and tick (✔) the box. There is one example.

Children listen and tick the correct picture.

Answers (Audioscript on p. 223)

1 b **2** c **3** c

3.1))) AB 3.2 Speaking. Look and listen to the example. Complete the questions.

Digital Resources

Student eBook, Digital Activity Book • Use the answer key, showing the answers all at once or one by one.

Teacher Resource Center • Print out Test Chapter 3 to use at the end of this lesson. The Test Generator allows you to create customized tests.

• Print out Festival Worksheet: Christmas to expand the children's knowledge of US culture.

Chapter 4
Eat, Sleep, Play!
Overview

The children will:

- use critical thinking skills to identify actions.
- ask and answer questions about what people are doing.
- read, understand, and act out a story.
- identify what people are doing.
- find out about world time.
- make a monster.

Key Vocabulary

Verbs in simple present: bark, eat, jump, sit, sleep, walk

Verbs in –*ing* form: doing my homework, going to bed, making, reading a book, watching TV, working

Key Grammar

- What are you doing? I'm playing.
- What's he doing? He's sleeping.
- Are you sleeping? Yes, I am. / No, I'm not.
- Is he jumping? Yes, he is. / No, he isn't.
- He isn't working.

Reading Skills

Story: *A New Pet for Trixie*
Genre: science fiction

Literacy Development

- predict story content from titles and pictures
- focus on the narrative text that sets the scene in the story
- think about what happens at the end of a story

Functional Language

- What time is it?
- It's 1 o'clock.
- Great! It's time for a story.

Phonics

The children practice pronunciation of the *ing* ending as in work*ing*.

CLIL: Geography—Different times around the world

The children find out about time in other countries. They work out time differences between places around the world.

Competency Focus

The children will:

use critical thinking skills to identify actions. (Lesson 1)	apply new grammar to previously learned vocabulary. (Lesson 2)	work in pairs to act out a dialogue. (Lesson 3)	predict what happens next in the story. (Lesson 4)	calculate the time difference between different places around the world. (Lesson 7)
predict the content of a story. (Lesson 3)	ask and answer about what people are doing. (Lesson 6)	work in groups to act out the story. (Lesson 8)	evaluate their own progress in the chapter. (Review)	
describe what they are doing. (Lesson 5)				

Digital Overview

Teacher Presentation

Student eBook and Digital Activity Book

- ASL Vocabulary Video 4.1: Verbs in simple present
- ASL Vocabulary Video 4.4: Verbs in –*ing* form
- Music Video 4.2 (4.3): *Stitch*
- Interactive versions of AB activities
- Integrated audio and answer key for all activities

Teacher resources for planning, lesson delivery, and homework

Teacher Resource Center

- Class Planner Chapter 4
- Worksheets to print out (including notes and answers):
  - Grammar Worksheet 4A: What are you doing? I'm …ing.
  - Grammar Worksheet 4B: Are you …ing? Yes/No, …
  - CLIL Graphic Organizer 4
  - Phonics Worksheet 4
  - Project Template 4
  - Test Chapter 4
- Test Generator
- Literacy Handbook

Watch the Music Video

Children's resources for consolidation and practice at home

Student eBook

- ASL Vocabulary Video 4.1: Verbs in simple present
- ASL Vocabulary Video 4.4: Verbs in –*ing* form
- Music Video 4.2 (4.3): *Stitch*

The Inks Student's App

Vocabulary games: Verbs in simple present and verbs in –*ing* form

Vocabulary

Lesson objective: identify actions
Key vocabulary: *bark, eat, jump, sit, sleep, walk*
Materials: Track 4.1; pet pictures (Warmer)

Warmer: Pets, pets, pets

Draw a Pets diagram and scramble the pet words.

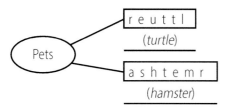

r e u t t l
(*turtle*)

Pets

a s h t e m r
(*hamster*)

Have the children copy and unscramble the letters. Invite children to write a pet word on the board and stick pictures next to the correct word. Leave the mind map on the board for the class survey (in Optional activity).

1 4.1 Listen and number. Then say.

- Ask the children to look at the pictures. Ask *What animals can you see?* (*dog, cat*) Point to the animals' body parts and ask *What's this?/What are these?* to elicit *ears, eyes, nose, legs, head, tail.*

- Focus attention on the small pictures and words. Give the children time to study them and match any they already know to the big pictures.

- Play Track 4.1 and have the children listen and match the actions to the pictures of the dog.

- Play Track 4.1 again, pausing for the children to repeat.

- Elicit answers and check with the class.

- Divide the class into pairs. Have them take turns being Fluffy and Fluffy's owner. The "owner" says *It can . . .* and "Fluffy" demonstrates the action. Invite pairs to show the class a few actions.

Audioscript

Girl: *Look, at my pet dog, Fluffy!*
Boy: *Wow! What can it do?*
Narrator: *1*
Girl: *It can walk.*
Narrator: *2*
Girl: *It can eat.*
Narrator: *3*
Girl: *It can sit. Sit, Fluffy.*
Narrator: *4*
Girl: *It can bark. Shh! Fluffy! Be quiet.*
Narrator: *5*
Girl: *It can jump.*
Narrator: *6*
Girl: *And it can sleep.*

Answers

3, 1, 6
5, 2, 4

Optional activity: Pet class survey

Have the children work in pairs. Allocate a pet for each pair. Have them mingle and ask their question, e.g. *Do you have a hamster?* Have them compare answers with their friend. Ask the children to report the results, e.g. *Three children in our class have a fish.*

Competency Focus

Think! Critical Thinking

The children use critical thinking skills to identify action verbs by using visual clues and processing the written and spoken forms.

1 Unscramble and write.

Have the children write the verbs. Elicit answers and check with the class.

Answers

1 walk **2** sit **3** eat **4** jump **5** sleep **6** bark

2 Write the words in three groups.

Ask the children to write the verbs from the box in the correct group. Elicit answers.

Answers (suggested)

in the park: walk, jump
in the park and at home: bark, sit
at home: sleep, eat

Cooler: Play "Simon Says"

Have the children play the game with verbs from the lesson (see Games Bank p. 222).

Digital Resources

Student eBook • Play ASL Vocabulary Video 4.1 to pre-teach key vocabulary as an alternative to the critical thinking approach.

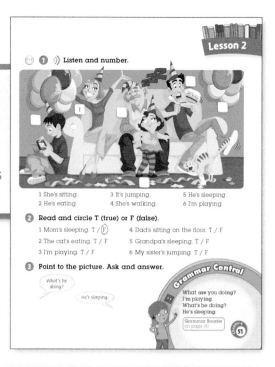

Grammar

Lesson objectives: ask and answer questions about what people are doing
Key grammar: *What are you doing? I'm (playing). What's he doing? He's (sleeping).*
Materials: Track 4.2; Grammar Worksheet 4A [TRC printout] (optional); pieces of paper with the action verbs from Lesson 1 (optional)

Warmer: family members

Revise family words (*mom, dad*, etc.). Invite individuals to call out a family word. Each time ask the class to write the word. Check answers by asking children to write them on the board.

1))) 4.2 Listen and number.

- Ask the children to look at the picture. Have them say what they can see. Pre-teach *baby sister*. Ask *What are they doing?* (*having a party*)
- Give the children time to read the sentences. Play Track 4.2 twice and have them listen and number.
- Elicit answers.
- In pairs, they take turns pointing to someone/the cat and saying what they/it is doing.

Audioscript

Boy: *Look! This is my family. It's my birthday party. This is my mom. She's sitting on the sofa. This is my dad.*
Narrator: *What's he doing?*
Boy: *He's eating. But, look! The cat is jumping on him. My baby sister is walking. And look at my grandpa! He's sleeping.*
Narrator: *And what are you doing?*
Boy: *I'm playing my new computer game.*

Answers

6, 1, 5, 4, 2, 3

Grammar Central

What are you doing? ...

Have children read the question and sentences aloud. Remind the class that in questions we put *you/he/she* between *are/is* and the verb ending in *ing*. Ask the children to practice the questions and answers in pairs. Monitor to check pronunciation.

For extra practice, try the **Grammar Booster** section in the Student Book (p. 60).

Answers p. 60

Activity 1: **1** doing **2** I'm **3** What's **4** eating **5** doing **6** jumping

Activity 2: **1** What's he doing? He's eating. **2** What's she doing? She's running. **3** What's he doing? He's sleeping. **4** What are you doing? I'm watching TV.

2 Read and circle T (true) or F (false).

- Have a child read the example and explain why it is false. (*She's sitting.*)
- Ask the children to read the rest of the sentences and look at the picture in Activity 1 to choose true or false.
- Elicit answers and check with the class. Invite children to correct the false sentences.

Answers

1 F **2** F **3** T **4** F **5** T **6** F

3 Point to the picture. Ask and answer.

- Divide the class into pairs and ask them to look at the picture in Activity 1. Choose a pair to model the example for the class, pointing to Grandpa.

- Write *What's he/she doing?* on the board to help the children. Monitor to ensure they use *he/she/it* correctly.

Optional activity: What are you doing?

Invite two children to the front and give them an action verb paper each. Have them mime their verb. The class ask *What are you doing?* and the children miming answer, e.g. *I'm barking.* Continue with different children and verbs.

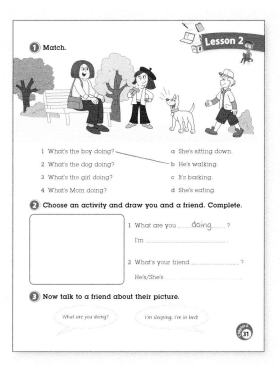

3 Now talk to a friend about their picture.

Have the children work in pairs, talking about their picture using the questions and answers from Activity 2.

Cooler: Chanting in a circle

Have the children stand in a circle and choose a child to stand in the middle. Chant with the children *What's he doing? What's she doing? What are you doing? Tell us!* Stop suddenly and have the child answer, e.g. *I'm jumping.* Everyone does the action and repeats *I'm jumping!* Repeat with different children and different actions.

Competency Focus

Learn

By identifying what people are doing in a different context with new grammatical structures, the children demonstrate their understanding of previously acquired vocabulary from Lesson 1.

1 Match.

Have the children look at the picture and match the questions to the answers. Elicit answers and check with the class.

Answers

1 b **2** c **3** d **4** a

2 Choose an activity and draw you and a friend. Complete.

Tell the children to choose an activity from Lesson 1 or 2 and a different activity for their friend. Have them draw and then complete the questions and answers.

Answers

Children's own answers.

Digital Resources

Digital Activity Book • Display AB page for Activity 2 review. Have children use *Pen* to draw themselves and a friend doing an activity. Have the class ask *What are you/ your friend doing?* for them to respond.

Teacher Resource Center • For extra grammar practice, print out Grammar Worksheet 4A.

Reading: Story Extract

Lesson objectives: ask and say what time it is; use the title and pictures to predict story content; read the extract from *A New Pet for Trixie* (middle)

Functional language: *What time is it? It's 1 o'clock. Great! It's time for a story.*

Secondary language: *barking, dark, hungry, lightning, thunder*

Materials: Tracks 4.3 and 4.4

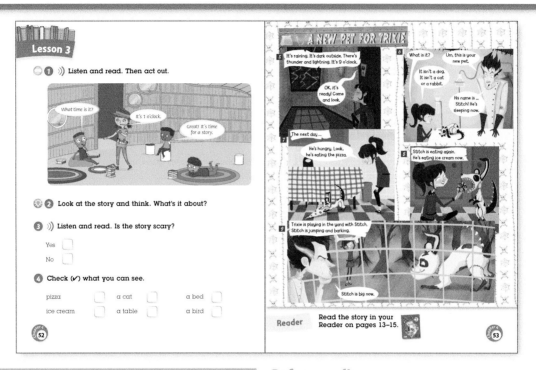

Warmer: Clock and watch

Draw a clock on the board. Start with the circle and have the children count 1–12 as you write the hours. Pre-teach *clock* and *watch*. Ask *Are you wearing a watch?* and have children show their watch to the class.

Functional language

1)) 4.3 Listen and read. Then act out.

- Have the children look at the picture and ask *Who's wearing a watch?* (*Libby*) Play Track 4.3 and ask them to listen and read. Play Track 4.3 again, pausing for them to repeat.
- Divide the class into pairs and have them act out the dialogue.

Before reading

2 Look at the story and think. What's it about?

- Tell the children to look at the title and pictures and ask *What pet can you see?* (*a dog*) *Whose is it?* (*the girl's*) *Does she like her dog?* (*yes*) Have a child read the title. Ask *What's the story about?* (*a girl and her dog*)
- Draw the children's attention to the pictures of the dog. Ask *Is it a different dog? Why?* (They might need to use L1.)

3)) 4.4 Listen and read. Is the story scary?

- Play Track 4.4 and have the children listen and read along. Then ask *What's the dog's name?* (*Stitch*)
- Ask the children to read the question. Explain *scary*, if necessary. Have them check yes or no. Check answers by having the children raise their hands if they think the story is scary.

- Play Track 4.4 again pausing after the first picture. Ask *What time is it?* (*It's 9 o'clock.*) Continue pausing after each picture and inviting children to say what Stitch is doing in each one. (You might need to use L1.)

Answers

Children's own answers.

4 Check (✔) what you can see.

- Choose a child to read the list of words. Have the children look at the pictures and check what they can see in the story.

- Elicit answers and check with the class. Have the children call out other things they can see. (e.g. *a dress, a door, a window, a bin*)

Answers

a pizza, an ice cream, a table

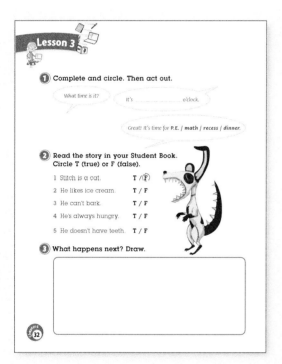

1 Complete and circle. Then act out.

Have the children complete the dialogue, saying the time on their watch/classroom clock. Then have them act out their dialogues in pairs. Ask pairs to act out for the class.

Answers

Children's own answers.

2 Read the story in your Student Book. Circle T (true) or F (false).

Have the children read the sentences and choose true or false. Tell them to read the story again if they are not sure.

Answers

1 F 2 T 3 F 4 T 5 F

3 What happens next? Draw.

Elicit ideas from the class about what happens next in the story. Then have the children draw a picture. Have them show and tell in pairs.

Cooler: Play "The Chain Game"

Play the game using *Look at Stitch! He's eating (pizza and an apple) now!* (see Games Bank p. 222).

Competency Focus

Collaborate and Communicate

The children work together, putting into practice new functional language by acting out a realistic dialogue.

Think! Critical Thinking

By looking at the story artwork, the children use prediction skills to help them engage with the story.

Digital Resources

Student eBook • Display the SB story extract and encourage the children to develop the reading skill of using details in the pictures. Use *Timer* and give the class one minute to look at the pictures. Then stop displaying the SB story extract. Elicit the detail.

Lesson objective: read and understand the science fiction story *A New Pet for Trixie* in the Reader

Materials: Track 4.5; Reader

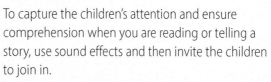

Warmer: Review story characters

Ask children to remember the story characters (*Trixie and Stitch*) and the food Stitch ate (*pizza and ice cream*). Explain that the extract comes from the middle of the story. Invite the children to guess what happened earlier. (You might need to use L1.)

Story Summary

A professor makes a pet dog named Stitch for his daughter, Trixie. Stitch eats everything and keeps growing bigger and bigger. The Professor is worried so he makes a drink for Stitch, and Stitch shrinks back to his normal size. But then Stitch starts to eat everything again …

Value: Be careful what you wish for!

))) **4.5 While reading**

- Ask the children to look at *A New Pet for Trixie* in their Reader. Give them time to study the picture on the first page carefully. Ask *Who's the man in the story?* (*Trixie's dad/the professor*)

- Play Track 4.5 and have the children listen and read along. Then check comprehension of the story by asking *Is Stitch a real dog?* (*No—Trixie's dad created him.*) *Does Stitch get very big?* (*yes*) *Is he big at the end of the story?* (*no*) *Why?* (*He drinks a special drink.*) (L1 may be necessary.)

- Play Track 4.5 again with children reading along and miming the actions, e.g. sleeping, eating, etc.

After reading: Reflect

- Have the children think about pets. Ask *Why is it nice to have a pet? Is it easy to have a pet? What do pets need? What are our responsibilities?* (They might need to use L1.)

Optional activity: Complete the phrase

Dictate part of some sentences from the story, e.g. … *is sitting on the sofa, … is eating pasta now.* Have the children write them and add the characters. Monitor and check spelling. Invite children to read a sentence aloud.

Story Time

Sound effects

To capture the children's attention and ensure comprehension when you are reading or telling a story, use sound effects and then invite the children to join in.

Reading Strategy

Visual Imagery

Using Visual Imagery is a very important strategy that good readers should apply while reading and listening to a story. It helps them personalize the story by building their own mental images as they read. It also offers good comprehension support.

For additional explanation and activities, see the Literacy Handbook on Teacher Resource Center.

Cooler: Aww! It's so small!

Have the children draw a small pet, e.g. a small fish. Write *Aww! It's so small!* on the board. Ask them to show each other their drawings. Have them exclaim *Aww! It's so small!* at each pet. If there is time, do the same for *Wow! It's so big!*

Digital Resources

Reader eBook • Display the Reader story on the board. Review the story extract. Elicit ideas on what happened before and after the story extract.

- TIP Show the Reader pictures as you play the audio.

- Children use *Pen* to find and circle Stitch in all the pictures. The class calls out *Very small./Small./Big./Very big.* as appropriate each time.

Reading Comprehension and Critical Literacy

Lesson objectives: focus on the narrative text; think about what happens next in a story

Materials: Track 4.5; Reader

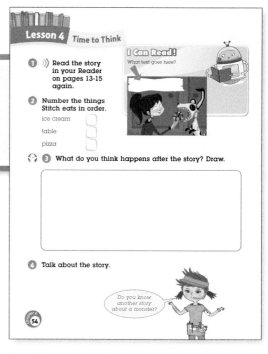

Note: Please ensure that your class has read the Reader story before you do this lesson.

Warmer: Stitch's teeth

Draw Stitch's open mouth (picture 8) on the board. Call out words from the story, e.g. *thunder, ice cream.* Have the children spell each word around the class (one letter each). The child to say the last letter of each word draws a tooth in Stitch's mouth.

1))) 4.5 Read the story in your Reader.

- Have the children read the story. (Alternatively, play Track 4.5 and have them read along.)
- Ask *What is Stitch doing here?* as you point to different pictures to elicit answers from the class.

I Can Read!

Ask the children to look at the text on the top left of the pictures in the story. Invite children to read a few. Ask them to say what this text does. (*It tells us when something happens—later …, the next day …—and what's happening—Trixie is playing in the yard with Stitch.*)

Answer

Stitch is eating again. He's eating ice cream now.

2 Number the things Stitch eats in order.

- Ask the children to think about the food/things Stitch eats in the story. Have them close their Reader and number the words in order. Then have them check.
- Ask them to add one more thing Stitch eats. (*pasta*)

Answers

ice cream 2, table 3, pizza 1

3 What do you think happens after the story? Draw.

- Have the children think what might happen next. Prompt them with a few questions, e.g. *What will Stitch eat next? Will he stay the same size or get smaller/ bigger?* (You might need to use L1.)
- Give them time to think and draw the next picture for the story. Monitor and ask children to explain what they are drawing. Invite fast finishers to write a sentence, e.g. *Trixie has a new pet. It's a cat!*

4 Talk about the story.

- Ask the children if they liked the story and why/why not. Have them say if they prefer the small or big Stitch.
- Have a child read Libby's question. Invite children to share other stories about monsters.

Optional activity: The last picture

Tell the children to look at the last picture and have them think of a short sentence to use as narrative text, e.g. *Stitch is hungry again.* Choose a sentence as a class and ask them to write it on the picture.

The worksheet image:

① Complete in story order.

Lesson 4
Time to Think

pasta
table
~~pizza~~
drink
ice cream

1 Stitch is small.
  He's eating ......pizza....... .

2 Now he's eating ....

3 It's lunch time. He's eating ....

4 He's eating the .... now! He's big!

5 The professor is making a ....
  Stitch is small again!

② Check (✔) the best description of the picture.

1 It's raining. It's dark outside.
  There's thunder and lightning.
  It's 9 o'clock.

2 It's 1 o'clock. It's lunch time.

3 The professor is working again.

③ What do you think about Stitch? Choose and check (✔).

He's funny. ☐   He's scary. ☐   He's cute. ☐

Competency Focus

Me: Critical Literacy

The children use critical literacy skills to reflect on the story and use their imagination to think about how the story continues.

---

1 Complete in story order.

Ask the children to complete the sentences according to the story, using the words supplied. Allow them to look in their Reader if necessary. Elicit answers and check with the class.

Answers

1 pizza **2** ice cream **3** pasta **4** table **5** drink

2 Check (✔) the best description of the picture.

The children practice the **I Can Read!** feature. Have them look at the picture and read the three descriptions. Then have them check the best description.

Answer

by 1

3 What do you think about Stitch? Choose and check (✔).

Tell the children to give their opinion of Stitch by checking a sentence. Elicit opinions.

Answers

Children's own answers.

Cooler: Find it and join in

Read out the captions from the story in jumbled order starting slowly, e.g. *Trixie is walking* ... (picture 4), etc. Have the children find it quickly in their Reader and read along.

Digital Resources

Reader eBook • Display the Reader on the board. Show Picture 4. Elicit what happened before and after this. Repeat with Pictures 9 and 14.

Student eBook, Digital Activity Book • TIP You can move the answer key pop-up window around the screen to have the activity and the answers side by side.

Vocabulary, Song, and Phonics

Lesson objectives: identify what people are doing; distinguish and practice the *ing* ending of verbs

Key vocabulary: *doing my homework, going to bed, making, reading a book, watching TV, working*

Secondary language: *dinner, lunch, notebook*

Materials: Tracks 4.6 and 4.7; soft ball (Warmer) ; Phonics Worksheet 4 [TRC printout] (optional)

Warmer: Catch and do

Pre-teach the new vocabulary using mimes. Then throw a soft ball (or crumpled paper) to a child and ask *What are you doing?* The child with the ball mimes one of the new items (e.g. *going to bed*) and the class say what it is. Repeat, with each child choosing a friend to throw the ball to.

1))) 4.6 Listen and number. Then sing.

- Have the children look at the new words in red in the song. Have them mime each action to check understanding. Then ask them to look at the pictures around the song.

- Play Track 4.6 and ask the children to listen and write numbers next to the red words, matching them to the pictures. Elicit answers and check with the class.

- Ask *Who's singing the song?* (*Trixie*) Explain *munch* is the sound we make when we eat.

- Then play Track 4.6 again and have the children sing along, pointing to the pictures as they sing.

Answers

working 2, making 5, doing my homework 3, reading a book 1, watching TV 4, going to bed 6

2 Play a miming game.

- Demonstrate the game with a child. Mime watching TV and ask *What am I doing?* Encourage the child to answer *You're watching TV.*

- Divide the class into pairs and ask them to look at the example question and answer and notice the structures.

- Give them time to play in pairs using the actions in Activity 1. Monitor and help.

3))) 4.7 Listen and say the chant.

- Play Track 4.7 and ask the children to listen to the chant. Ask them which sentence matches the picture. (*I'm going to bed.*)

- Write *ing* on the board and ask them to say the words ending with it. Play Track 4.7 again, pausing for them to repeat the phrases.

- Practice the chant a few times with the class. When they have learned it, ask them to chant it on their own, miming the actions.

Optional activity: Play "Hot Potato"

Have the children play the game with verbs ending in –*ing* (see Games Bank p. 222).

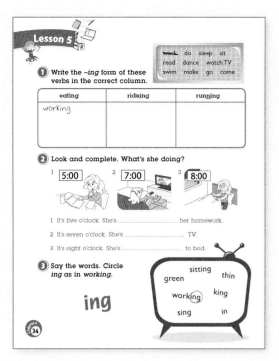

Cooler: Point to the picture

Divide the class into pairs. Have the children take turns pointing to a picture in Activity 1. Have their friend say the correct –*ing* verb/phrase.

Competency Focus

Think! Critical Thinking

By matching the words to the pictures, the children use critical thinking skills to identify the actions and assimilate the written and spoken forms.

1 Write the –*ing* form of these verbs in the correct column.

Have the children complete the table with the –*ing* form of the verbs. Elicit answers and check with the class.

Answers

eating: working, doing, sleeping, reading, watching TV, going *riding:* dancing, making, coming
running: sitting, swimming

2 Look and complete. What's she doing?

Ask the children to look at the pictures and complete the sentences.

Answers

1 doing **2** watching **3** going

3 Say the words. Circle *ing* as in *working*.

Have the children circle the *ing* endings of the words. Divide the class into small groups to practice saying the *ing* words.

Answers

Circled: **ing** in work**ing**, sitt**ing**, k**ing**, s**ing**

Digital Resources

Student eBook • Play ASL Vocabulary Video 4.4 to pre-teach key vocabulary, pausing for the children to repeat the word and copy the sign.

• For SB Activity 1, play Music Video 4.2 (4.3) and encourage the children to dance and sing along. The lyrics appear on screen for support. Pause the video for the children to continue dancing and singing.

Teacher Resource Center • For phonics practice, print out Phonics Worksheet 4.

Grammar and Reading

Lesson objectives: ask and answer about what people are doing
Key grammar: *Are you sleeping? Yes, I am. / No, I'm not.*
Is he jumping? Yes, he is. / No, he isn't. He isn't working.
Secondary language: *battery, feel well, full, low*
Materials: Track 4.8; Grammar Worksheet 4B [TRC printout]
(optional)

Warmer: Memory test

Ask the children to look at the picture in Activity 1 on
Student Book p. 39 for ten seconds, then close their book.
Ask *What's Mom/Dad/the boy/his sister/Grandpa/the cat
doing?* Ask children to answer a question.

1)) 4.8 Listen and read.

- Tell the children to look at the first two pictures in
  Activity 1. Ask *What's the matter?* and elicit ideas.
  (They might need to use L1.)

- Play Track 4.8 and ask them to listen and read along. Ask
  Where's Libby? (*at home*) *Why?* (*She's isn't well.*) *Why
  is Biblio jumping?* (*His battery is low.*) *Who solves the
  problem?* (*Tom*)

- Play Track 4.8 again, pausing for them to repeat. Ask
  children to read out the online dialogue in picture 3 and
  mime typing on a keyboard.

2 Write about Libby and Biblio.

- Call on a child to read the first sentence. Do the next
  question with the class as an example.

- Give the children time to complete the questions and
  answers. Tell them to look at Grammar Central if they
  need help. Elicit answers.

Answers

1 isn't, Is she, She's **2** working, Is, he is

Grammar Central

Are you sleeping? ...

Have the children read the questions and answers. Then
ask them to read the sentence and explain we use *isn't* in
the negative sentence. Tell them that we cannot say *Yes,
I'm.* or *Yes, he's.* Have the children practice the questions
and answers in pairs. Say the last sentence for the class to
repeat.

For extra practice, try the **Grammar Booster** section in the
Student Book (p. 61–63).

Answers p. 61

Activity 1: **1** Are **2** I am **3** playing **4** is **5** isn't

Activity 2: **1** Is Tim Walking? No, he isn't. **2** Is he sitting
down? Yes, he is. **3** Is he playing the violin? Yes he is. **4** Is he
eating? No he isn't. **5** Is he reading a book? No, he isn't.

p. 62

Activity 1: doing **2** I'm **3** sleeping **4** Are **5** isn't **6** running

Activity 2: **1** It's watching the cat. **2** What's, doing **3** Yes, it is.
4 Yes, it is. **5** Is, sleeping **6** It's running.

p. 63

Activity 1: He's watching TV. **2** What's Lily doing? **3** No, he
isn't. **4** Yes, she is. **5** He's brushing his teeth. **6** Is Lily brushing
her teeth?

Activity 2: **1** What are you doing? **2** I'm eating lunch. **3**
What's the weather like? **4** What are you wearing?

Optional activity: Four questions

Write two questions on the board, e.g. *Are you jumping? Are you sleeping?* Have the children copy, then check one and cross the other. Have them ask and answer in pairs saying, *Yes, I am./No, I'm not.* Ask children about their friend, e.g. *Is he jumping?* (*Yes, he is./No, he isn't.*)

3 What are you doing now? Complete the text message.

Tell the children to complete the text message. Then have them practice their dialogue in pairs. Invite pairs to demonstrate for the class.

Answers

Children's own answers.

Cooler: Ellie's message

Ask the children to look at the last picture in Activity 1. Brainstorm ideas about what Ellie wrote next, e.g. *OK, Libby! Get well soon.* Write a few options on the board. Have the children write one in the picture.

Competency Focus

Learn

The children demonstrate their understanding of the new grammatical patterns by reading the text and completing the activity.

1 Circle the answers for Biblio.

Ask the children to look at the picture of Biblio. Have them read the questions and circle the correct answers. Invite pairs of children to read a question and answer for the class.

Answers

1 No, he isn't. **2** No, he isn't. **3** Yes, he is. **4** No, he isn't.

2 Write sentences about Libby using the correct verb forms.

Have the children write sentences about Libby and what she is doing in the picture using the verbs supplied. Ask children to read a sentence for the class.

Answers

1 She isn't working. **2** She's reading. **3** She isn't feeling well. **4** She isn't sleeping.

Digital Resources

Student eBook • Display the SB page. Use *Highlighter* to show the grammar structures in the Story Central story.

Teacher Resource Center • For extra grammar practice, print out Grammar Worksheet 4B.

CLIL: Geography—Different times around the world

Lesson objective: find out about time in other countries
Materials: Track 4.9; CLIL Graphic Organizer 4 [TRC printout] (optional); a globe/world map (Find Out More!)

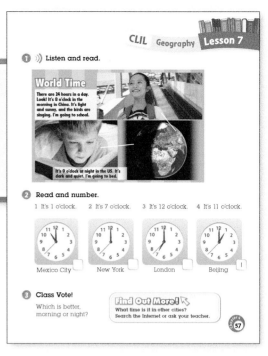

Warmer: Play "Tic-Tac-Toe"

Have the children play the game with action verbs from the chapter (see Games Bank, p. 222).

1))) 4.9 Listen and read.

- Ask the children to look at the pictures. Ask them to guess where the girl and boy are from and find the places on the map in Activity 2. (*China and the USA*)

- Play Track 4.9 and have the children listen and read along. Ask *How many hours are there in a day?* (*24*) *Where's she going?* (*to school*) *What's he doing?* (*reading, going to bed*)

- Play Track 4.9 again and ask the children to underline the times. (*8 o'clock in the morning and 9 o'clock at night*) Make sure they understand time difference and how many hours apart they are (13).

2 Match.

- Ask the children to read the different times. Remind them that the big hand points to minutes and the little hand to the hour. Read the cities aloud and point them out on the map (or on your globe). Give them time to match the times to the clocks. Choose individuals to give their answers and check with the class.

Answers

1 Beijing **2** London **3** New York **4** Mexico City

3 Class Vote!

- Organize your class vote. Read out the question. Have the children stand on one side of the room if they prefer the morning and on the other side if they prefer the night. Invite children to say why. (They might need to use L1.)

- Count the children and write the totals on the board, e.g. *13 children think morning is best.* Elicit the result of the vote.

Find Out More!

Use the globe or a map to find Mexico City, New York, London, Singapore, and Sydney. Ask the children to write these in their notebook and find out what time it is there when it is 8 o'clock in the morning in their country. Suggest appropriate resources, e.g. Internet, library books, etc., or provide the information yourself. The children will need to complete this research before doing the follow-up activity in the Activity Book. (It could be set as homework.)

Optional activity: Morning vs. night

Write *morning* and *night* on the board. Brainstorm words for each, e.g. *wake up* (morning); *watch TV* (night). Have the children copy these. Then ask them to work in groups and add two more words. Have them draw a smiley face (☺) next to the things they like.

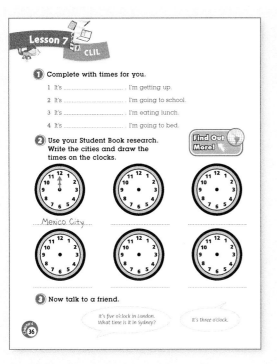

Competency Focus

Act

The children carry out research to find out about the time in other countries. This helps them expand their learning and relate it to their world, both inside and outside the classroom.

1 Complete with times for you.

Have the children complete the sentences with times that reflect their own routine. Ask children to read a sentence for the class.

Answers

Children's own answers.

2 Use your Student Book research. Write the cities and draw the times on the clocks.

Ask the children what they know or found out about time in other countries. Then ask them to draw the time on the clocks. Elicit answers and check with the class.

Answers

Clock hands drawn to show times calculated from **12** a.m. in Mexico City.

3 Now talk to a friend.

Demonstrate the example dialogue with a child. Have the children practice in pairs with the times from Activity 2.

Cooler: Play "Time Race"

Draw two big clocks on the board. Divide the class into two teams. Call out a child from each team and say an "o'clock" time. Have them race to draw the time on their clock. Whoever does it first correctly wins a point for their team.

Digital Resources

Student eBook • Use the SB for an alternative "heads-up" introduction to the topic (TE Activity 1 point 1). Point to the SB to help the children follow the text as you play the audio.

Teacher Resource Center • Print out CLIL Graphic Organizer 4 for the children to use in collating their Find Out More! research.

CLIL eBook • The children can use the CLIL eBook to expand their knowledge of the lesson topic.

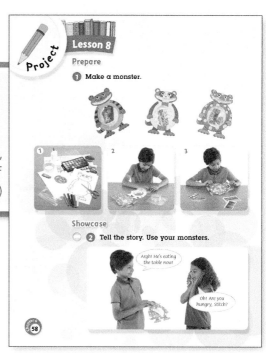

Project

Lesson objectives: review language from Chapter 4; complete a craft project—making a monster; act out the story from the Reader

Materials: Reader; Project Template 4 [TRC printout]; scissors, glue, sticky tape, paintbrush, watercolors, colored markers, paper, plastic bags, small pictures of food and school objects; stuffed toys (Alternative craft activity); music (Cooler)

Warmer: Play "Ready, Set, Draw!"

Have the children play the game with words from the chapter (see Games Bank p. 222).

Prepare

1 Make a monster.

- Have the children look at the completed monsters. Ask *Which do you like best?* Tell them they are going to make their own monster.

- Hold up the materials to show the class. Point to the pictures and explain the stages. (You might need to use L1.)

- Demonstrate how to make a monster, stage by stage.

- Divide the class into pairs or groups if it is necessary to share materials. Give out the materials.

- As the children make their monsters, monitor and give help as necessary.

- Have the children choose three food/school objects pictures and cut them out.

Alternative craft activity

A simpler option would be to have the children use a stuffed toy as a monster and draw food/school objects on a piece of paper and cut them out. Make sure their drawings are small enough to fit through the "monster's" mouth.

Showcase

2 Tell the story. Use your monsters.

- Ask the children to hold up their monsters and pictures. Then divide your class into pairs.

- Have them look at the story again. The children then take turns being Trixie (holding the monster) and her dad. Give them time to practice the story.

- Monitor and encourage children to change the food in the story depending on the pictures they have.

- Call out pairs to the front of the class to perform part of the story using their monster.

Optional activity: Play "The Chain Game"

Play the game, starting the chain off with *In my monster's tummy, there's a bike . . .* (see Games Bank p. 222).

1 Play "The Memory Game."

Tell the children to look at the picture for two minutes. Then ask them to close their books and work in pairs. Have them say sentences about what the people are doing in the picture. Their friend corrects the sentence if they think it is incorrect. Then have them open their books to check.

Cooler: Musical monsters

Ask the children to place their monster on their desk with the food pictures in its "tummy." Play music and have them walk around and stop at different desks. When you stop the music, invite children to say what the monster on the desk they have stopped at is eating.

Competency Focus

Collaborate and Communicate

By acting out the story, the children consolidate their understanding in a fun and engaging way. They also demonstrate their ability to work with friends and use interpersonal skills.

Digital Resources

Student eBook • Show the Prepare photos, stage by stage, as you talk the class through the activity process.

Digital Activity Book • Give prompts, e.g. *She's eating cake.* Children use *Highlighter* to identify the correct person in AB Activity 1.

• To review grammar, point to the people in AB Activity 1 and ask questions, e.g. *Is she riding a bike?* to elicit *Yes, she is. / No, she isn't.*, as appropriate.

Teacher Resource Center • Print out Project Template 4 for the SB craft activity.

Language Review

Lesson objective: review language from Chapter 4
Materials: Tracks 4.10 and AB 4.1; pictures of people doing everyday actions (Warmer), monsters from Lesson 8

Warmer: Disappearing pictures

Put or draw action pictures on the board. Point to elicit sentences, e.g. *He's walking. He's watching TV.* Remove a picture and have the children repeat the sequence, including the missing action. Continue until there are no pictures left.

1)) 4.10 Listen and draw the times. Then write.

- Ask the children to look at the pictures. Point out that the clocks have only the minute hand.
- Play Track 4.10 twice and have the children listen and draw the hour hand in each clock. Elicit answers.
- The children use the pictures to write sentences. Elicit answers.

Audioscript

Narrator: 1 It's 4 o'clock. What are you doing?
Boy: I'm walking. I'm walking home from school.
Narrator: 2 It's 5 o'clock. What are you doing?
Boy: I'm watching TV.
Narrator: 3 It's 6 o'clock. What are you doing?
Boy: I'm doing my homework.
Narrator: 4 It's 7 o'clock. What are you doing?
Boy: I'm eating my dinner.
Narrator: 5 It's 8 o'clock. What are you doing?
Boy: I'm reading a book.
Narrator: 6 It's 9 o'clock. What are you doing?
Boy: I'm going to bed.

Answers

1 He's walking. 4 o'clock
2 He's watching TV. 5 o'clock
3 He's doing his homework. 6 o'clock
4 He's eating his dinner. 7 o'clock
5 He's reading a book. 8 o'clock
6 He's going to bed. 9 o'clock

2 What's happening now? Write.

- Children read out the questions.
- Give them time to write their answers. Check answers.

Answers

Children's own answers.

3 Think about Chapter 4. Color the books.

- Children color the book which represents how they feel about their own progress.

Treasure Hunt!

Ask the children to look at Student Book pp. 4–5 and find someone sitting on a toadstool.

Cooler: Play "Word Ladders"

Divide the class into two teams. Draw a big ladder in front of each team. On the bottom step of each ladder write *b*. The first child writes a word starting with b, e.g. *bark*. The next child writes a word on the next step beginning with the last letter of the previous word, e.g. *kangaroo*. The game continues until the top of their ladder.

Chapter 4 Exam Booster

1 Reading and Writing

Read this. Choose a word from the box. Write the correct word next to numbers 1–5. There is one example.

Parks

Most towns have one or two parks. Parks are big green places. There's ...grass... and there are (1) .... There aren't many cars or (2) .... In the parks in my city, you can see people (3) .... their dog or (4) .... their lunch and watching birds. Sometimes you can see someone (5) .... a book under a tree, or children playing. Parks are great places to do and see many things.

Example

grass	reading	trees	buses
eating	walking	skating	café

(87)

2 Listening

Read the question. Listen and write a name or a number. There are two examples.

Examples

What's the family name?	Clark
How many bedrooms are there?	4

Questions

1 How many pets do they have?
2 What's the brother's name?
3 How old is he?
4 What's the dog's name?
5 How many sisters does David have?

(88)

3 Reading and Writing

Read this. Choose a word from the box. Write the correct word next to numbers 1–5. There is one example.

Dogs

There are many different kinds of dogs – big dogs and small dogs, dogs with long ...tails..., and dogs with short tails. You can teach your dog to (1) .... down and to jump. You can (2) .... or run with your dog in the park. This is Tom's dog, Bongo. Bongo has a (3) .... in the kitchen where he sleeps. The weather is not good today. It's (4) .... , so Bongo is wearing a (5) .... Bongo and Tom are best friends.

Example

tail	walk	sit	bed
raining	coat	sunny	shoes

Exam Tip
Read the paragraph before you write the words.

(89)

---

1 Reading and Writing. Read this. Choose a word from the box. Write the correct word next to numbers 1–5. There is one example.

Children complete the text, using the words supplied.

Answers

1 trees **2** buses **3** walking **4** eating **5** reading

2))) AB 4.1 Listening. Read the question. Listen and write a name or a number. There are two examples.

Children listen and write a name or number. Play Track AB 4.1 twice, then elicit answers.

Answers (Audioscript on p.223)

1 9 **2** Eric **3** 7 **4** Rex **5** 1

3 Reading and Writing. Read this. Choose a word from the box. Write the correct word next to numbers 1–5. There is one example.

Have the children complete the text, using the words supplied. Check answers.

Answers

1 sit **2** walk **3** bed **4** raining **5** coat

Competency Focus

Me: Self-evaluation

The children reflect on the chapter and express their opinions about their own progress. This encourages them to evaluate and make decisions about how they learn and what they need to revisit.

Digital Resources

Teacher Resource Center • Print out Test Chapter 4 to use at the end of this lesson. The Test Generator also allows you to create customized tests.

Student's App • Encourage the children to play the games on their smartphone/tablet. Have a class vote on which of the three games they played is their favorite. (*The Inks* Apps are free and available on the App Store and Google Play.)

The children will:

- use critical thinking skills to identify sports.
- ask and answer questions about what sport people are doing and which ones they are good at.
- read, understand, and act out a story.
- identify and use verbs related to sports.
- compare athletes' abilities to animals.
- make medals.

Key Vocabulary

Activities and sports: do gymnastics, do judo, play basketball, play ping-pong, play tennis, play volleyball

Action verbs: bounce, catch, score, shout, throw, win

Key Grammar

- What are they doing?
- They're playing (ping-pong).
- They aren't playing (tennis).
- Are you good at (running)?
- Yes, I am. / No, I'm not.
- I'm not very good at (catching).

Reading Skills

Story: *The Animal Olympics*
Genre: modern animal story

Literacy Development

- predict story content from title and pictures
- identify words ending in *–ing*
- reflect on the story theme and choose characters to support

Functional Language

- Great job.
- Thank you.

Phonics

The children practice the pronunciation of the letter *a* as in *all*.

CLIL: Science—Human and animal abilities

The children find out about human athletes' abilities compared to animals' abilities.

Competency Focus

The children will:

use critical thinking skills to identify sports. (Lesson 1)	apply new grammar to previously learned vocabulary. (Lesson 2)	work in pairs to act out a dialogue. (Lesson 3)	personalize their response to the story by choosing their favorite character in the story. (Lesson 4)	relate the abilities of athletes to animal abilities. (Lesson 7)
predict the content of a story. (Lesson 3)	ask and answer about what they are good at. (Lesson 6)	work in groups to act out the story. (Lesson 8)	evaluate their own progress in the chapter. (Review)	
identify different action verbs related to sports. (Lesson 5)				

Digital Overview

Teacher Presentation
Student eBook and Digital Activity Book
- ASL Vocabulary Video 5.1: Activities and sports
- ASL Vocabulary Video 5.3: Action verbs
- Oral Storytelling Video 5.2: *The Animal Olympics*
- Interactive versions of AB activities
- Integrated audio and answer key for all activities

Teacher resources for planning, lesson delivery, and homework
Teacher Resource Center
- Class Planner Chapter 5
- Worksheets to print out (including notes and answers):
  - Grammar Worksheet 5A: What are they doing? They're …ing.
  - Grammar Worksheet 5B: Are you good at …ing? Yes, I am.
  - Oral Storytelling Video Worksheet 5: *The Animal Olympics*
  - Phonics Worksheet 5
  - CLIL Graphic Organizer 5
  - Test Chapter 5 and Mid-year Test
- Test Generator
- Literacy Handbook

Watch the Oral Storytelling Video

Children's resources for consolidation and practice at home
Student eBook
- ASL Vocabulary Video 5.1: Activities and sports
- ASL Vocabulary Video 5.3: Action verbs

Student eBook and Reader eBook
- Oral Storytelling Video 5.2: *The Animal Olympics*

The Inks **Student's App**
Vocabulary games: Activities/sports and action verbs

Vocabulary

Lesson objective: identify sports
Key vocabulary: *do gymnastics, do judo, play basketball, play ping-pong, play tennis, play volleyball*
Materials: Track 5.1; sentences on pieces of paper (Warmer)

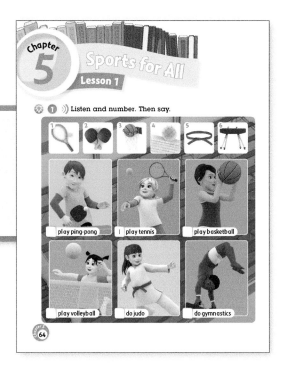

1)) Listen and number. Then say.

play ping-pong | play tennis | play basketball

play volleyball | do judo | do gymnastics

64

Warmer: Play "Running Dictation"

Write sentences on separate pieces of paper, and stick them on the wall around the classroom (or outside): *Can you ride a bike? Yes, I can. I can rollerblade and swim too. My brother can't swim. He can run and he likes soccer.* Divide the class into pairs. One child runs to read the text and dictates it a sentence at a time to their friend. Pairs swap to check each other's work.

1))) 5.1 Listen and number. Then say.

- With books closed, have the children underline the sports in the Warmer text. Encourage them to brainstorm other sports they know as a class.

- Then have them look at the pictures in their book and find any sports they did not mention.

- Play Track 5.1 and have the children listen and point.

- Then have them match the sports items to the phrases, writing the numbers. Play Track 5.1 again, pausing for them to repeat. Tell them to compare answers, then check as a class.

- Say *Come on, everyone! Let's play tennis!* and invite the children to repeat and mime the sport. Repeat with two more sports. In small groups, have the children take turns saying different sports, e.g. *Let's (do judo).* Have them all repeat and mime the sport.

Audioscript

Boy 1: *What's that?*
Girl 1: *It's my new game. Look everyone, it's really cool! You can play different sports. What sport would you like to play?*
Narrator: 1
Boy 1: *Let's play tennis.*
Narrator: 2
Boy 2: *No, let's play ping-pong.*
Narrator: 3
Girl 2: *I like basketball.*
Boy 3: *OK, let's play basketball.*
Narrator: 4
Boy 1: *Come on, everyone. Let's play volleyball!*
Boys & Girls: *Yes! Let's play.*
Narrator: 5
Boy 1: *Can you do judo?*
Narrator: 6
Girl 1: *No, but I can do gymnastics!*

Answers

play ping-pong 2, play tennis 1, play basketball 3, play volleyball 4, do judo 5, do gymnastics 6

Optional activity: Sports categories

Draw two circles on the board with the headings *Ball Sports* and *Other Sports.* Invite children to write a phrase in one of the circles, e.g. *play tennis* or *run.* Have them copy and draw a picture for each sport.

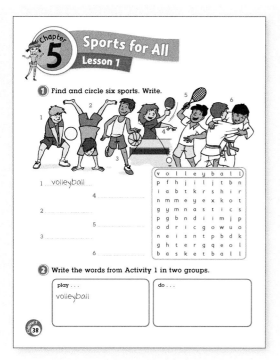

1 Find and circle six sports. Write.

2 Write the words from Activity 1 in two groups.

Competency Focus

Think! Critical Thinking

The children use critical thinking skills to identify sports by using visual clues and processing the written and spoken forms.

1 Find and circle six sports. Write.

Have the children find and circle the words in the wordsearch. Then have them label the numbered pictures.

Answers

Horizontal: volleyball, gymnastics, basketball
Vertical: ping-pong, tennis, judo

1 volleyball **2** gymnastics **3** basketball **4** ping-pong
5 tennis **6** judo

2 Write the words from Activity 1 in two groups.

Ask the children to write the sports from Activity 1 in the *play* or *do* group. Elicit answers and check with the class.

Answers

play: volleyball, ping-pong, basketball, tennis
do: judo, gymnastics

Cooler: Can you ...? mingle

Ask *Can you play ping-pong?* to elicit *Yes, I can.* or *No, I can't.* Have the children write three sports on a piece of paper. Then they mingle, asking and answering *Can you ...?* questions. Have children report their findings, e.g. *Sandra can do gymnastics.*

Digital Resources

Student eBook • Play ASL Vocabulary Video 5.1 to pre-teach key vocabulary as an alternative to the critical thinking approach.

• Play "Kim's Game" with the new vocabulary. Display the SB page. Have the class read the phrases aloud. Use *Timer* to give the class one minute to memorize the pictures, then one minute to recall them (with SB page closed). Repeat several times.

Grammar

Lesson objectives: ask and answer questions about what sport people are doing

Key grammar: *What are they doing? They're playing* (ping-pong). *They aren't playing* (tennis).

Materials: Track 5.2; Grammar Worksheet 5A [TRC printout] (optional)

Warmer: Sports revision

Invite individual children to mime a sport from Lesson 1 or other sports that they wrote in their notebook. Ask *What's he/she doing?* (e.g. *He's/She's playing tennis.*)

1))) 5.2 Listen and point. Then say.

- Ask the children to identify the sports in the pictures. Say the picture number and ask *What are they doing?* (*They're playing/doing …*)

- Play Track 5.2 and have them listen and point to the pictures for the correct sport. Play Track 5.2 again, pausing after each question and sentence for the children to repeat.

Audioscript

Narrator: 1
Girl: What are they doing?
Boy: They're playing tennis.
Narrator: 2
Boy: Umm … They aren't playing tennis. They're playing volleyball.
Narrator: 3
Girl: What are they doing?
Boy: They're doing judo.
Narrator: 4
Girl: What are they doing?
Boy: They're playing basketball. They aren't playing volleyball.
Narrator: 5

Girl: What are they doing?
Boy: They're doing gymnastics.
Narrator: 6
Girl: What are they doing?
Boy: They're playing ping-pong.

Grammar Central

What are they doing? …

Have children read the question and sentences aloud. Explain that we use *What are they …ing?* and *They're/They aren't …ing* to ask and talk about what two or more people are doing right now. Then divide your class into pairs and have them practice the question and answers. Monitor and check they are pronouncing the *ing* ending correctly.

For extra practice, try the **Grammar Booster** section in the Student Book (p. 74).

Answers p. 74

Activity 1: **1** doing **2** They're **3** doing **4** are **5** playing **6** aren't

Activity 2: **1** doing, They aren't playing volleyball. They're playing ping-pong. **2** What, They aren't playing tennis. They're playing basketball. **3** are, They aren't playing soccer. They're doing judo. **4** What are they doing? They aren't swimming. They're doing gymnastics.

2))) Track 5.2 Listen again and circle. What are they doing?

- Play Track 5.2 again, pausing after the example. Have a child read the example sentence for picture 1.

- Play the rest of the track. Have the children listen and circle the correct word. Ask them to compare answers with a friend.

Answers

1 tennis **2** volleyball **3** judo **4** basketball **5** gymnastics
6 ping-pong

3 Point to the picture. Ask and answer.

- Ask *What are they doing?*, pointing to picture 1 in Activity 1. Call on a child to read the example.

- Divide the class into pairs. Have the children take turns pointing and asking *What are they doing?*, and responding with an affirmative and negative sentence. Monitor and help.

Optional activity: Mime and write

Invite two children to the front. Show them a picture of a sport in Activity 1 and have them mime it. Tell the class to write a sentence describing the sport, e.g. *They're doing judo*. Repeat with pairs/groups of children for each sport.

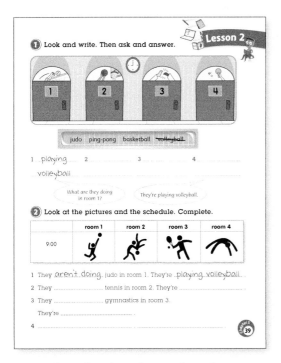

1 Look and write. Then ask and answer.

Using clues in the picture, the children write *playing* or *doing* and the correct sport from the box. Then they practice asking and answering about the pictures in pairs.

Answers

1 playing volleyball **2** playing basketball **3** doing judo
4 playing ping-pong

2 Look at the pictures and the schedule. Complete.

Have the children complete the sentences looking at the schedule. Elicit answers and check with the class.

Answers

1 aren't doing; playing volleyball **2** aren't playing; doing judo **3** aren't doing; playing tennis **4** They aren't doing/playing (children's own answer) in room 4. They're doing gymnastics.

Cooler: Listen and jump

Draw a check and a cross on either side of the board. Have the children stand at the front. Say *They're doing judo*. and *They aren't playing ping-pong*. and have them jump to the "check" side for a positive sentence and to the "cross" side for negative sentences. Continue, calling on individual children to say a sentence.

Competency Focus

Learn

By identifying people doing sports in a different context with new grammatical structures, the children demonstrate their understanding of previously acquired vocabulary from Lesson 1.

Digital Resources

Teacher Resource Center • For extra grammar practice, print out Grammar Worksheet 5A.

Reading: Story Extract

Lesson objectives: give and accept praise; use the title and pictures to predict story content; read the extract from *The Animal Olympics* (middle)

Functional language: *Great job. Thank you.*

Secondary language: *cheetah, message, Olympics, ostrich*

Materials: Tracks 5.3 and 5.4; pictures related to the Olympics (e.g. Olympic rings or medal award ceremony) (Warmer)

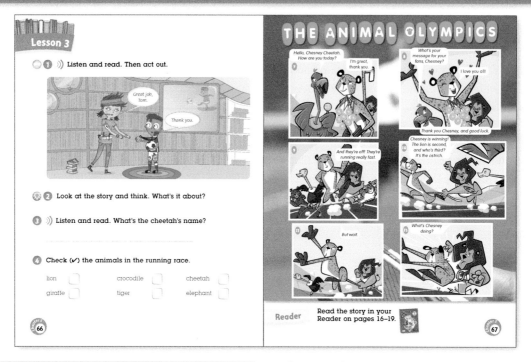

Warmer: Olympics

Show the pictures you have and elicit *Olympics.* Write it on the board and ask *When do they happen?* (*every four years*) *Where?* (*in different countries*) *When/Where were the last Olympics? And the next?* (You might need to use L1.)

Functional language

1)) 5.3 Listen and read. Then act out.

- Have the children look at the picture and ask *What sport does Tom play?* (*soccer*)

- Play Track 5.3 and ask them to listen and read. Pre-teach *medal* using the picture. Ask *Why is Libby giving Tom a medal?* (*because he played well/scored goals*) (They might need to use L1.)

- Play Track 5.3 again, pausing after each sentence for the children to repeat.

- Have the class act out the dialogue in pairs.

Before reading

2 Look at the story and think. What's it about?

- Call on a child to read the title of the story. Point to the pictures and ask *What sport is it?* (*running*)

- Ask *What's the story about?* (*a race*) *Who are the main characters?* Check understanding of *ostrich* and *cheetah.*

3)) 5.4 Listen and read. What's the cheetah's name?

- Play Track 5.4 and have the children listen and read along. They write the cheetah's name. Elicit answers.

- Play Track 5.4 again, pausing after picture 9 to ask *Who's winning?* (*Chesney*) *What's the lion doing?* (*pulling the cheetah's tail*) At the end, check understanding by asking if the lion does anything wrong. (You might need to use L1.)

Answer

Chesney/Chesney Cheetah

4 Check (✔) the animals in the running race.

- Choose a child to read the list of animals. Have the children check the animals in the race.

- Have individual children say an animal. Ask them to say which other animals they can see that are not in the list. (*leopard, ostrich*)

- Have a quick class survey asking the children to raise their hand for the animal they like most.

Answers

lion, tiger, cheetah

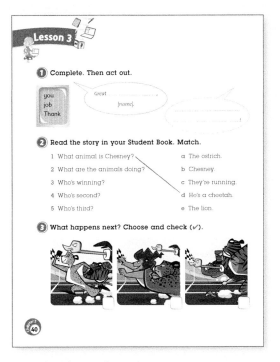

1 Complete. Then act out.

Have the children complete the dialogues. Then have them practice in pairs. Ask pairs to act out for the class.

Answers

job, (children's own answer), Thank you!

2 Read the story in your Student Book. Match.

Tell the children to read the story again and match the questions to the answers. Elicit answers.

Answers

1 d 2 c 3 b 4 e 5 a

3 What happens next? Choose and check (✔).

The children think about who is going to win the race. Have them check a picture. Elicit ideas.

Answers

Children's own answers.

Cooler: More sports and animals

Ask *What do you think happens next? Do you think the cheetah will win?* Have them brainstorm other sports and animals they might see in the story. Keep a note of their ideas for the next lesson.

Competency Focus

Collaborate and Communicate

The children work together, putting into practice new functional language by acting out a realistic dialogue.

Think! Critical Thinking

By looking at the story artwork, the children use prediction skills to help them engage with the story.

Digital Resources

Student eBook • After you have completed the book activities, display the SB page and show the story extract. Use *Timer* to give the children one minute to study the pictures. Then close or cover the page and ask questions to elicit details in the pictures, e.g. *How many medals does Chesney have in the first picture? Which animals are running in the race? Who's winning?*.

Lesson objective: read and understand the modern animal story
The Animal Olympics in the Reader
Materials: Track 5.5; Reader; Oral Storytelling Video Worksheet 5 [TRC printout] (optional)

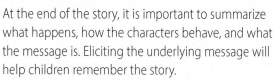

Warmer: Story recap

Write key words from the story on the board, e.g. *medals, winner, sports*, etc. Have the children say what they remember about the story. (They might need to use L1.) Then ask them to call out the animals and sports they brainstormed at the end of the previous lesson and write these on the board.

Story Summary

The Animal Olympics feature penguins, dolphins, giraffes, kangaroos, crocodiles, pandas, monkeys, an ostrich, a lion, a leopard, and a tiger—but the star is Chesney Cheetah! Chesney runs a race but the lion cheats to stop him winning. Chesney wins a gold medal for gymnastics instead.

Value: Play fairly with friends.

))) 5.5 While reading

- Ask the children to look at *The Animal Olympics* in their Reader. Give them time to study the pictures (only on the first two pages) and have children check the animals and sports on the board that appear in the story.

- Play Track 5.5 and have the children listen and read along. Ask *Who comes first/second/third in the race?* (*the ostrich, the leopard, and the tiger*) *Who's the winner of the Olympics?* (*Chesney*)

- Play Track 5.5 again. Encourage the children to mime the sports on the first page, the lion pulling the tail on the second page, and Chesney celebrating on the last page. For the third page, encourage them to make noises as Chesney would.

After reading: Reflect

- Ask the children to say why the lion did not compete well. Ask *Is it more important to win a race or take part fairly and enjoy it?* Invite children to talk about their own experiences. (The conversation may need to take place in L1.)

Optional activity: What happens next?

Have the children imagine what the lion and cheetah did after the award ceremony. Ask them to draw a picture of the lion and cheetah. Have them add speech bubbles. Have pairs of children present their drawings and act out the scene.

Story Time

The underlying message

At the end of the story, it is important to summarize what happens, how the characters behave, and what the message is. Eliciting the underlying message will help children remember the story.

Reading Strategy

List–Group–Label

With this strategy, children brainstorm words related to the story before they read it. They also organize the words in meaningful chunks which helps them build up their vocabulary. In addition, they practice their critical thinking and communication skills, and engage with the story before reading it.

For additional explanation and activities, see the Literacy Handbook on Teacher Resource Center.

Cooler: Group miming

Divide the class into animal groups using the animals from the story. Say *The penguins are running!* and have the penguin group run on the spot. Repeat with other animal groups and sports. Do this faster to make it more fun.

Digital Resources

Reader eBook • Show the the Reader story, as you play the audio.

- Watch Oral Storytelling Video 5.2 together before you do the After reading: Reflect activity.

- As an alternative Cooler, children take turns miming different animals from the story. Choose a different child each time to highlight the animal being mimed and identify it.

Teacher Resource Center • Print out Oral Storytelling Video Worksheet 5 to help you get the most out of the video.

Reading Comprehension and Critical Literacy

Lesson objectives: focus on words ending in *ing*; reflect on the story theme and choose characters to support

Materials: Track 5.5; Reader; pieces of paper for *1st, 2nd, 3rd* (Cooler); Oral Storytelling Video Worksheet 5 [TRC printout] (optional)

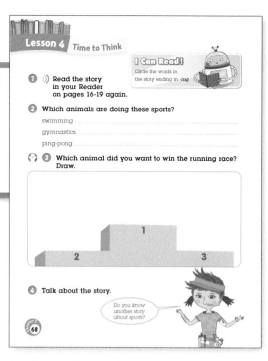

Note: Please ensure that your class has read the Reader story before you do this lesson.

Warmer: Animals and sports

Ask the children to recall the animals that appear in the story and write them on the board. Then ask them to work in pairs and say the sport each animal did in the story. Check as a class.

1))) 5.5 Read the story in your Reader.

- Have the children read the story. (Alternatively, play Track 5.5 and have them read along.)
- Have them count Chesney's medals in picture 6. (*8 in total*) Ask *What sport does Chesney win a gold medal for?* (*gymnastics*)

I Can Read!

Ask the children to look at the story and circle the words ending in *ing*. Have them compare with a friend. Have the children work in pairs and write a sentence using an *–ing* word, e.g. *We're playing ping-pong.* Then have children act out their sport.

Answers

swimming, playing, jumping, doing, running, winning, flying

2 Which animals are doing these sports?

- Have the children look at the pictures in their Reader and find the animals that do each sport. Ask them to write the animals or a full sentence, e.g. *The penguins and the dolphins are swimming.*
- Elicit answers and check with the class. Ask them what the other animals are doing, e.g. *The horse and the flamingo are asking questions.*

Answers

swimming: penguins and dolphins
gymnastics: monkeys (and Chesney Cheetah)
ping-pong: crocodiles and pandas

3 Which animal did you want to win the running race? Draw.

- Elicit the order of the animals in the race. (*ostrich—first, leopard—second, tiger—third*) Elicit the other two animals that ran. (*the cheetah and the lion*)
- Tell the children to choose and draw the three animals they wanted to come first, second, and third. Monitor and help.
- Call out the animals and have the children raise their hand if they chose that animal as the winner.

4 Talk about the story.

- Ask the class if they like the story. Have them choose their favorite picture.
- Ask a child to read Libby's question. Have the children share stories about sports, e.g. *The Hare and the Tortoise.*
- Invite children to talk about their own experiences with competitions. (They might need to use L1.)

Optional activity: Interview Chesney

Tell the children they are going to interview Chesney. Have them work in pairs to write two questions, e.g. *How do you feel?* Monitor and help. Ask children to take turns being Chesney answering the class's questions. Have them stand up with a "microphone" (pen).

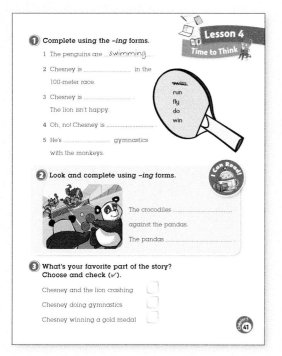

1 **Complete using the -ing forms.**

Have the children complete the sentences. Allow them to look back at the story if necessary. Elicit answers and check with the class.

Answers

1 swimming **2** running **3** winning **4** flying **5** doing

2 **Look and complete using -ing forms.**

The children practice the **I Can Read!** feature by completing the sentences, looking at the picture from the story. Elicit answers and check with the class.

Answers

are playing (ping-pong); are winning.

3 **What's your favorite part of the story? Choose and check (✔).**

Have the children read the three scenes and check their favorite one. Do a class vote to find out the most popular scene.

Answers

Children's own answers.

Cooler: First, second, third

Write *1st*, *2nd*, and *3rd* on three pieces of paper. Invite three children to the front and give them a piece of paper. Ask them to stand in a running pose in order (according to their paper). Elicit their positions, e.g. (*Pedro*) *is first!*

Competency Focus

Me: Critical Literacy

The children use critical literacy skills to reflect on the meaning of the story and decide what they wanted to happen.

Digital Resources

Student eBook • TIP As you monitor the children's progress, use *Add personal note* to keep a note of weaknesses in vocabulary, grammar, or pronunciation so you can review in later lessons.
• If you haven't already, show Oral Storytelling Video 5.2.

Teacher Resource Center • If you haven't already, print out Oral Storytelling Video Worksheet 5 to do the support activities.

Vocabulary, Song, and Phonics

Lesson objectives: use action verbs for sports; practice the sound of *a* in tall

Key vocabulary: *bounce, catch, score, shout, throw, win*

Secondary language: *fun, game, point, we all love*

Materials: Tracks 5.6 and 5.7; photo of a kangaroo (Warmer) ; Phonics Worksheet 5 [TRC printout] (optional)

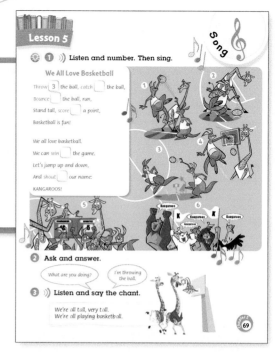

Warmer: We're kangaroos!

Quickly show the photo of a kangaroo and ask *What is it?* Alternatively, draw a kangaroo slowly on the board. Explain that the song is about kangaroos who are very good at basketball. Pre-teach the new vocabulary using mimes. Say the words for the children to do the actions as though they were kangaroos playing basketball.

1))) 5.6 Listen and number. Then sing.

- Have the children look at the pictures and ask *Who's the winner?* (*the kangaroos*) *What's the score?* (*10–5*) *How do the giraffes feel?* (*sad*)

- Then call out the red words one by one and mime them with the class. Play Track 5.6 and have them listen and number the words to match them with the pictures. Choose individual children to give their answer to the class.

- Play Track 5.6 again and have the class sing, miming the action words. Call out the number of the pictures at random and have the class say the action.

Answers

Throw 3, catch 1, Bounce 2, score 4, win 5, shout 6

2 Ask and answer.

- Mime one of the actions from Activity 1 (e.g. throw) and have the children ask you *What are you doing?* Say *I'm throwing the ball.* Have a pair of children demonstrate once more if necessary.

- In pairs or small groups, have the children take turns miming an action and asking, for the child miming to say what they are doing. Monitor and help.

3))) 5.7 Listen and say the chant.

- Have the children look at the picture and ask *What are the giraffes doing?* (*playing basketball*) *Are they short or tall?* (*tall*)

- Then ask them to look at the chant and notice the letter *a* in red. Play Track 5.7 and have the children listen and follow in their books, paying particular attention to the highlighted *a* sounds.

- Play Track 5.7 again, pausing for them to repeat the phrases. Practice the chant a few times with the class.

Optional activity: New verses

Brainstorm other ball games, e.g. tennis, etc. Divide the class into small groups. Have them choose a ball game and an animal, e.g. *soccer, penguins*. Play the song and have them sing in their groups, replacing *basketball and kangaroos* with their choices.

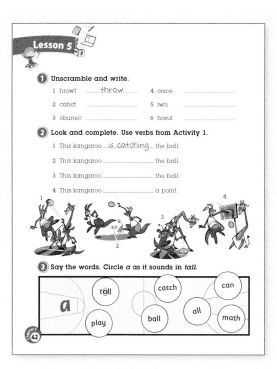

Competency Focus

Think! Critical Thinking

By matching the words to the pictures, the children use critical thinking skills to identify the action verbs related to sports and assimilate the written and spoken forms.

1 Unscramble and write.

Ask the children to write the words. Elicit answers and check with the class.

Answers

1 throw **2** catch **3** bounce **4** score **5** win **6** shout

2 Look and complete. Use verbs from Activity 1.

Have the children look at the pictures and complete each sentence with a verb from Activity 1. Ask children to read a sentence for the class.

Answers

1 is catching **2** is throwing **3** is bouncing **4** is scoring

3 Say the words. Circle *a* as it sounds in *tall*.

Tell the children to circle the *a* with the long sound as in *tall*. Check answers and have the class repeat the words after you.

Answers

Circled: **a** *in* t**a**ll, b**a**ll, **a**ll

Cooler: Disappearing chant

Write the chant on the board. Chant as a class, each time erasing one of the words. Continue until there are no words left on the board and the class are chanting with no prompt.

Digital Resources

Student eBook • Play ASL Vocabulary Video 5.3 to pre-teach key vocabulary. Play it again, pausing to elicit the word when the picture and sign are shown.

Student's App • Encourage the children to play the games on their smartphone/tablet. They could do this with a friend as a fun way to review the chapter vocabulary together. (*The Inks* Apps are free and available on the App Store and Google Play.)

Teacher Resource Center • For phonics practice, print out Phonics Worksheet 5.

Grammar and Reading

Lesson objectives: ask and answer about what they are good at
Key grammar: *Are you good at (running)? Yes, I am. / No, I'm not. I'm not very good at (catching).*
Secondary language: *throw the ball, Wait!*
Materials: Track 5.8; Grammar Worksheet 5B [TRC printout] (optional); cardboard, paper and colored pens for poster (Cooler)

Warmer: Imaginary ball

Show the class an imaginary ball, the size of a soccer ball. Mime bouncing and say *Bounce!* Then throw it to a child as you say *Throw/Catch!* Have the children repeat the actions and phrases. Do the same with different sized balls.

1))) 5.8 Listen and read.

- Point to the first picture. Ask *Where are Tom and Ellie?* (*the gym*) Point to Tom's outfit and ask *What color and number is it?* (*red and white, 9*)

- Play Track 5.8 and have the children listen and read along. Play Track 5.8 again, pausing for them to repeat.

- Elicit what Tom is doing. (*bouncing, throwing*) Ask *Who's good at scoring?* (*Biblio*) Why? (*He has long arms.*)

2 Write about you.

- Ask the children to look at Activity 1 again and say what Tom is and is not good at. (*He's good at throwing the ball, but he's not good at scoring.*) Do the same for Ellie and Biblio. (*She's not good at catching. He's good at scoring.*)

- Ask the example question around the class, eliciting *Yes, I am.* or *No, I'm not.* Have the children complete the answers and write about themselves. Monitor and help.

- Have the children compare answers in pairs. Ask children to read sentences 3 and 4 to the class.

Answers

1 good, (children's own answer) **2** Are you (children's own answer)? **3–4** children's own answer

Grammar Central

Are you good at running? …

Have the children look at the patterns. Explain that we use *be/not be good at* + *–ing* verb to talk about things we do well or not so well. Model the question, answers and negative sentence for the class to repeat. Have the children practice questions and answers in pairs.

For extra practice, try the **Grammar Booster** section in the Student Book (p. 75–77).

Answers p. 75

Activity 1: **1** good **2** I'm not **3** good at **4** I am **5** I'm not

Activity 2: Children's own answers.

p. 76

Activity 1: **1** d **2** c **3** a **4** e **5** b

Activity 2: **1** What are they doing? **2** They're playing ping-pong. **3** They're not playing tennis. **4** Are you good at ping-pong? **5** No, I'm not.

p. 77

Activity 1: **1** c **2** b **3** b **4** c **5** a **6** c

Activity 2: Children's own answers.

Activity 3: Children's own answers.

Optional activity: Are you good at … ? mingle

Write *Are you good at …?* on the board and elicit ideas, e.g. *playing ping-pong, swimming*, etc. Have the children write two questions. Set a time limit to mingle and ask questions. When they finish, have them write a sentence in response to each question, e.g. *Carla isn't good at jumping.*

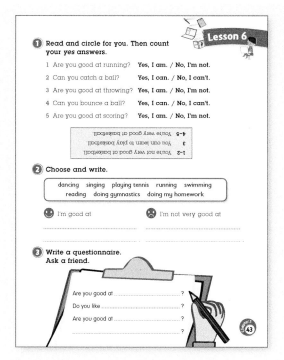

1 Read and circle for you. Then count your *yes* answers.

Have the children read the questions and circle the answer that is true for them. Then have them count their *yes* answers and read the result in the upside-down box. Ask children to say how many *yes* answers they have.

Answers

Children's own answers.

2 Choose and write.

Have the children choose two things they are good at and two they are not good at from the options supplied. They complete the sentences, then compare in pairs. Elicit responses.

Answers

Children's own answers.

3 Write a questionnaire. Ask a friend.

Have the children complete their questionnaire. Then tell them to ask their questions in pairs or in bigger groups if there is time. Ask children to say what they found out about their friend(s).

Cooler: We're good at speaking English!

Have the children find phrases in their book that they use/like, e.g. *How are you today?* etc. Assign pairs of children a phrase and have them write it on a piece of paper and decorate it. Stick the phrases on the poster.

Competency Focus

Learn

The children demonstrate their understanding of the new grammatical patterns by reading the text and completing the activity about themselves.

Digital Resources

Student eBook • Using *Timer*, give the class one minute to look at SB Activity 1. Cover the speech bubbles. Elicit the missing text. Repeat with different speech bubbles.

• Show the Grammar Central box. Children use *Highlighter* to identify questions and answers in SB Activity 1 text.

Teacher Resource Center • For extra grammar practice, print out Grammar Worksheet 5B.

CLIL: Science—Human and animal abilities

Lesson objective: learn about human athletes' abilities compared to animals' abilities

Materials: Track 5.9; CLIL Graphic Organizer 5 [TRC printout] (optional)

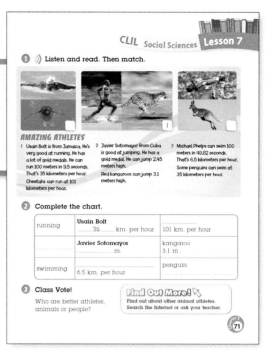

Warmer: Play "The Shark Game"

Play the game with *penguin*, *cheetah*, and *kangaroo* (see Games Bank p. 222).

1))) 5.9 Listen and read. Then match.

- With books closed, ask *What's (the penguin) good at?* Invite the class to answer. Repeat with *cheetah* and *kangaroo*. Pre-teach *athletes*.

- Have the children open their books and look at the pictures of the animals and athletes. Check if they know who the sportspeople are.

- Play Track 5.9 and have the children listen, read, and number the pictures. Elicit answers.

- Play Track 5.9 again, pausing after each paragraph and asking a comprehension question, e.g. *What's (Usain Bolt) good at? How fast can he (run)?*

Answers

3, 1, 2

2 Complete the chart.

- Ask the children to look at the chart and complete it, referring to Activity 1. Monitor and, if necessary, explain that the first column is the sports column, the second for the athletes and the third for the animals.

- Have the children compare answers in pairs before you check as a class.

Answers

running	Usain Bolt **35 km. per hour**	**cheetah** 101 km. per hour
jumping	Javier Sotomayor **2.45 m.**	kangaroo 3.1 m.
swimming	**Michael Phelps** 6.5 km. per hour	penguin **35 km. per hour**

3 Class Vote!

- Organize your class vote. Ask *Who are better at sports: animals or people?*

- Give the children a minute to think. Then write *Animals* and *People* on the board.

- Have the children raise their hand for each answer. Count the votes and write the totals on the board. Elicit the result of the vote.

Find Out More!

Ask the children if they know other animals that are very good at something, e.g. *The ostrich is the fastest bird running.* Then ask them to find out how fast two animals are. Suggest appropriate resources, e.g. Internet, library books, etc., or provide the information yourself. The children will need to complete this research before doing the follow-up activity in the Activity Book. (It could be set as homework.)

Optional activity: My favorite athlete

Have the children think about a sportsperson they admire and find information, e.g. where they are from, what they are good at, etc. Ask them to write a short paragraph on a piece of paper and decorate it. Display work around the class.

Have the children read the texts in Activity 1. Ask them to stand in a line. Say true/false sentences about the text. Have the children take two steps forward for "true" and one step back for "false." Continue until they reach the board.

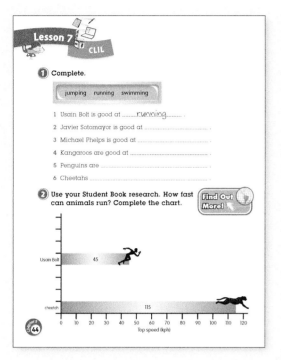

Competency Focus

Act

The children carry out research to find out about other animal athletes. This helps them expand their learning and relate it to their world, both inside and outside the classroom.

1 Complete.

Have the children complete the sentences about the sportspeople and the animals. Elicit answers and check with the class.

Answers

1 running **2** jumping **3** swimming **4** jumping
5 good at swimming **6** are good at running

2 Use your Student Book research. How fast can animals run? Complete the chart.

Ask the children what they know or found out about other animal athletes. Have the children share their information in small groups. Then they complete the chart.

Answers

(estimated speeds)
elephant: **25** km/h; *cat:* **45** km/h; *lion:* **80** km/h;
ostrich: **70** km/h; *leopard:* **100** km/h

Digital Resources

Student eBook • Show the pictures (from left to right) and have the children predict the topic. Ask them to identify any sports/animals they recognize.

• TIP Remember—you can use *Add personal note* to log the results of the class vote. Involve the children in tallying the results and writing the scores on the board.

Teacher Resource Center • Print out CLIL Graphic Organizer 5 for the children to use in collating their Find Out More! research.

CLIL eBook • The children can use the CLIL eBook to expand their knowledge of the lesson topic.

Project

Lesson objectives: review language from Chapter 5; complete a craft project—making medals; act out the story from the Reader

Materials: Reader; scissors, glue, paintbrush, silver and gold paint, paper (silver, gold, and brown), red ribbon; sticky labels, yellow/gray/brown pens or pencils (Alternative craft activity); two game pieces and a dice for each group; microphone (optional); camera (Cooler)

Warmer: Medals

Write *Medals* on the board. Have the children look through Chapter 5 quickly and find who won medals, e.g. *Chesney Cheetah, the monkeys, Phelps, Bolt, Sotomayor*. Then elicit the types of medals. (*gold—1st, silver—2nd, bronze—3rd*)

Prepare

1 Make medals.

- Have the children look at the completed medals. Tell them they are going to make their own medals.
- Hold up the materials to show the class. Point to the pictures and explain the stages. (You might need to use L1.)
- Demonstrate how to make a medal, stage by stage.
- Divide the class into pairs or groups if it is necessary to share materials. Give out the materials.
- As the children make their medals, monitor and give help as necessary.

Alternative craft activity

A simpler option would be to give the children sticky labels to decorate as medals, writing *1st, 2nd, 3rd* and coloring them yellow, gray, and brown.

Showcase

2 Tell the story. Use your medals.

- Choose three children to act out the flamingo, the cheetah, and the lion in pictures 7–12. Have the "cheetah" wear a gold medal.
- Divide the class into groups. Give them time to practice the extract of the story using their medals. Walk around, monitor, and give help with pronunciation.
- Call out groups to the front to perform their story using their medals.

Optional activity: More acting

Choose other sections of the story, e.g. pictures 1–3, and allocate the role of the horse/reporter to a child. They read out the text using a microphone if you have one (or a pen) and the class mime being the animal athletes. You could also use pictures 13–20 with different children reading the flamingo's part.

1 Play "Racetrack."

Read the game instructions with the class. Have the children play in groups. Give each group a dice. Make sure the children color the squares in their own books when they answer a question or do a task correctly. At the end, elicit how four children have "run".

Cooler: Team "photo"

Choose a child to be the "photographer." Ask the class to get together or in groups wearing their (gold) medals. Have them call out *We are the champions!* as they take photos. (Alternatively, use a real camera and display the photo in class.)

Competency Focus

Collaborate and Communicate

By acting out the story, the children consolidate their understanding in a fun and engaging way. They also demonstrate their ability to work with friends and use interpersonal skills.

Digital Resources

Student eBook • Show the Prepare photos, stage by stage, as you talk the class through the activity process.

Digital Activity Book • For AB Activity 1, as you monitor children's progress, use *Add personal note* to keep a note of weaknesses so you can review them in later lessons.

Language Review

Lesson objective: review language from Chapter 5
Materials: Tracks 5.10, AB 5.1 and AB 5.2

Warmer: Play "The Chain Game"

Have the children play the game using sports and action verbs from the lesson (see Games Bank p. 222).

1 Look and write the question or the answer.

- Ask the children to look at the pictures. Ask the example question and elicit the answer. Have the children write the questions/answers. Then have them compare in pairs before checking as a class.

Answers

1 They're swimming. **2** What are the monkeys doing?
3 They're playing ping-pong. **4** What are the crocodiles doing?

2))) 5.10 Listen and circle the things these animals are good at.

- Write *penguins*, *kangaroos*, *crocodiles*, and *cheetahs* on the board. Ask *What are the (kangaroos) good at?* Elicit ideas for all the animals from the class.

- Give the children time to read the sentences. Play Track 5.10, pausing after the example. Have a child say the answer.

- Play the rest of Track 5.10 through once for the class to listen and circle the correct words. Play Track 5.10 again for the children to check their answers.

- Elicit answers for the class to confirm.

Audioscript

1 Penguins are interesting birds. They can't fly but they're good at running and they're good at swimming.
2 Kangaroos can't run, but they're good at jumping.
3 Crocodiles are good at swimming.
4 Cheetahs are good at running, but they don't like water. They aren't very good at swimming.

Answers

1 swimming **2** jumping **3** swimming **4** running

3 Think about Chapter 5. Color the books.

- Have the children look back at Chapter 5. Elicit their favorite parts. The children then color the book which represents how they feel about their own progress (self-evaluation).

Treasure Hunt!

Ask the children to look at Student Book pp. 4–5 and find a basketball. Have the children raise their hands when they find it.

Cooler: Stand up, sit down

Call out verbs in the base form and *–ing*, e.g. *run, running, swim, swimming*. Have the children stand up for the *–ing* verbs and sit down for the base form. Call out the forms randomly and faster to make it fun.

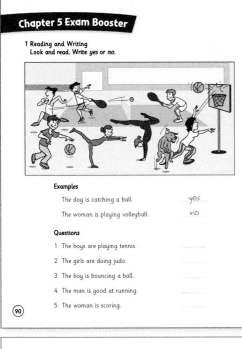

Chapter 5 Exam Booster

1 Reading and Writing
Look and read. Write *yes* or *no*.

Examples

The dog is catching a ball. ...yes...

The woman is playing volleyball. ...no...

Questions

1 The boys are playing tennis. ....

2 The girls are doing judo. ....

3 The boy is bouncing a ball. ....

4 The man is good at running. ....

5 The woman is scoring. ....

(90)

2 Listening
)) Listen and draw lines. There is one example.

Alex   Ben   Kim

Tony   Grace   Ann

(91)

3 Listening
)) Listen and draw lines. There is one example.

Alex   Katy   Ben

Sally   Ann   Peter

Exam Tip
Listen carefully for the names and descriptions.

(92)

1 Reading and Writing. Look and read. Write *yes* or *no*.

Have the children read the sentences and use the picture to respond *yes* or *no* to each one. Check answers.

Answers

1 yes **2** no **3** yes **4** yes **5** no

2))) AB 5.1 Listening. Listen and draw lines. There is one example.

Children listen and match the names to the characters.

Answers (Audioscript on pp. 223)

Lines from: Alex—boy jumping, Ben—boy bouncing the ball, Kim—girl scoring, Tony—boy shouting, Grace—girl sitting

3))) AB 5.2 Listening. Listen and draw lines. There is one example.

Children listen and match the names to the characters.

Answers (Audioscript on p. 223)

Lines from: Ann - girl eating sandwich, Katy - girl eating with fork, Ben - boy eating sandwich, Sally - girl eating apple, Peter - boy eating with fork

Competency Focus

Me: Self-evaluation

The children reflect on the chapter and express their opinions about their own progress.

Digital Resources

Teacher Resource Center • Print out Test Chapter 5 and Mid-year Test to use at the end of this lesson. The Test Generator also allows you to create customized tests.

• For the Exam Booster activities on the AB page, choose the audio button to access the recordings.

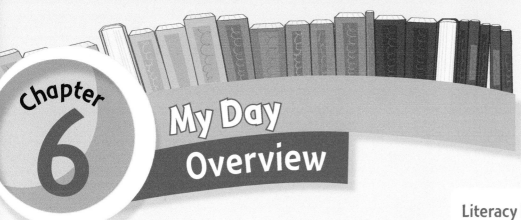

Chapter 6 — My Day Overview

The children will:

- use critical thinking skills to identify daily routines
- ask and answer questions about daily routines.
- read, understand, and act out a story.
- talk about daily routines and the time.
- do a quiz about the use of water.
- make a clock.

Key Vocabulary

Daily routine activities: brush my teeth, comb my hair, eat breakfast, get dressed, get up, go to bed, go to sleep, make my bed, take a shower, wake up, wash my face

Times: (nine) thirty, quarter after (nine), quarter to (nine)

Key Grammar

- What do you do (in the morning)?
- I get up. I brush my teeth. I don't take a shower.
- What time do you go to (bed)?
- I go to (bed) at (nine o'clock).
- Do you wake up early/late?
- Yes, I do. / No, I don't.

Reading Skills

Story: *I'm Late, Late, Late!*
Genre: modern rhyming story

Literacy Development

- predict story content from title and pictures
- focus on words that rhyme
- think about ways to help others

Functional Language

- Can I use the bathroom?
- Yes, sure.
- Thank you.

Phonics

The children practice the pronunciation of *k* sound as in loo*k* and clo*ck*.

CLIL: Math—Water use

The children find out about the importance of water and saving it by doing a quiz.

Competency Focus

The children will:

use critical thinking skills to identify daily routines. (Lesson 1)	apply new grammar to previously learned vocabulary. (Lesson 2)	work in pairs to act out a dialogue. (Lesson 3)	personalize their response to the story by thinking of their daily routines. (Lesson 4)	do a quiz to find out how much water they use every day. (Lesson 7)
predict the content of a story. (Lesson 3)	ask and answer what time they do daily routines. (Lesson 6)	work in groups to act out the story. (Lesson 8)	evaluate their own progress in the chapter. (Review)	
identify more daily routines and the time. (Lesson 5)				

Digital Overview

Teacher Presentation

Student eBook and Digital Activity Book

- ASL Vocabulary Video 6.1: Daily routine activities
- ASL Vocabulary Video 6.4: Times
- Music Video 6.2 (6.3): *Hush Little Baby*
- Interactive versions of AB activities
- Intergrated audio and answer key for all activities

Teacher resources for planning, lesson delivery, and homework

Teacher Resource Center

- Class Planner Chapter 6
- Worksheets to print out (including notes and answers):
  - Grammar Worksheet 6A: What do you do …? I get up.
  - Grammar Worksheet 6B: What time do you …? I … at …
  - Phonics Worksheet 6
  - CLIL Graphic Organizer 6
  - Festival Worksheet: Mother's Day
  - Test Chapter 6
- Test Generator
- Speaking Assessment: Cambridge English Young Learners Exams

Watch the Music Video

- Literacy Handbook

Children's resources for consolidation and practice at home

Student eBook

- ASL Vocabulary Video 6.1: Daily routine activities
- ASL Vocabulary Video 6.4: Times
- Music Video 6.2 (6.3): *Hush Little Baby*

***The Inks* Student's App**

Vocabulary games: Daily routine activities and times

Chapter 6 My Day

Lesson 1

Vocabulary

Lesson objective: identify daily routines
Key vocabulary: *brush my teeth, comb my hair, eat breakfast, get dressed, get up, make my bed, take a shower, wash my face*
Materials: Track 6.1

1)) Listen and number. Then say.

Warmer: Good morning!

Draw a sun on the board and write *Good morning!* Have the children wave and say *Good morning!* Then call on individual children to mime something they do in the morning. Elicit any morning routines they already know.

1))) 6.1 Listen and number. Then say.

- Have the children look at the picture of Buck. Pre-teach *cowboy.* Have them point to the daily routines they mimed/mentioned in the Warmer.

- Give them time to study the pictures and phrases in the game. Say *Howdy!* and wave. Tell them this means *Hello.* Point to the small pictures and ask *What does Buck do in the morning?* Elicit answers with the phrases. (They might need to use L1.)

- Play Track 6.1 and ask the children to listen and point.

- Then have them match the phrases to the small pictures of Buck, writing the numbers.

- Play Track 6.1 again, pausing for the children to repeat. Ask children to give an answer and check with the class.

- Divide the class into pairs or small groups. Have them take turns miming a morning routine for their friends to guess. Walk around and help with pronunciation.

Audioscript

Howdy! I'm Buck. Let's play! Look what I can do …
I can …
get up in the morning
wash my face and brush my teeth.
I can take a shower and comb my hair.
I can get dressed.
And make my bed.
And look! I can eat my breakfast.

Answers

bottom left, clockwise: 4, 2, 6, 3, 5, 7, 1, 8

Optional activity: Mime the routines

Invite pairs to mime a morning routine. Have the other children raise their hand if they know the phrase. Wait until all the children know (encourage them to help each other). Then say *1, 2, 3!* and have the children say the phrase.

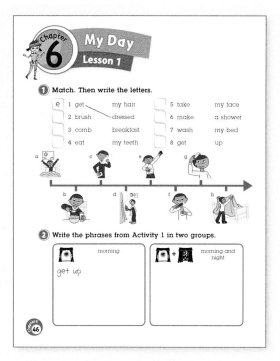

1 Match. Then write the letters.

Have the children match the words to make phrases. Then have them match the routines to the pictures, writing the correct letters. Elicit answers and check with the class.

Answers

e **1** get dressed
f **2** brush my teeth
g **3** comb my hair
b **4** eat breakfast
d **5** take a shower
h **6** make my bed
c **7** wash my face
a **8** get up

2 Write the phrases from Activity 1 in two groups.

Ask the children to write the phrases in the correct group. Elicit answers and check with the class.

Answers (suggested)

morning: get up, get dressed, comb my hair, eat breakfast, make my bed

morning and night: brush my teeth, take a shower, wash my face

Cooler: Clap, clap, clap!

Clap three times, say a phrase from Activity 1, and clap again three times. Call on a child to say a different phrase. Continue calling on children and encourage the children to clap with you. If someone repeats a phrase, start again.

Competency Focus

Think! Critical Thinking

The children use critical thinking skills to identify daily routines by using visual clues and processing the written and spoken forms.

Digital Resources

Student eBook • Play ASL Vocabulary Video 6.1 to pre-teach key vocabulary as an alternative to the critical thinking approach.

Digital Activity Book • Use the AB page to give feedback on activities, using the built-in interactive activity or answer key, as appropriate.

Grammar

Lesson objectives: ask and answer questions about daily routines
Key grammar: *What do you do* (*in the morning*)?
I get up. I brush my teeth. I don't take a shower.
Materials: Track 6.2; Grammar Worksheet 6A [TRC printout] (optional); small pieces of paper for mini-flashcards (optional), small ball (Cooler)

---

1))) **Listen and check (✔) for Sophie.**

Morning Routine		Sophie	Me
	I get up.	✔	
	I get dressed.		
	I take a shower.		
	I wash my face.		
	I eat breakfast.		
	I brush my teeth.		
	I comb my hair.		
	I make my bed.		

2 Now check (✔) for you. What do you do in the morning?

3 Talk to a friend.

What do you do in the morning?

I brush my teeth. I don't make my bed.

Grammar Central

What do you do in the morning?
I get up. I brush my teeth. I don't take a shower.
Grammar Booster on page 88

79

Warmer: Draw, say, mime

Draw a routine from Lesson 1 slowly on the board. Ask the children to call out and mime the phrase. Continue with all the routines. Invite individual children to draw on the board for the class to say and mime the routine.

---

1))) **6.2 Listen and check (✔) for Sophie.**

- Ask the children to open their books and look at the photo. Tell them they are going to listen to Sophie talk about her morning routine. Have them cover the second column and elicit the routines from the pictures.
- Play Track 6.2 and have them listen and check the things Sophie does.
- Play Track 6.2 again, pausing for the children to check answers.

Audioscript

Man: What do you do in the morning, Sophie?
Sophie: I get up. I get dressed. I don't take a shower. I wash my face. I eat breakfast. I brush my teeth. I comb my hair. I don't make my bed.

Answers

✔ *by:* get up, get dressed, wash my face, eat breakfast, brush my teeth, comb my hair

Grammar Central

What do you do in the morning? ...

Have the children focus on the patterns of the questions and the positive and negative sentences. Point out that the first *do* is a word that helps us make questions. Then divide your class into pairs and have them take turns asking the question and answering with a sentence as if they were Sophie.

For extra practice, try the **Grammar Booster** section in the Student Book (p. 88).

Answers p. 88

Activity 1: **1** do **2** get **3** take **4** do you do **5** I brush **6** I don't comb

Activity 2: **1** I get up. **2** I don't make my bed. **3** I wash my face. **4** I don't take a shower. **5** I get dressed. **6** What do you do in the morning?

2 Now check (✔) for you. What do you do in the morning?

- Ask the children to think about what they do every morning. Tell them to check the things they do in the Me column of the chart in Activity 1. Monitor and help.

Answers

Children's own answers.

3 Talk to a friend.

- Demonstrate the task with a child. Ask the question and call on a child to say what they do and do not do in the morning.

- Divide the class into pairs. Have them practice asking and talking about their morning routine.

Optional activity: Mini-flashcards

In pairs, the children make mini-flashcards for daily routines. Demonstrate and hold a set of mini-flashcards in specific order. Describe your morning routine according to this. Invite children to order their flashcards on the desk as you talk about your morning routines. Check that routines are in the same order.

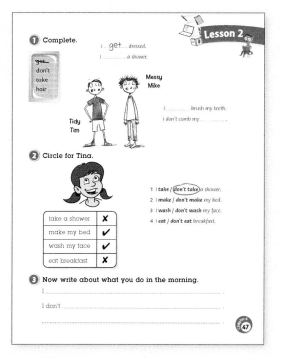

Cooler: Questions in a circle

Have the children stand in a big circle. Throw a ball to a child and ask *What do you do in the morning?* Have them answer and throw the ball to another child, repeating the question. The next child has to answer with a different morning routine. Continue like this to elicit all the morning routines, then start again.

Competency Focus

Learn

By identifying daily routines in a different context with new grammatical structures, the children demonstrate their understanding of previously acquired vocabulary from Lesson 1.

1 Complete.

Have the children complete the sentences with the words supplied. Elicit answers and check with the class.

Answers

get, take; don't, hair

2 Circle for Tina.

Ask the children to circle the correct words using the information in the table.

Answers

1 don't take **2** make **3** wash **4** don't eat

3 Now write about what you do in the morning.

Have the children write about their morning routine. Ask children to tell the class about their typical morning.

Answers

Children's own answers.

Digital Resources

Student eBook • Show the Grammar Central box. Use *Highlighter* to focus on key grammar structures.

Teacher Resource Center • For extra grammar practice, print out Grammar Worksheet 6A.

Reading: Story Extract

Lesson objectives: ask permission; use the title and pictures to predict story content; read the extract from *I'm Late, Late, Late!* (end)

Functional language: *Can I use the bathroom? Yes, sure. Thank you.*

Secondary language: *afternoon, evening, juice*

Materials: Tracks 6.3 and 6.4

Warmer: Rooms in the house

Review the rooms (*bedroom, kitchen,* etc.). Draw a few objects you can find in each room to help children, e.g. bed, sofa. Call on children to write a room next to the object and ask the class to help with spelling.

Functional language

1))) 6.3 Listen and read. Then act out.

- Have the children look at the picture and ask *What are they doing?* (*reading a story*)
- Play Track 6.3 and have the children listen and read along. Ask *Which room does Tom want to use?* (*the bathroom*) Play Track 6.3 again, pausing for the children to repeat.
- Choose two children to model the dialogue. "Libby" can use a book as a prop. Then have the children act out the dialogue in pairs.

Before reading

2 Look at the story and think. What's it about?

- Read the title of the story and point to the pictures. Ask *Where are they?* (*kitchen*) Point to the first picture and ask *What's Sonny doing?* (*eating breakfast*) Then point to the next picture and ask *Is he happy?* (*no—worried*)
- Ask *What's the story about?* (*a boy being late for school*)

3))) 6.4 Listen and read. Is the story funny?

- Play Track 6.4 and have the children listen and read along. They check *yes* or *no*. Ask *Is the story funny?* Invite children to answer and explain why. (They might need to use L1.)
- Play Track 6.4 again, pausing after the first picture and ask *Who is she?* (*Sonny's aunt*) Have them say what Sonny needs to do. (*comb his hair, wash his face*)

Answer

Children's own answer.

4 Check (✔) what time of day it is.

- Explain that morning is when we eat breakfast, afternoon is lunchtime, and evening is when it starts getting dark.
- Ask *What time of day is it in the story?* Elicit the answer.

Answer

morning

Optional activity: Drawing and guessing

Have the children write *morning, afternoon, evening* on pieces of paper. Then have them draw themselves doing something at that time of day on the other side. They take turns in groups showing their drawings. The first group guesses, e.g. *It's morning.* The second group shows the word and says *No.* or *Yes! I'm (sleeping).*

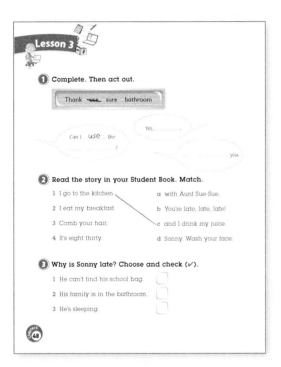

1 Complete. Then act out.

Have the children complete the dialogue and act it out in pairs. Ask pairs to act out for the class.

Answers

use, bathroom; sure; Thank

2 Read the story in your Student Book. Match.

Have the children match the sentences from the story. Check with the class. Ask them who says each sentence.

Answers

1 c 2 a 3 d 4 b

3 Why is Sonny late? Choose and check (✔).

Have the children read and check why they think Sonny is late. Elicit ideas.

Answers

Children's own answers.

Cooler: What happened before?

Explain that the extract is the end of the story. Have the children imagine what happened before. Elicit ideas. (They might need to use L1.)

Competency Focus

Collaborate and Communicate

The children work together, putting into practice new functional language by acting out a realistic dialogue.

Think! Critical Thinking

By looking at the story artwork, the children use prediction skills to help them engage with the story.

Digital Resources

Student eBook • Use *Highlighter* to draw attention to Pictures 11 and 12. Focus on Sonny in each picture. Elicit how he is feeling. Ask the children to predict what happened before this in the story and why Sonny feels like this.

Lesson objective: read and understand the modern rhyming story
I'm Late, Late, Late! in the Reader
Materials: Track 6.5; Reader

Warmer: Story characters

Ask the children to remember the characters from the extract (Sonny, his Aunt Sue-Sue, and his mom). Tell them there are three more people in the story. Encourage them to guess who.

Story Summary

Sonny, a young boy, is late for school. He tries to use the bathroom but someone in his family is always in there! He manages to eat breakfast but does not manage to comb his hair or wash his face.

Value: Don't be late.

)) 6.5 While reading

- Have the children look at the pictures in their Reader and identify the rooms.

- Play Track 6.5 and have the children listen and read along. Elicit the new characters in the story: Papa, Jay-Jay, and Gran-Gran.

- Play Track 6.5 again, pausing after pictures 3, 6, and 10 to ask *Who's in the bathroom (now)?*

- Read the story to the children yourself slowly, using different voices for each character and knocking on the table when appropriate. Have the children mime the actions of the characters as you read along.

- Check comprehension of the story by asking *Who's late? (Sonny) Are his dad, brother, or grandma late? (No, they aren't.)* Then have the children consider whether or not it is Sonny's fault. (They might need to use L1.)

After reading: Reflect

- Ask *Did you like the story? Why or why not? Do you feel sorry for Sonny?* Then have them say if they are usually late or on time. Encourage them to think about the importance of being on time. Do they like waiting for other people? (You might need to use L1.)

Optional activity: Knock, knock, knock!

Have the children stand in pairs, back to back. Ask one child to mime knocking, saying *Knock, knock, knock. Who's in there?* (Knock on the table at the same time.) Have the other child walk to face their friend and say *It's me! (Pedro)!*

Story Time

Repetition and chants

Some children may get distracted when they are listening passively. To encourage active participation, choose key phrases (featuring repetition and rhyming) for the children to repeat or supply as you tell the story.

Reading Strategy

Choral Reading

In Choral Reading, the children read aloud as a group or as a whole class. It is a useful strategy particularly for young and less confident readers. It helps develop their fluency, pronunciation, and intonation.

For additional explanation and activities, see the Literacy Handbook on Teacher Resource Center.

Cooler: The "Lesson's Over" chant

Have the class chant *I pack my bag. It's time to go home. I'm late, I'm late. Come on! Come on!,* miming the action of packing a bag. Once the children have memorized the chant, have them chant it at the end of class in other lessons too.

Digital Resources

Reader eBook • For the Warmer, children identify the other characters in the story. Ask them to try to figure out from the Reader pictures what these people all have in common. (*They all use the bathroom and make Sonny late.*)

Reading Comprehension and Critical Literacy

Lesson objectives: focus on rhyming words; think about ways to help the main character

Materials: Track 6.5; Reader

Lesson 4 Time to Think

1))) Read the story in your Reader on pages 20–21 again.

I Can Read! What words rhyme with "wait"?

2 Number the things Sonny does in order.
get dressed ☐   eat breakfast ☐   make the bed ☐

3 Help Sonny. How can he make sure he isn't late?

4 Talk about the story.

Do you know another story with repetition?

82

Note: Please ensure that your class has read the Reader story before you do this lesson.

Warmer: Order story characters

Elicit the story characters and write them on the board. Have the children work in pairs and say them in order of appearance. Call on children to write a number next to each character. Have them check in their Reader.

1))) 6.5 Read the story in your Reader.

- Have the children read the story. (Alternatively, play Track 6.5 and have them read along.) Ask *Why is Sonny not happy in the last picture?* (*He's late.*)
- Draw two clocks on the board with different times: quarter to eight and eight thirty. Have the children calculate how much time passes in the story. (*45 minutes*) (You might need to use L1.)

I Can Read!

Ask the question and have the children repeat *wait*. Write *tail*, *late*, *nose* on the board and have them identify which word rhymes with *wait*. (*late*) Tell them to find other words in the story that rhyme with *wait*. Call on children to say a word.

Answer

late, eight

2 Number the things Sonny does in order.

- Ask the children to number the routines in order of the story. Have them compare in pairs before checking as a class.

Answers

2, 3, 1

3 Help Sonny. How can he make sure he isn't late?

- Ask *Why is Sonny late?* (*He can't get into the bathroom.*) (They might need to use L1.)
- Then ask *What can he do to be on time?* Brainstorm ideas, e.g. *Wake up at seven thirty. Comb his hair in his bedroom. Wash his face in the kitchen.*
- Write their ideas on the board and help if necessary.

Answer

Children's own answer.

4 Talk about the story.

- Ask the children if they liked the story. Have a class vote, asking them to raise their hands for *yes* or *no*. Encourage them to give reasons why/why not. (They might need to use L1.)
- Have a child read Libby's question. Have children share other stories featuring repetition with the class.

Optional activity: More routines

Have the children look at Activity 2 again. Ask them to copy the routines and add more of them from the story that are missing, e.g. *wash my face, open my curtains.* Have them check the ones they did this morning.

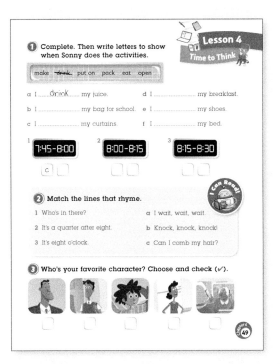

Cooler: Do they rhyme?

Write the following words in random order on the board: *May, play, say, they; these, please, cheese, peas; Sue, blue, shoe, you.* Have the children work in pairs or small groups to make three groups of four rhyming words. Call on children to draw lines to match the words on the board.

Competency Focus

Me: Critical Literacy

The children use critical literacy skills to reflect on the story and give the main character advice.

1 Complete. Then write letters to show when Sonny does the activities.

Have the children imagine they are Sonny. Tell them to complete the sentences, using the words supplied. Then they match them to the correct times, writing the letters under the clocks. Elicit answers and check with the class.

Answers

a drink **b** pack **c** open **d** eat **e** put on **f** make
1 c f **2** b e **3** a d

2 Match the lines that rhyme.

Ask the children to read the lines and focus on the last words and how they sound. They practice the **I Can Read!** feature by matching the lines, then check in pairs before you check as a class.

Answers

1 c **2** a **3** b

3 Who's your favorite character? Choose and check (✔).

Tell the children to choose their favorite character. Ask children to tell the class who it is and explain why.

Answers

Children's own answers.

Digital Resources

Reader eBook • Use *Timer* to give the children one minute to study the Reader story. Then minimize it and ask them to remember the members of Sonny's family in story order. Show the page again. Children confirm the answer by using *Pen* to link the people in order and identify them by name.

Student eBook, Digital Activity Book • TIP You can move the answer key pop-up window to show the answers next to the activity.

Vocabulary, Song, and Phonics

Lesson objectives: talk about daily routines and the time; practice the *k* sound with a chant

Key vocabulary: *go to bed, go to sleep, wake up; quarter after* (*nine*), *quarter to* (*nine*), (*nine*) *thirty*

Secondary language: *cry, hush*

Materials: Tracks 6.6 and 6.7

Warmer: Human clock 1

Pre-teach the new vocabulary using mimes/drawings. Say *go to bed, go to sleep,* and *wake up* for the children to mime. Then draw a big clock on the board (without hands). Stand in front of the clock. Invite the class to say times with *a quarter after, a quarter to,* and *thirty.* Place your arms accordingly.

1)) 6.6 Listen and number. Then sing.

- Point to the pictures as you ask *Is the baby asleep or awake?* Pre-teach *hush* and *tick-tock.*

- Ask them to look at the phrases in red and mime them as a class. Explain the difference between *wake up* and *get up.* Then play Track 6.6 and have them number the phrases, matching them to the pictures.

- Elicit answers and check with the class.

- Play Track 6.6 again and have the class sing along. Teach them gestures (rocking baby in arms). For the times, mark them with your arms in the air—right arm for nine and left arm marking the minutes.

Answers

go to bed 4, quarter to nine 3, go to sleep 6, wake up 1, quarter after nine 5, nine thirty 2

2 Do a class survey. Ask and answer.

- Ask the children to read the question. Elicit other times of day. (*morning, afternoon*)

- Divide the class into pairs to practice asking and answering *What do you do in the evening?*

- Say *Do a class survey with the same question.* Ask them to note down one thing each friend does. Set a time limit.

- Elicit answers from the class and write the actions on the board, e.g. *brush my teeth,* and the number of children for each.

3)) 6.7 Listen and say the chant.

- Ask *What time is it?* pointing to the picture. (*nine o'clock*)

- Play Track 6.7 and have the children listen to the chant. Then play Track 6.7 again, pausing for them to repeat.

- Focus on the spellings of the sound *k: ck* and *k.*

- Practice the chant with the class. Repeat each phrase and build up the rhythm.

Optional activity: Dictation with times

Have the children draw four clock faces in their notebook. Dictate four times (using *o'clock, thirty, a quarter after,* and *a quarter to*). Ask them to draw and write the times. Have them compare in pairs before you check as a class.

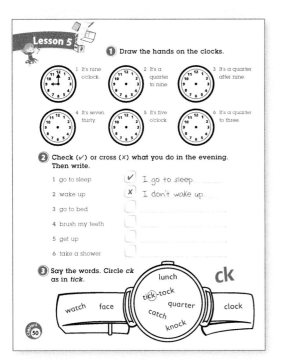

Cooler: Chant the different times

Draw a big clock on the board (without hands). Ask a child to draw a time. Repeat the chant from Activity 3, changing the time to the one that is on the board. Invite more children to choose a different time and repeat the chant.

Competency Focus

Think! Critical Thinking

The children use critical thinking skills to identify the meaning of routine activities and times by processing the written and spoken forms, and matching them to the correct picture.

1   Draw the hands on the clocks.

Ask the children to read the sentences and draw the time on each clock. Check with the class by having children draw the time on the board.

Answers

Clocks with the following times drawn on:
1 9:00 **2** 8:45 **3** 9:15 **4** 7:30 **5** 5:00 **6** 2:45

2   Check (✔) or cross (✗) what you do in the evening. Then write.

Have the children read the activities and put a check or a cross so that it is true for them. Then have them write sentences. Elicit responses.

Answers

1 I go to sleep. **2** I don't wake up. **3** I go to bed. **4** I brush my teeth. **5** I don't get up. **6** I take/don't take a shower.

3   Say the words. Circle *ck* as in *tick*.

Ask the children to circle *ck* in the words. Check answers.

Answers

Circled: **ck** *in* ti**ck**-to**ck**, kno**ck**, clo**ck**

Digital Resources

Student eBook • Play ASL Vocabulary Video 6.4 to pre-teach key vocabulary. Play it again, pausing to elicit the word when the picture and sign are shown.

• Play Music Video 6.2 (6.3). Encourage the children to dance and sing along. The lyrics appear on screen for support. Pause the video for the children to continue dancing and singing.

Teacher Resource Center • For phonics practice, print out Phonics Worksheet 6.

Grammar and Reading

Lesson objectives: ask and answer about what time they do daily routines

Key grammar: *What time do you go to (bed)? I go to (bed) at (nine o'clock). Do you wake up early/late? Yes, I do. / No, I don't.*

Secondary language: *hours of sleep, survey*

Materials: Tracks 6.6 and 6.8; Grammar Worksheet 6B [TRC printout] (optional); strips of paper (optional)

Warmer: Hush, little baby

)) 6.6

Divide the class into pairs; one child is Sonny and the other is the baby. Play the song from Lesson 5 and have "Sonny" sing and the baby cry/go to sleep in each pair. Play the song again and have them change roles.

1)) 6.8 Listen and read.

- Ask the children to look at the first picture. Call on a child to read the title and mime *to be asleep*. Then have the children look at the other pictures and identify who takes part in the survey. (*Ellie, Libby, and Biblio*)

- Play Track 6.8 and ask them to listen and read along.

- Play Track 6.8 again, pausing for them to repeat.

- Draw the times for Ellie on the board (nine o'clock and eight o'clock) and show them how to count the hours of sleep. (*11 hours*) Do the same for Libby. Point to Biblio and ask *Is he asleep?* (*yes*)

Grammar Central

What time do you go to bed? …

Have the children look at the patterns and point out the word order for questions and short answers. Point out that we say *at* before the time. Divide the class into pairs and have them practice the questions and answers.

For extra practice, try the **Grammar Booster** section in the Student Book (p. 89–91).

Answers p. 89

Activity 1: **1** do **2** go **3** don't go **4** take **5** at **6** Do

Activity 2: **1** Yes, I do. **2** I get up at 5 o'clock. **3** No, I don't. **4** Do you eat **5** What time do you **6** Do you go

p. 90

Activity 1: **1** What time **2** I go **3** do you **4** What do **5** I don't go

Activity 2: **1** b **2** c **3** e **4** a **5** d

p. 91

Activity 1: **1** What time do you get up? **2** What are you doing now? **3** Do you make your bed? **4** Are you good at swimming? **5** Do you eat breakfast at 8:30? **6** What time do you go to bed? **7** What do you do in the evening? **8** Do you wake up early?

Activity 2: Children's own answers.

2 Complete the answers for Tom.

- Point to the clocks next to the sentences and elicit the times.

- Ask the class to complete the questions and the sentences about Tom, referring to these clocks.
- Give them time to complete their answers, referring back to Grammar Central. Elicit answers and check with the class.

Answers

1 do, go, nine **2** do, o'clock

Optional activity: Choose a time

Distribute two strips of paper to each child and have them write a different time on each. Collect the strips and distribute them again. Divide the class into pairs and give four strips of paper face down to each pair. Have them take turns saying *Do you wake up/go to bed early/late?* Have them choose a strip of paper and answer with that time.

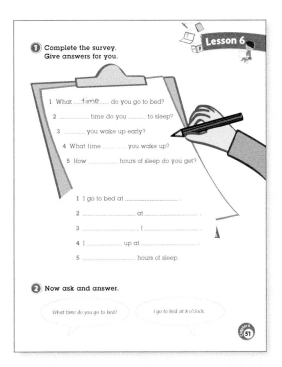

2 Now ask and answer.

In pairs, the children practice asking and answering the questions in Activity 1. Encourage them to answer without reading the sentence on the page.

Cooler: Role-play

In pairs, the children take turns being Tom and Ellie/Libby and do a role-play. Encourage them to use a pen and pretend to take notes. If there is time, have the children act out a role-play between Tom and Biblio too. Have each pair calculate Biblio's hours of sleep and compare in class.

Competency Focus

Learn

The children demonstrate their understanding of the new grammatical patterns by reading the text and completing the activity.

1 Complete the survey. Give answers for you.

Have the children complete the questions first. Elicit answers and then have them complete the sentences for themselves.

Answers

Questions: **1** time **2** What, go **3** Do **4** do **5** many
Answers: **1** children's own answer **2** I go to sleep, children's own answer **3** Yes/No, do/don't **4** wake, children's own answer **5** I get + children's own answer.

Digital Resources

Digital Activity Book • Have children do the AB interactive digital activities or set them for homework.

Teacher Resource Center • For extra grammar practice, print out Grammar Worksheet 6B.

CLIL: Math—Water use

Lesson objective: find out about the importance of water and saving it by doing a quiz

Materials: Track 6.9; CLIL Graphic Organizer 6 [TRC printout] (optional); 1 liter bottle of water, construction paper for poster (optional)

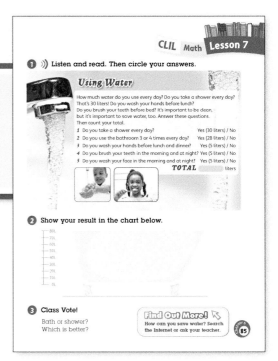

Warmer: Missing vowels

Write *W_t_r _s _mp_rt_nt!* on the board and have the children work in small groups to solve. (*Water is important!*) Provide the vowels on the board if necessary. Elicit what the children and their family use water for at home.

1)) 6.9 Listen and read. Then circle your answers.

- Have the children look at the pictures and ask *What are they doing?* (*washing hands, brushing teeth*)
- Play Track 6.9 and have the children listen and read along.
- Then have the children read questions 1 to 5 again and circle *yes/no* for them.
- When they have circled their answers, ask the questions again and elicit *yes/no* from the class. Show them a 1 liter bottle of water to help them understand the quantity of water for each *yes* answer.
- Ask the children to calculate the total number of liters they use every day. Walk around and help. Elicit answers from the class.

Answers

Children's own answers.

2 Show your results in the chart below.

- Point to the chart and have the children mark their result according to their total in Activity 1. Have them color the bathtub blue up to their mark.

- Ask children to show the class their bathtub and say *I use (45) liters of water a day.* Find out who uses the smallest and biggest amount in the class.

Answers

Children's own answers.

3 Class Vote!

- Organize your class vote. Ask children if they prefer taking a bath or a shower. Then have them think which is better for the environment. Give the children a minute to think. Then write *bath* and *shower* on the board. Have the children raise their hand for each answer. Count the votes and write the totals on the board. Elicit the result of the vote.

Find Out More!

Ask the children if they know of ways to save water, e.g. *turn off the tap while you are washing your face/brushing your teeth.* (They might need to use L1.) Ask the children to find out more ideas. Suggest appropriate resources, e.g. Internet, library books, etc., or provide the information yourself. The children will need to complete this research before doing the follow-up activity in the Activity Book. (It could be set as homework.)

Optional activity: Class Poster—Save water

Create a "Save water" poster with the class. Ask the children to write advice/ideas on the poster, find pictures, or draw to decorate the class poster. Display it in class or in the school.

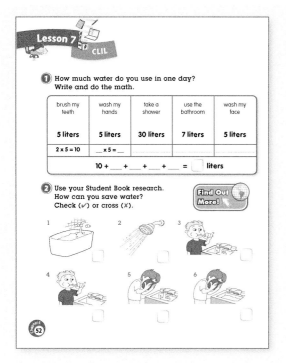

Competency Focus

Act

The children carry out research to find out ways to save water. This helps them expand their learning and relate it to their world, both inside and outside the classroom.

1 How much water do you use in one day? Write and do the math.

Have the children count how many times they do each activity a day. Then help them do the math if necessary. Tell them to write the liters of water and add up the final amount. Find out who uses the most water in class.

Answers

Children's own answers.

2 Use your Student Book research. How can you save water? Check (✔) or cross (✗).

Ask the children to share ideas on how to save water. Then have them look at the pictures and put a check (if the activity saves water) or a cross (if it does not). Check answers with the class.

Answers

✔ by 2, 4, 6
✗ by 1, 3, 5

Cooler: Play "Whisper It!"

Have the children play the game with actions and routines from the lesson (see Games Bank p. 222).

Digital Resources

Student eBook, Digital Activity Book • TIP Remember—do not be afraid to turn off the screen! Children benefit from variety of pace and focus.

Digital Activity Book • Use *Pen* to create a model answer for AB Activity 1. Write in your amounts and have children do the math.

Teacher Resource Center • Print out CLIL Graphic Organizer 6 for the children to use in collating their Find Out More! research.

CLIL eBook • The children can use the CLIL eBook to expand their knowledge of the lesson topic.

Project

Lesson objectives: review language from Chapter 6; complete a craft project—making a clock; act out the story from the Reader

Materials: Reader; black and white construction paper, black marker, felt-tip pens, watercolors, paintbrush, paper fastener; paper plates (Alternative craft activity)

Warmer: Times in the story

Ask the children to look at the story in their Reader and underline the times. (*a quarter to eight—picture 1, eight o'clock—picture 5,* etc.) Elicit the times from the class in order.

Prepare

1 Make a clock.

- Have the children look at the completed clocks. Ask *Which do you like best?* Tell them they are going to make their own clock.

- Hold up the materials to show the class. Point to the pictures and explain the stages. (You might need to use L1.)

- Demonstrate how to make a clock, stage by stage.

- Divide the class into pairs or groups if it is necessary to share materials. Give out the materials.

- As the children make their clocks, monitor and give help as necessary. Make sure one hand is clearly longer than the other.

Alternative craft activity

A simpler option would be to give the children paper plates to use for their clocks.

Showcase

2 Tell the story. Use your clocks.

- Choose a child to help you act out the first part of the story (pictures 1–6). Act out Dad and Jay-Jay, and the child can be Sonny. Hold the child's clock and invite them to show the time.

- Divide the class into pairs to act out the story. Have them take turns being Sonny and the other characters. Give them time to practice using their Reader. Monitor and give help during rehearsal time.

- Ask pairs to perform their story using their clocks.

Optional activity: What time is it?

Divide the class into small groups. Have a child in each group show a time on their clock (secretly). Their group asks *What time is it?* and they answer, then show their clock for the group to confirm.

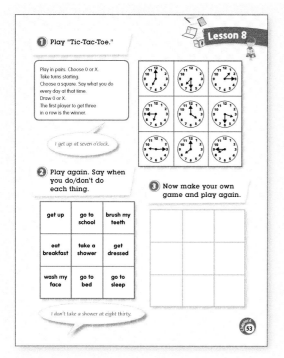

Competency Focus

Collaborate and Communicate

By acting out the story, the children consolidate their understanding in a fun and engaging way. They also demonstrate their ability to work with friends and use interpersonal skills.

1 Play "Tic-Tac-Toe."

Read the instructions with the class. Demonstrate the game on the board with a child. Then have the children play in pairs.

2 Play again. Say when you do/don't do each thing.

Have the children play the game with a different friend and the new prompts. Make sure they use the affirmative and negative form of the verbs. Have them draw 0 or X.

3 Now make your own game and play again.

Tell the children to complete the Tic-Tac-Toe grid with their own ideas, e.g. times and/or verbs. In different pairs, have them play each other's game making correct sentences with the words/phrases/times in the grid.

Cooler: Clock gallery

Have the children place their clocks on their desks face up. Have them walk around the desks in pairs. Tell them to look at the clocks and ask and answer with their friend, e.g. *What time is it?* (e.g. *It's seven o'clock.*)

Digital Resources

Student eBook • Show the Prepare photos, stage by stage, as you talk the class through the activity process.

Language Review

Lesson objective: review language from Chapter 6
Materials: Tracks 6.10, AB 6.1, AB 6.2 and AB 6.3; clocks from Lesson 8 (optional)

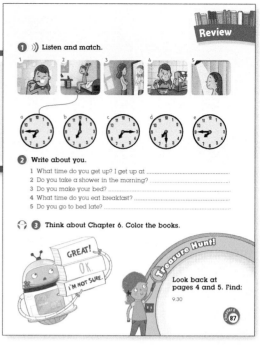

Warmer: Human clock 2

Draw a big clock on the board (without hands). This time, invite children to stand and mark the time with their arms. The class says what time it is.

1))) 6.10 Listen and match.

- Ask the children to look at the pictures. Elicit what the girl is doing in each one. Then point to the clocks and elicit the times.
- Play Track 6.10 and have the children match the pictures and clocks. Play Track 6.10 again for them to check their answers before checking with the class.

Audioscript

Man: What time do you get up?

Girl: I get up at a quarter to seven. I take a shower at seven o'clock. I eat breakfast at a quarter past seven. Then at seven thirty, I brush my teeth. I get dressed at a quarter to eight and I go to school.

Answers

1 d 2 a 3 e 4 c 5 b

2 Write about you.

- Have children read the questions one by one, eliciting model answers from different children.
- Give them time to write their own answers. Walk around and encourage them to write full sentences.

- Divide the class into pairs and have them ask and answer.

Answers

Children's own answers.

3 Think about Chapter 6. Color the books.

- Have the children look back at Chapter 6. Elicit their favorite parts. The children then color the book which represents how they feel about their own progress (self-evaluation).

Treasure Hunt!

Ask the children to look at Student Book pp. 4–5 and find a clock showing 9:30. Have the children raise their hand when they find it.

Cooler: Is it the same for you?

Invite a child to read one of their answers from Activity 2. Have the children stand up if they answered the same thing. Repeat with different children prompting.

Competency Focus

Me: Self-evaluation

The children reflect on the chapter and express their opinions about their own progress. This encourages them to evaluate and make decisions about how they learn and what they need to revisit.

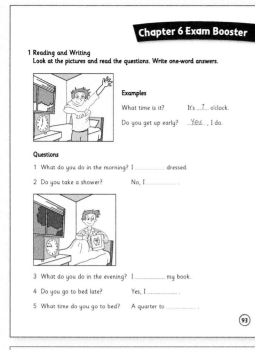

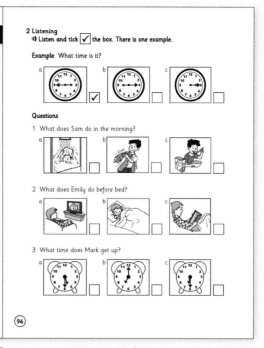

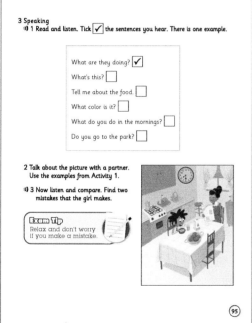

1 Reading and Writing. Look at the pictures and read the questions. Write one-word answers.

Children look at the pictures and complete the answers.
Answers

1 get **2** don't **3** read **4** do **5** eleven

2))) AB 6.1 Listening. Listen and tick (✔) the box. There is one example.

Children listen and tick the correct pictures. Play Track AB 6.1 twice, then elicit answers.
Answers (Audioscript on p. 223)

1 b **2** c **3** a

3.1))) AB 6.2 Speaking. Read and listen. Tick (✔) the sentences you hear. There is one example.

Children listen and tick the correct pictures. Play Track AB 6.2 twice, then elicit answers.
Answers (Audioscript on p. 223)

What are they doing?; Tell me about the food.; What do you do in the mornings?

3.2 Speaking. Talk about the picture with a partner. Use the examples from Activity 1.

Have the children talk about the picture.

3.3))) AB 6.3 Speaking. Now listen and compare. Find two mistakes that the girl makes.

Ask the children to listen and compare their answers.
(Audioscript on p. 223)

Digital Resources

Teacher Resource Center • Print out Test Chapter 6 to use at the end of this lesson.

- For the Cambridge English Young Learners exam preparation activities, there are Speaking prompts available for this chapter.
- Print out Festival Worksheet: Mother's Day to expand the children's knowledge of US culture.

Student's App • Encourage the children to play the games on their smartphone/tablet. Ask them to record their scores to compare in the next lesson. (*The Inks* Apps are free and available on the App Store and Google Play.)

Chapter 7

Busy Lives
Overview

The children will:

- use critical thinking skills to identify professions.
- ask and answer questions about what people do and where they work.
- read, understand, and act out a story.
- talk about what people do at work.
- find out about people who help others.
- make a mask.

Key Vocabulary

Professions: cleaner, chef, doctor, firefighter, office worker, police officer, teacher, vet
Verbs that describe professions: catch, clean, cook, put out, take care, teach, travel

Key Grammar

- What does she do?
- She's a (doctor).
- Where does she work?
- She works in (a hospital).
- He doesn't (cook).
- Does he go (to school)?
- Yes, he does. / No, he doesn't.

Reading Skills

Story: *The Secret Life of Shelly the Chef*
Genre: superhero story

Literacy Development

- predict story content from title and pictures
- focus on the visual clues in the story
- personalize the main character's actions

Functional Language

- What do you want to be?
- I want to be a superhero.

Phonics

The children practice pronunciation of *sh* sound as in *she* and *s* sound as in *super*.

CLIL: Social sciences—People who help

The children find out how people help in their community.

Competency Focus

The children will:

use critical thinking skills to identify professions. (Lesson 1)	apply new grammar to previously learned vocabulary. (Lesson 2)	work in pairs to act out a dialogue. (Lesson 3)	personalize their response to the story by imagining themselves as the main character. (Lesson 4)	think about how people help in their community. (Lesson 7)
predict the content of a story. (Lesson 3)	ask and talk about what people do at work. (Lesson 6)	work in groups to act out the story. (Lesson 8)	evaluate their own progress in the chapter. (Review)	
describe what people do at work. (Lesson 5)				

Digital Overview

Teacher Presentation

Student eBook and Digital Activity Book

- ASL Vocabulary Video 7.1: Professions
- ASL Vocabulary Video 7.3: Verbs that describe professions
- Oral Storytelling Video 7.2: *The Secret Life of Shelly the Chef*
- Interactive versions of AB activities
- Integrated audio and answer key for all activities

Teacher resources for planning, lesson delivery, and homework

Teacher Resource Center

- Class Planner Chapter 7
- Worksheets to print out (including notes and answers):
  - Grammar Worksheet 7A: What does she do? She's a ...
  - Grammar Worksheet 7B: He doesn't ...
  - Oral Storytelling Video Worksheet 7: *The Secret Life of Shelly the Chef*
  - Phonics Worksheet 7
  - CLIL Graphic Organizer 7
  - Project Template 7
  - Test Chapter 7
- Test Generator
- Literacy Handbook

Watch the Oral Storytelling Video

Children's resources for consolidation and practice at home

Student eBook

- ASL Vocabulary Video 7.1: Professions
- ASL Vocabulary Video 7.3: Verbs that describe professions

Student eBook and Reader eBook

- Oral Storytelling Video 7.2: *The Secret Life of Shelly the Chef*

***The Inks* Student's App**

Vocabulary games: Professions and verbs that describe professions

Vocabulary

Lesson objective: identify professions
Key vocabulary: *chef, cleaner, doctor, firefighter, office worker, police officer, teacher, vet*
Materials: Track 7.1; Reader; "Pelmanism" cards (optional)

Warmer: Professions review

Show the children the story in the Reader for Chapter 2 (*Hilltop School for Young Detectives*). Point to the teacher, the cleaner, and the jeweler in the pictures in turn. Elicit the professions and have the children call out other professions they know.

1))) 7.1 Listen and number. Then say.

- Ask the children to open their books and look at the pictures of the people. Have them identify the professions they know. For the professions they do not know, point out clues in the picture (the clothes/uniform or other objects, e.g. the sponge and spray for cleaner, etc.). Then give them time to study the pictures of the objects.

- Play Track 7.1 and have them listen and match the pictures of the objects with the correct professions.

- Have the children check in pairs, then ask individual children to give an answer and check with the class.

- Play Track 7.1 again, pausing after each sentence. Have the children repeat and point to the correct person.

Audioscript

Narrator: 1
Girl: She's a teacher. . . . (Teacher.)
Narrator: 2
Girl: She's a vet. . . . (Vet.)

Narrator: 3
Girl: She's a police officer. . . . (Police officer.)
Yes!
Narrator: 4
Girl: He's a doctor. . . . (Doctor!)
Yay!
Narrator: 5
Girl: He's a cleaner. . . . (Cleaner.)
Narrator: 6
Girl: He's a chef. . . . (Chef.)
Narrator: 7
Girl: She's an office worker. . . . (Office worker.)
Yes!
Narrator: 8
Girl: He's a fire fighter. . . . (Fire fighter.)
Hooray!

Answers

4, 1, 6, 5
7, 2, 8, 3

Optional activity: Play "Pelmanism"

Make two sets of cards for each group. You can photocopy the pictures on Student Book p. 68 and make separate cards with just the words. Divide the class into groups. They set out the cards face down. The children take turns turning over two cards to find a matching picture/word pair. They keep any pairs they find or turn the cards back over if they do not match. The child with the most pairs wins.

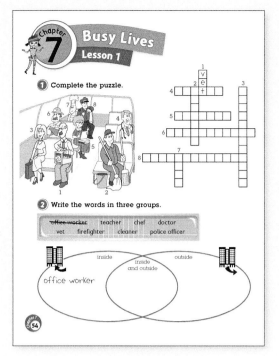

Competency Focus

Think! Critical Thinking

The children use critical thinking skills to identify the professions by using visual clues and processing the written and spoken forms.

1 Complete the puzzle.

Have the children look at the jobs in the pictures and complete the puzzle. Elicit answers and check with the class.

Answers

1 vet **2** cleaner **3** office worker **4** doctor **5** teacher **6** firefighter **7** chef **8** police officer

2 Write the words in three groups.

Ask the children to put the words from the box in the correct group. Elicit answers and check with the class.

Answers (suggested)

inside: office worker, cleaner, teacher, doctor, chef
inside and outside: vet, police officer
outside: firefighter

Cooler: Mime the profession

Mime a profession, e.g. firefighter, to elicit *You're a firefighter.* Invite children to mime a profession for the class to guess. With bigger classes, have them mime in groups.

Digital Resources

Student eBook • Play ASL Vocabulary Video 7.1 to pre-teach key vocabulary as an alternative to the critical thinking approach.

• Play "Kim's Game" with the new vocabulary. Display the SB page and point to the labeled pictures in Activity 1. Use *Timer* to give the class one minute to memorize the pictures, then one minute to recall them (with SB page closed). Repeat several times.

Reader eBook • Use the Reader for Chapter 2 to do the Warmer activity.

Grammar

Lesson objectives: ask and answer questions about what people do and where they work

Key grammar: *What does she do? She's a (doctor). Where does she work? She works in (a hospital).*

Materials: Track 7.2; Grammar Worksheet 7A [TRC printout] (optional); wordcards (Cooler)

Warmer: Multiple miming

Invite three children to the front and allocate a different profession each from Lesson 1. Then say *One, two, three and mime!* The children mime their profession. Then say *Freeze!* The class work in pairs/small groups to identify each person's profession.

1))) 7.2 Listen and point. Then draw lines.

- Ask the children to look at the pictures and identify the places and professions.

- Play Track 7.2 and have them listen and draw lines to match each person to the place they work in.

- Play Track 7.2 again for them to check. Elicit answers and check with the class.

- Divide the class into pairs. Have them take turns saying a place, e.g. *Hospital!*, for their friend to say the corresponding profession, e.g. *Doctor!*

Audioscript

Man: What does she do?
Girl: She's a doctor.
Man: Where does she work?
Girl: Um … She works in a hospital. Look! Here's the hospital. She's a teacher. She works in a school. Here's the school. He's a chef.
Man: Yes. Where does he work?
Girl: He works in a restaurant. This is the restaurant. He's a police officer. He works in a police station. Here.

She's a cleaner.
Man: Where does she work?
Girl: Umm … she works in a hotel. Here. Look. He's an office worker. He works in an office.
Man: That's right.

Answers

1 hospital **2** school **3** restaurant **4** police station **5** hotel **6** office

Grammar Central

What does she do? …

Have the children read the question and answers. Point out the *–s* in *She works in a hospital.* Then explain that we use *does* in questions with *he/she* and that the final *–s* is not used: *Where does she work?* Have the children practice in pairs.

For extra practice, try the **Grammar Booster** section in the Student Book (p. 102).

Answers p. 102

Activity 1: **1** does **2** does **3** do **4** He's **5** work **6** works

Activity 2: **1** Where does she work? **2** She works in a restaurant. **3** She works in the kitchen. **4** What does she do? **5** chef

2 Look at the picture. Circle T (true) or F (false).

- Tell the children that the sentences refer to the people in Activity 1. Read the example and elicit the correct profession. (*She's a doctor.*)

- The children read the sentences and choose true or false. Have them compare with a friend before you check as a class. Have children correct the false statements.

Answers

1 F **2** T **3** F **4** T

3 Point to the picture. Ask and answer.

- Invite two children to demonstrate the example.

- Divide the class into pairs. Have them take turns pointing to a person in Activity 1 and asking *What does he/she do? Where does he/she work?* for their friend to answer. Monitor and check that they use *he/she* and *work/works* correctly.

Optional activity: **Guess the profession**

Divide the class into groups. They take turns to write a profession, keeping it secret. The group ask each child in turn *Do you work in a … ?* When the child answers *Yes, I do.*, they name his/her profession.

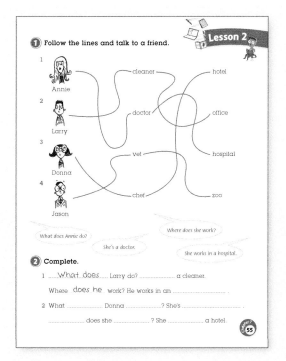

1 Follow the lines and talk to a friend.

Demonstrate the example with a child. Have the children ask and answer questions in pairs about the people pictured, following the lines to find out the information to give.

2 Complete.

Tell the children to complete the questions and answers about Larry and Donna, using the information in Activity 1. Elicit answers and check with the class.

Answers

1 What does; He's; does he; office. **2** does, do; a chef; Where, work; works in

Cooler: Police line-up

Prepare wordcards using the professions in Activity 1 (or reuse the cards you made for "Pelmanism" in Lesson 1). Invite three children to stand at the front. Give each a card and have them say, e.g. *I'm a chef!* Ask the class to say where each child works, e.g. In a restaurant.

Competency Focus

Learn

By identifying people's professions and where they work in a different context with new grammatical structures, the children demonstrate their understanding of previously acquired vocabulary from Lesson 1.

Digital Resources

Digital Activity Book • TIP The interactive activities in the AB can be done again and again, giving different children the chance to participate.

Teacher Resource Center • For extra grammar practice, print out Grammar Worksheet 7A.

Reading: Story Extract

Lesson objectives: say what you want to be; use the title and pictures to predict story content; read the extract from *The Secret Life of Shelly the Chef* (start)

Functional language: *What do you want to be? I want to be a superhero.*

Secondary language: *cape, mask, news, puts out fires, rescues, superhero*

Materials: Tracks 7.3 and 7.4

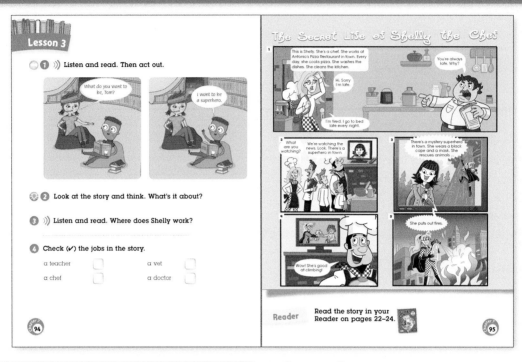

Warmer: Superhero

Have a class vote to choose the most popular superhero. Ask children to say why they like the particular character. (They might need to use L1.)

Functional language

1))) 7.3 Listen and read. Then act out.

- Have the children look at the book cover Tom is holding. Ask *What does Shelly do?* (*She's a chef.*)

- Play Track 7.3 and have the children listen and read along. Ask *What does Tom want to be?* (*a superhero*)

- Play Track 7.3 again, pausing for them to repeat.

- Choose two children to act out the dialogue for the class. Then divide your class into pairs and have them act out the dialogue. They can replace superhero with a profession.

Before reading

2 Look at the story and think. What's it about?

- Ask the children to look quickly at the picture and find the chefs. Then read the title. Ask *What's the story about?* Elicit ideas.

3))) 7.4 Listen and read. Where does Shelly work?

- Play Track 7.4 and have the children listen and read along.

- Then ask *Who's Shelly?* and have the children point to Shelly in their books. Ask *Where does she work?* Have the children write the answer and check with the class.

- Play Track 7.4 again, pausing to ask comprehension questions, e.g. *What does Shelly do every day?* (*She is a chef.*) *Who's the man with the mustache?* (*the owner*) *Who's the superhero? What does she do?* (They might need to use L1.)

Answer

She works in a restaurant/at Antonio's Pizza Restaurant.

4 Check (✔) the jobs in the story.

- Have the class read out the list of jobs/professions. They check the ones that appear in the extract.
- Elicit answers and check with the class. Ask *How many chefs are there?* (*two*)

Answers

a chef

Optional activity: Shelly's weekend

Brainstorm things the children do on the weekend, e.g. *eat breakfast, play soccer*, etc. Then divide your class into pairs and have them write four things Shelly does. Have them compare with another pair by saying, e.g. *Shelly gets up late. She eats breakfast.*

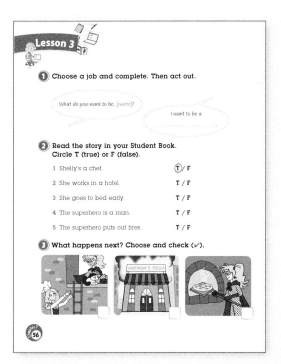

1 Choose a job and complete. Then act out.

Tell the children to complete the sentence so that it is true for them. Then have them act out the dialogue in pairs. Ask pairs to act out for the class.

Answers

Children's own answers.

2 Read the story in your Student Book. Circle T (true) or F (false).

Have the children read the sentences, look at the story extract, and choose true or false. Elicit answers and check with the class. Ask children to correct the false sentences.

Answers

1 T 2 F 3 F 4 F 5 T

3 What happens next? Choose and check (✔).

Ask the children to imagine what happens next in the story. Tell them to choose one of the three pictures. Ask children to share their ideas with the class.

Answers

Children's own answers.

Cooler: What do you want to be?

Have the children choose their favorite job from Lesson 1. Write on the board *What do you want to be? I want to be a(n)* … Have them mingle, asking and answering the question. They pair up/get into groups with people who have the same answer.

Competency Focus

Collaborate and Communicate

The children work together, putting into practice new functional language by acting out a realistic dialogue.

Think! Critical Thinking

By looking at the story artwork, the children use prediction skills to help them engage with the story.

Digital Resources

Student eBook • Display the SB story extract and play a game to encourage the children to develop the reading skill of using picture details. Use *Timer* to give the class one minute to look at the pictures. Then stop displaying the SB story extract. Elicit the detail.

Lesson objective: read and understand the superhero story
The Secret Life of Shelly the Chef in the Reader
Materials: Track 7.5; Reader; Oral Storytelling Video Worksheet 7 [TRC printout] (optional)

Warmer: Recap extract

Have the children remember Shelly's name and where she works. Ask children to recall what happens in the extract. (e.g. *She rescues animals and puts out fires.*)

Story Summary

Shelly, a chef in a pizzeria, is secretly a superhero. She is good at climbing and can put out fires. When a thief in the restaurant steals a woman's purse, Shelly uses her superhero powers to catches him. When she returns to the busy restaurant, everyone realizes that she is really the superhero!

Value: We are all good at different things.

)) 7.5 While reading

- Have the children look at *The Secret Life of Shelly the Chef* in their Reader and identify other characters. Pre-teach *thief* and *catch thieves*.

- Play Track 7.5 and have the children listen and read along.

- Ask the children to say three things that Shelly does. (*She rescues animals, catches thieves, and cooks fantastic pizza.*)

- Play Track 7.5 again, pausing to ask comprehension questions, e.g. *Who robs the bank? (a thief) Can Shelly catch him? (No, she can't.) Why is she surprised? (because the thief is in the restaurant) Can she catch the thief now? (yes) What does she do after she catches the thief? (returns to work/the restaurant)*

After reading: Reflect

- Ask *What does Shelly do at the restaurant?* Elicit ideas. (e.g. *she cooks, cleans, cuts onions, makes pizza*) Point out that in many professions you have to be good at different things. (They might need to use L1.)

Optional activity: We're superheroes!

List the things Shelly can do on the board, e.g. *Can: climb trees, put out fires*, etc. Then ask the children to be superheroes. In pairs, they take turns saying and acting out what they can do, e.g. *I can put out fires.*

Story Time

Encouraging comments

The children might make comments about characters or things happening in the story. Take this opportunity to encourage them and rephrase their comments in English to extend their language.

Reading Strategy

Story Sequence

By using the Story Sequence strategy, children put their critical and visual literacy skills into practice. They think about the logical order of events by looking at pictures from the story.

For additional explanation and activities, see the Literacy Handbook on Teacher Resource Center.

Cooler: True or false?

Have the children look through the story in their Reader and write a true and a false sentence. Divide the class into small groups. The children take turns to read a sentence. The group decides if it is true or false and explains why.

Digital Resources

Reader eBook • Display the Reader on the board. Show Picture 7. Elicit what happened before and after this. Repeat with Pictures 10 and 15.

• Watch Oral Storytelling Video 7.2 together before you do the After reading: Reflect activity.

Teacher Resource Center • Print out Oral Storytelling Video Worksheet 7 to help you get the most out of the video.

Reading Comprehension and Critical Literacy

Lesson objectives: focus on the visual clues in a story; personalize the main character's actions

Materials: Track 7.5; Reader; numbers between 0–100 on pieces of paper (optional); Oral Storytelling Video Worksheet 7 [TRC printout] (optional)

Note: Please ensure that your class has read the Reader story before you do this lesson.

Warmer: Exclamations

Write the following exclamations in jumbled order: *Wow!*, *Help, help!*, *Hey!*, *Ouch!*, *Ha!*, *OK, OK, I'm here!* Divide the class into pairs. Have them find the exclamations in their Reader and say them in order. Check intonation.

1))) 7.5 Read the story in your Reader.

- Have the children read the story. (Alternatively, play Track 7.5 and have them read along.) Ask *Why are the people surprised in the last picture?* (*They realize that Shelly is the superhero.*) Ask *How does Shelly feel?* Elicit their answers. (They might need to use L1.)

I Can Read!

Have the children look at the pictures of the story again. Ask *How do we know Shelly is the superhero?* Elicit the visual clues from the class. (They might need to use L1.)

Answer

She's wearing checked pants. The superhero has long blond hair and blue eyes like Shelly. In picture 10, she's putting on her mask. In picture 16, Shelly is still wearing her mask.

2 What does Shelly do when she's a chef or a superhero? Circle C (chef) or S (superhero).

- Do the first sentence as an example with the class. Ask them to find the corresponding part in the story.

- Give them time to read the rest of the sentences and refer to the story to circle C or S. Have them compare answers with a friend before checking as a class.

Answers

1 S 2 S 3 C 4 C 5 S

3 What are you good at? Check (✔) your superhero job.

- Tell the children to imagine they are superheroes. Ask *Are you good at rescuing animals/putting out fires/ catching thieves?* Invite the class to call out *yes* or *no*.

- Have the children check their superhero job. Elicit their superhero jobs and what else they are good at.

Answers

Children's own answers.

4 Talk about the story.

- Ask the children if they liked the story. Do a class vote, asking them to raise their hands for *yes* or *no*. Encourage them to give reasons why/why not. (They may need L1.)

- Have a child read Libby's question. Elicit answers. (e.g. *Superman—reporter*)

- Discuss the theme of the story. Use simple prompt questions to guide the children to understanding, e.g. *Is she brave?* (*yes*) *Does she always succeed?* (*no*) *Does she always try to help?* (*yes*) (You might need to use L1.)

Optional activity: A pizza for table 12!

Write some numbers from 0–100 on a piece of paper (one for each child). Distribute the numbers randomly. Write on the board *A tomato pizza for table . . .!* Invite a "waiter" and a "restaurant owner" to the front. Prompt a third child to say *A pizza, please!* The "waiter" serves the "pizza" on a "tray" and the owner says *A tomato pizza for table (56)!*, using the number written on the third child's paper. Repeat with different children.

1 Check (✔) the facts about Shelly the Superhero.

Have the children check the information that is true about Shelly. Allow them to look back to the story if they need to. Elicit answers and check with the class.

Answers

✔ *by:* **1** a mask, a cape, boots **2** rescues animals, catches thieves, cooks pizza **3** climbing, running, cooking

2 Find in the story and write the frame number.

The children practice the **I Can Read!** feature by finding the pictures in the story and writing the frame numbers in the boxes. Elicit answers and check with the class.

Answers

10, 12, 16

3 What do you think about this story? Choose and check (✔).

Have the children choose the description they agree with. Ask children to say what they think of the story and why.

Answers

Children's own answers.

Cooler: A superhero portrait

Say *You are superheroes!* Have the children draw a picture of themselves doing something heroic. Have them write a superhero name and a caption. Set a time limit and monitor. Have them show their pictures in small groups.

Competency Focus

Me: Critical Literacy

The children use critical literacy skills to reflect on the story and compare themselves to the main character.

Digital Resources

Reader eBook • Display the Reader story. Ask children to find the superhero in different pictures and act out the superhero's part for the class.

Student eBook, Digital Activity Book • TIP Use the forward and backward arrows to navigate to previous or later lessons.

Student eBook, Reader eBook • If you haven't already, show Oral Storytelling Video 7.2.

Teacher Resource Center • If you haven't already, print out Oral Storytelling Video Worksheet 7 to do the support activities.

Vocabulary, Song, and Phonics

Lesson objectives: talk about what people do at work; practice the *sh* and *s* sounds

Key vocabulary: *catch, clean, cook, put out, take care, teach, travel*

Secondary language: *restaurant, take care of, thieves*

Materials: Tracks 7.6 and 7.7; pictures for Key vocabulary (Warmer) ; Phonics Worksheet 7 [TRC printout] (optional)

Warmer: Work mimes

Pre-teach the vocabulary using pictures or mimes. Say the words in random order for the class to mime.

1))) 7.6 Listen and number. Then sing.

- Ask the children to look at the pictures and study the words in red. Read the title and ask *Is Shelly a superchef or a superhero?* (*both*)

- Play Track 7.6 and have the children listen and match the words to the pictures, writing the numbers. Choose individual children to say a word and the number of the picture.

- Play Track 7.6 again and have the class sing along.

- Sing the song again as a class, miming each verb/action.

Answers

cooks 6, cleans 2, puts out 5, takes care 1, travel 7, teaches 3, catches 4

2 Talk to a friend.

- Ask the children to underline the professions in the song. (*superchef, firefighter, doctor, vet, teacher, police officer*) Choose two children to read the example. Point out the word order in the question and the answer.

- Then divide your class into pairs. Have them take turns asking and answering about the professions in Activity 1 using language from the lyrics. Monitor and make sure they answer with the 3rd person singular *–s/–es.*

3))) 7.7 Listen and say the chant.

- Ask the children to say what Shelly is doing in the picture. (*putting out a fire*)

- Play Track 7.7 and have the children listen to the chant.

- Play Track 7.7 again, pausing for them to repeat.

- Focus on the sounds in *chef* and *super*. Point out that their mouth is rounder when they make the *sh* sound and that it is the sound we make when we want people to be quiet. Practice the chant a few times with the class. Explain that two words can be written differently but have the same sound, as in *chef* and *Shelly*.

Optional activity: Memory test

Give the children time to study the pictures and verbs in Activity 1. Then have them cover the lyrics. They work in pairs to remember the verb for each picture. Have pairs recall the verbs for the class.

① Write the words in the correct place. Add –s or –es.

cook   put out   teach   take care of
wash   travel   wear   catch   clean

he / she … + s

he / she … + es

cooks

teaches

② Complete using the words from Activity 1.

1 A firefighter puts out fires.
2 A chef .... in a restaurant.
3 A doctor .... you.
4 A child .... to school by bus.
5 A teacher .... in a school.
6 A police officer .... thieves.

③ Say the words. Circle sh as in Shelly. Underline s as in super.

sh   s

bus
Shelly
rescue
shoe
zoo
super
she

Cooler: Pronunciation practice

Write two headings on the board: *sh* and *s*. Call out words and ask individual children to write each word under the correct heading, e.g. *sh: sure, shower, short, shelf; s: pencil, science, skirt*. Then point to words for the class to say.

Competency Focus

Think! Critical Thinking

The children use critical thinking skills to identify the meaning of verbs related to professions by processing the written and spoken forms and matching them to the correct picture.

1 Write the words in the correct place. Add –s or –es.

Have the children write the verbs in the correct place, according to the correct ending: *–s* or *–es*. Elicit answers and check with the class.

Answers

he/she …+s: cooks, puts out, takes care of, travels, wears, cleans
he/she …+es: teaches, washes, catches

2 Complete using the words from Activity 1.

Have the children complete the sentences using the verbs from Activity 1.

Answers

1 puts out **2** cooks **3** takes care of **4** travels **5** teaches **6** catches

3 Say the words. Circle *sh* as in *Shelly*. Underline *s* as in *super*.

Have the children say the two sounds and words before they do the task. Elicit answers and check with the class.

Answers

Circled: **sh** in **Sh**elly, **sh**oe, **sh**e
Underlined: **s** in bu**s**, re**s**cue, **s**uper

Digital Resources

Student eBook • Play ASL Vocabulary Video 7.3 to pre-teach key vocabulary.

• Choose the audio button to hear the song. Point to the SB page to help the children follow the song lyrics.

Student's App • Encourage the children to play the games on their smartphone/tablet. They could arrange to do this with a friend as a fun way to review the chapter vocabulary together. (*The Inks* Apps are free and available on the App Store and Google Play.)

Teacher Resource Center • For phonics practice, print out Phonics Worksheet 7.

Grammar and Reading

Lesson objectives: ask and talk about what people do and don't do
Key grammar: *He doesn't (cook). Does he go (to school)?*
Yes, he does. / No, he doesn't.
Secondary language: *article, guitar, That's cool!, travels, world*
Materials: Track 7.8; Grammar Worksheet 7B [TRC printout] (optional)

Warmer: Pop stars!

Write the name of a popular pop star/band that children will recognize on the board. Elicit other names and add them on the board. Ask children to say who their favorite pop star/band is.

1))) 7.8 Listen and read.

- Have the children look at the first picture and ask what Ellie and Tom are doing. (*reading a magazine and a book*) Then ask them who the boy in picture 3 is.

- Play Track 7.8 and ask them to listen and read along. Elicit who Dustin Fever is. (*a pop star*) Ask *Who likes him a lot?* (*Ellie*) *What does Ellie want to be?* (*Dustin's chef*) (You might need to use L1.)

- Play Track 7.8 again, pausing for the children to repeat.

2 Write about Dustin Fever.

- Ask the class to look at the story in Activity 1 again and recap the information on Dustin Fever.

- Then ask the children to complete the sentences and questions for Dustin, referring back to Grammar Central as necessary.

- Elicit answers and check with the class. Point out the example sentences again and remind the children of the final –*s* in affirmative sentences.

Answers

1 travels **2** doesn't **3** Does, he doesn't **4** do, he does

Grammar Central

He doesn't cook. . . .

Have the children look at the patterns. Read them out and have the children repeat. Explain that we use *doesn't* in the negative for *he*, *she*, and *it*. Point out the short answers and practice the pronunciation of *does* and *doesn't*.

For extra practice, try the **Grammar Booster** section in the Student Book (p. 103–105).

Answers p. 103

Activity 1: **1** does **2** takes **3** doesn't **4** Does **5** does **6** doesn't

Activity 2: **1** Does she teach, she does, She teaches, She's a **2** Does he catch, he doesn't, does he do, He's a

p. 104

Activity 1: Does **2** takes **3** work **4** works **5** do **6** teaches

Activity 2: **1** What does, **2** Where does he **3** Does he travel **4** he doesn't **5** Does he catch **6** he does

p. 105

Activity 1: **1** work, vet **2** go, office worker **3** get up, teacher **4** cooking, chef **5** don't, cleaner

Activity 2: **1** chef **2** teacher **3** vet **4** Yes, he is. **5** She works in a school. **6**. No, she doesn't.

Optional activity: Further practice

Have the children think of two more questions they want to ask Ellie about Dustin Fever, e.g. *Does he clean his bedroom? Does he go to bed early?* Divide the class into pairs. Have them take turns asking and answering their questions.

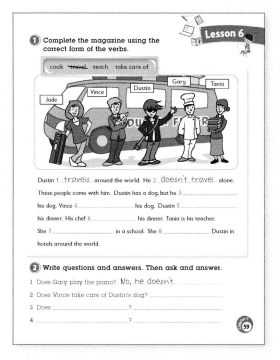

Write on the board question prompts about people at work, e.g. *Does a police officer …?* Give a few examples, e.g. *… catch thieves?* (*Yes, he/she does.*) *… cook in a restaurant?* (*No, he/she doesn't.*) In pairs, the children write questions, then ask and answer.

Competency Focus

Learn

The children demonstrate their understanding of the new grammatical patterns by reading the text and completing the activity.

1 Complete the magazine using the correct form of the verbs.

Have the children look at the picture and complete the text with the verbs supplied. Explain that they will need to use each verb twice, once in the positive form and once in the negative. Elicit answers and check with the class.

Answers

1 travels **2** doesn't travel **3** doesn't take care of **4** takes care of **5** doesn't cook **6** cooks **7** doesn't teach **8** teaches

2 Write questions and answers. Then ask and answer.

Have the children complete the questions and answers, and write two of their own. Then have them practice asking and answering the questions in pairs.

Answers

1 No, he doesn't. **2** Yes, he does. **3–4** Children's own answers.

Digital Resources

Student eBook • Point to only Pictures 1 and 2. Elicit ideas on who Dustin Fever is. (*He's a pop star.*) Elicit ideas on what he does. Refer the children to the whole story. Ask the children if their ideas were correct.

- Use *Highlighter* to identify key grammar structures in the SB Activity 1 story text.

Teacher Resource Center • For extra grammar practice, print out Grammar Worksheet 7B.

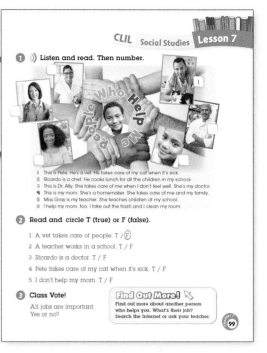

CLIL: Social sciences—People who help

Lesson objective: find out how people help in their community
Materials: Track 7.9; CLIL Graphic Organizer 7 [TRC printout] (optional)

Warmer: People who help me

Write on the board *People who help me*. Encourage the children to think of people who help/have helped them. Elicit the people and the ways in which they help/have helped the children. (They might need to use L1.)

1))) 7.9 Listen and read. Then number.

- Ask the children to look at the pictures and spot any people they mentioned in the Warmer, e.g. *doctor*.
- Play Track 7.9. The children listen, read, and number the pictures. Elicit answers and check with the class.
- Play Track 7.9 again and ask the children to raise their hand if they know someone similar. Pause and have the children explain who.

Answers

From top to bottom, left: **5**, **3**, **4**

From top to bottom, right: **1**, **2**, **6**

2 Read and circle T (true) or F (false).

- Choose a child to read the example sentence. Elicit from the class why it is false. (*A vet takes care of animals.*)
- The children read the sentences about Activity 1 and circle T (true) or F (false). Elicit answers including the correct versions of the false sentences.

Answers

1 F **2** T **3** F **4** T **5** F

3 Class Vote!

- Organize your class vote. Ask children if they think all jobs are important or not. Give them a minute to think. Then write *Yes* and *No* on the board. Have the children raise their hand for each answer.
- Count the votes and write the totals on the board. Elicit the result of the vote.

Find Out More!

Ask the children to think of a person with a different job that helps them. (e.g. *The P.E. teacher helps us stay healthy.*) Tell them to find out more about the person's job. Suggest appropriate resources, e.g. Internet, library books, etc., or provide the information yourself. The children will need to complete this research before doing the follow-up activity in the Activity Book. (It could be set as homework.)

Optional activity: Draw a picture

Have the children draw a picture of themselves helping other people or animals. Tell them it can be something that actually happened or something they would like to do, e.g. rescue a cat, etc. Tell them to title their drawing *I help people/animals.*

Competency Focus

Act

The children carry out research to find out about people and their professions. This helps them expand their learning and relate it to their world, both inside and outside the classroom.

1 Read and match.

Ask the children to read the problems and match each to the person who can help. Elicit answers and check with the class.

Answers

1 b **2** e **3** d **4** a **5** f **6** c

2 Check (✔) who helps you this week. Use your Student Book research. Write more jobs and check (✔).

Ask the children who has helped them this week. Ask children to talk about other jobs they found out about. Then give the children time to write and check the jobs of the people who helped them.

Answers

Children's own answers.

Cooler: Chant in a circle

Have the children stand up in a circle and hold wrists like the photo in Activity 1. Have them move their hands up and down gently as they chant *People help me. I help people.* With bigger classes, have them form smaller circles.

Digital Resources

Student eBook, Digital Activity Book • TIP When using the board for "heads-up" teaching, remember to give the children as much opportunity as possible to participate. Make sure you ask plenty of questions to give them the chance to engage with the text.

Teacher Resource Center • Print out CLIL Graphic Organizer 7 for the children to use in collating their Find Out More! research.

CLIL eBook • The children can use the CLIL eBook to expand their knowledge of the lesson topic.

Project

Lesson objectives: review language from Chapter 7; complete a craft project—making a superhero mask; act out the story from the Reader

Materials: Track 7.6 Reader; Project Template 7 [TRC printout]; scissors, glue, coloring pens, elastic cord; white construction paper, white tissue paper, tape (Alternative craft activity); two game pieces and a dice for each pair/group

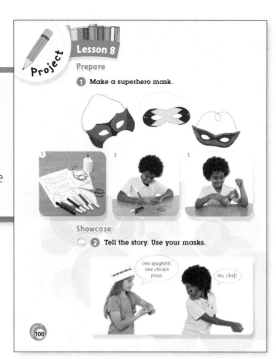

Warmer: Shelly is a superhero!

Recap the story of Shelly by having the children remember the things she does as a superhero, e.g. *rescue a cat, put out fires, catch thieves*, etc. Ask them to say what her superhero uniform is. (*checked outfit and mask, black cape*)

Prepare

1 Make a superhero mask.

- Have the children look at the completed masks. Ask *Which do you like best?* Tell them they are going to make their own mask.

- Hold up the materials to show the class. Point to the pictures and explain the stages. (You might need to use L1.)

- Demonstrate how to make a mask, stage by stage.

- Divide the class into pairs or groups if it is necessary to share materials. Give out the materials.

- As the children make their masks, monitor and give help as necessary.

Alternative craft activity

A simpler option would be to have the children make a chef's hat. Use white construction paper to cut a thick strip long enough to fit around a child's head when stapled/taped together. Then take a sheet of white tissue paper and tape the edges to the construction paper. Fluff up the tissue and fit the hat on the child's head.

Showcase

2 Tell the story. Use your masks.

- Ask the children to show you their masks. Divide the class into three groups and allocate each group a part of the story.

- Have the children practice their part of the story. In each part, one child is Shelly, another child is the chef(s)/waiter(s)/the thief, and the third child plays the other roles, e.g. reporter or police officer/customer, etc. Walk around, monitor, and give help with pronunciation.

- Call out groups to the front of the class to perform their part of the story using their masks.

Optional activity: Be a superhero!

))) **7.6**

Have the children wear their masks and stand up. Play Track 7.6 and sing the song from Lesson 5 again. Invite the children to sing and pretend they are superheroes too.

1 Play "What Do They Do?"

Have the children read the instructions and look at the questions. They play in pairs or in groups. Monitor and make sure the children answer the questions correctly. Tell children to look carefully at *he/she* and the picture.

Answers

1 She's a police officer. **2** Yes, she does. **3** cleaner
4 in a restaurant **5** She's an office worker. **6** teacher
7 Yes, he does. **8** No, she doesn't. **9** at a police station
10 chef **11** Yes, he does. **12** He's a doctor.
13 No, she doesn't. **14** in a hotel

Cooler: Colorful masks

Ask the children to stand and put on their mask. Call out colors at random. The children whose mask has that color mime their favorite superhero action.

Competency Focus

Collaborate and Communicate

By acting out the story, the children consolidate their understanding in a fun and engaging way. They also demonstrate their ability to work with friends and use interpersonal skills.

Digital Resources

Student eBook • Show the Prepare photos, stage by stage, as you talk the class through the activity process.

• The children vote to select a topic to review. Play the relevant ASL Vocabulary Video (from 1.1 to 7.3) to review vocabulary from previous chapters.

Digital Activity Book • Use *Timer* for AB Activity 1. Set a time limit of five minutes. The person in each pair who has traveled farthest on the board wins.

Teacher Resource Center • Print out Project Template 7 for the SB craft activity.

Language Review

Lesson objective: review language from Chapter 7
Materials: Tracks 7.1, 7.10 and AB 7.1

Warmer: Dictation

))) 7.1

Play Track 7.1 (Lesson 1, Activity 1). Have the children listen with Student Book closed. Pause for them to write the professions. Ask them to compare answers with a friend, then ask children to write the words on the board.

1))) 7.10 Listen and circle their jobs.

- Ask the children to look at the pictures. Have them describe each woman and guess what her job is.
- Play Track 7.10 twice and have the children circle the correct word. Elicit answers and check with the class. Ask questions, e.g. *Where does Annie work?* (*in a school*)

Audioscript

Annie works in a school. She doesn't teach children. She cooks their lunch. She works in the school kitchen. She cleans the kitchen, too. She's a chef.
Betty doesn't take care of pets. She takes care of tigers and monkeys. She works in a zoo. She's a vet.

Answers

1 chef **2** vet

2 Complete the questions. Then write A (Annie) or B (Betty).

- Have a child read the example question and answer. Remind the children that the –s in *works* is not used in the question.

- Give them time to read the answers and complete the questions. Allow them to look back through the chapter and check in pairs.
- Call on pairs to read a question and answer. Then elicit who they refer to.

Answers

1 does she work—A **2** does she do—A **3** Where does she work—B **4** does she do—B **5** take care—B **6** Does she—A

3 Think about Chapter 7. Color the books.

- Have the children look back at Chapter 7. Elicit their favorite parts. The children then color the book which represents how they feel about their own progress (self-evaluation).

Treasure Hunt!

Ask the children to look at Student Book pp. 4–5 and find a purple notebook. Have the children raise their hand when they find it.

Cooler: Betty the vet

Brainstorm other animals Betty (from Activity 1) takes care of. Divide the class into pairs. Have them take turns being Betty and an animal saying, e.g. *Betty works in the zoo. She takes care of giraffes.* Have them mime being, and taking care of, a giraffe.

Chapter 7 Exam Booster

1 Reading and Writing
Look at the pictures. Look at the letters. Write the words.

Example

d o c t o r

| c | d | o |
| o | r | t |

Questions

1 _ _ _ _ | f | h |
               | e | c |

2 _ _ _ _ _ _ _ | t | a |
                     | e | c |
                     | e | h |

3 _ _ _ _ _ _ _ _ _ | h | l | i |
                         | e | e |
                         | f | f | t |

4 _ _ _ _ _ _ | n | e | l |
                   | r | c | e |
                   | a |

5 _ _ _ _ _ _ _ _ _ _ _ _ | f | f | w |
                                | i | e | r |
                                | c | r | e |
                                | o | o | k |

96

2 Listening
Read the question. Listen and write a name or a number. There are two examples.

Examples

How many children are there? 100

What's your teacher's name? Miss Evans

Questions

1 What's the boy's friend's name? _____

2 What class is the boy in? _____

3 What's the cleaner's name? _____

4 How old is the chef? _____

5 What's the chef's name? _____

97

3 Reading and Writing
Look at the pictures. Look at the letters. Write the words.

Example

p u t   o u t | t | u |
                   | o | t | p |
                   | u |

Questions

1 _ _ _ _ | o |
               | c | k |
               | o |

2 _ _ _ _ _ | n | a |
                 | e | c |
                 | l |

3 _ _ _ _ _ _ | v | e |
                   | t | l | r |
                   | a |

4 _ _ _ _ | h | e |
               | c | t |
               | a |

Exam Tip
Say and write the word first.
Does it have all the letters?

98

---

1 Reading and Writing. Look at the pictures. Look at the letters. Write the words.

Have the children write the words. Check answers.

Answers

1 chef **2** teacher **3** firefighter **4** cleaner **5** office worker.

2))) AB 7.1 Listening. Read the question. Listen and write a name or a number. There are two examples.

Give the children time to read the questions. They then listen and write a name or number for each one. Play Track AB 7.1 twice, then elicit answers and check with the class.

Answers (Audioscript on p. 224)

1 Kenny **2** 4 **3** Jack **4** 21 **5** Amelia

3 Reading and Writing. Look at the pictures. Look at the letters. Write the words.

Have the children write the words. Check answers.

Answers

1 cook **2** clean **3** travel **4** teach

Competency Focus

Me: Self-evaluation

The children reflect on the chapter and express their opinions about their own progress. This encourages them to evaluate and make decisions about how they learn and what they need to revisit.

Digital Resources

Teacher Resource Center • Print out Test Chapter 7 to use at the end of this lesson. The Test Generator also allows you to create customized tests.

Chapter 8

Habits and Habitats
Overview

The children will:

- use critical thinking skills to identify animal body parts.
- ask and answer questions about wild animals and their body parts.
- read, understand, and act out a story.
- identify geographical features.
- find out about animal habitats.
- make a boomerang.

Key Vocabulary

Animal body parts: beak, feathers, fins, fur, pouch, scales, tail, teeth, wings
Geographical features: cave, forest, jungle, ocean, river, sky

Key Grammar

- Fish have (fins). They don't have (wings).
- Do they have (wings)?
  Yes, they do. / No, they don't.
- What do they eat? They eat (grass).
- Where do they live?
  They live in (Australia).
- When do they sleep?
  They sleep (in the day).

Reading Skills

Story: *The Kangaroo's Pouch*
Genre: Australian aboriginal myth

Literacy Development

- predict story content from title and pictures
- focus on the titles *Mr.* and *Mrs.*
- interpret the theme of the story

Functional Language

- Let me help you.
- Thank you.
- You're welcome.

Phonics

The children practice pronunciation of *s* sound as in *snake* and *z* sound as in *lizard*.

CLIL: Science—Animals and their habitats

The children find out about animal habitats.

Competency Focus

The children will:

use critical thinking skills to identify animal body parts. (Lesson 1)

predict the content of a story. (Lesson 3)

identify geographical features. (Lesson 5)

apply new grammar to previously learned vocabulary. (Lesson 2)

ask and answer about animals and their habits. (Lesson 6)

work in pairs to act out a dialogue. (Lesson 3)

work in groups to act out the story. (Lesson 8)

personalize their response to the story by thinking about their own relationships. (Lesson 4)

evaluate their own progress in the chapter. (Review)

find out about other wild animals and their habitats. (Lesson 7)

Digital Overview

Teacher Presentation

Student eBook and Digital Activity Book

- ASL Vocabulary Video 8.1: Animal body parts
- ASL Vocabulary Video 8.4: Geographical features
- Music Video 8.2 (8.3): *Birds Fly in the Sky*
- Interactive versions of AB activities
- Integrated audio and answer key for all activities

Teacher resources for planning, lesson delivery, and homework

Teacher Resource Center

- Class Planner Chapter 8
- Worksheets to print out (including notes and answers):
    - Grammar Worksheet 8A: Fish have … They don't have …
    - Grammar Worksheet 8B: What do they …? They …
    - Phonics Worksheet 8
    - CLIL Graphic Organizer 8
    - Project Template 8
    - Test Chapter 8
- Test Generator
- Literacy Handbook

Watch the Music Video

Children's resources for consolidation and practice at home

Student eBook

- ASL Vocabulary Video 8.1: Animal body parts
- ASL Vocabulary Video 8.4: Geographical features
- Music Video 8.2 (8.3): *Birds Fly in the Sky*

The Inks Student's App

Vocabulary games: Animal body parts and geographical features

Habits and Habitats

Lesson 1

Vocabulary

Lesson objectives: identify wild animals and their body parts
Key vocabulary: *beak, feathers, fins, fur, pouch, scales, tail, teeth, wings*
Materials: Track 8.1; wordcards (Warmer); ball (optional)

Warmer: I'm a giraffe!

Make wordcards with wild animals from Level 1 (e.g. *giraffe, elephant, crocodile, monkey, lion, tiger*) on pieces of paper. Divide the class into two groups. Call on a child from each group to choose one piece of paper. Have them draw the animal for their group to guess.

1))) 8.1 Listen and number. Then say.

- Have the children look at the pictures and identify the animals. Give them time to study the words for the different body parts. Then draw their attention to the pictures down the side.

- Play Track 8.1 and have the children listen and match the small pictures to the body parts, writing the numbers.

- Play Track 8.1 again, pausing where appropriate for the children to repeat the body parts. Tell them to compare answers.

- Check answers. Ask children to say a word and number. Ask extra comprehension questions, e.g. *Where are kangaroos from?* (*Australia*) *What color is the snake?* (*black and yellow*)

- Then have the children practice in pairs. Have them take turns pointing to a body part for their friend to say the word.

Audioscript

These animals are from Australia.
This bird is a parrot.
It has two wings.
It has a big beak.
It has red and green feathers.

This is a kangaroo.
Its fur is brown. It has a long tail.
Look! There's a baby in its pouch.

Wow! Look at this amazing snake. It's very long. It has black and yellow scales. They are beautiful.

This is a great white shark. It has big fins and a strong tail. Look at those scary teeth!

Answers

beak 2, feathers 3, wings 1; fur 4, pouch 5; scales 6; fins 7

Optional activity: Do you like kangaroos?

Ask *Do you like kangaroos?* Have the children stand up if they do. Throw a ball to a standing child. Everyone else sits down. Have them ask about a different animal, e.g. *Do you like penguins?* The children stand up for *yes* or sit down for *no*. A different child gets the ball and continues.

Write and explain *Land creatures* and *Ocean creatures* on the board. Ask the children to add the animals from Activity 1 in the correct category in their notebooks. Have the children work in pairs and write more animals.

Competency Focus

Think! Critical Thinking

The children use critical thinking skills to identify wild animals and their body parts by using visual clues and processing the written and spoken forms.

1 Look and write P (parrot), K (kangaroo), S (snake), or F (fish).

Have the children complete the table looking at the picture. Elicit answers and check with the class.

Answers

wings: P
a tail: P, K, F
a beak: P
a pouch: K
fur: K
feathers: P
fins: F
scales: F, S

2 Write the words from Activity 1 in two groups.

Ask the children to write each word from Activity 1 in one of the groups, easy or difficult. Say each word and invite children to say if it is difficult and why.

Answers

Children's own answers.

Digital Resources

Student eBook • Play ASL Vocabulary Video 8.1 to pre-teach key vocabulary as an alternative to the critical thinking approach.

• The SB Warmer can be done using *Pen*. Children draw their animal for the class to guess.

Student eBook, Digital Activity Book • TIP As you monitor the children's progress, use *Add personal note* to keep a note of weaknesses in vocabulary, grammar, or pronunciation so you can review in later lessons.

Grammar

Lesson objectives: ask and answer questions about wild animals and their features

Key grammar: *Fish have fins. They don't have wings. Do they have wings? Yes, they do. / No, they don't.*

Materials: Track 8.2; Grammar Worksheet 8A [TRC printout] (optional)

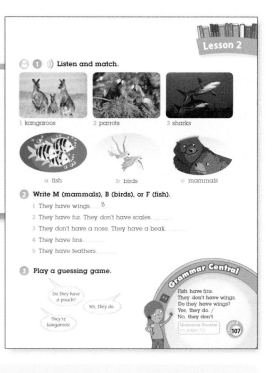

Warmer: Class dictation

Have the children write four columns in their notebooks: *parrot, kangaroo, shark, snake*. Have children call out one of the body parts from Lesson 1. The class writes the word in the correct column. Continue, checking each answer with the class as you go.

---

1))) **8.2 Listen and match.**

- Ask the children to identify the animals in the photos.
- Then play Track 8.2 and have them listen and match the animals in the photos with the correct animal types. Elicit answers and check with the class.
- Make sure children understand the differences between fish, birds, and mammals, e.g. *Fish and birds lay eggs, but mammals do not.* Explain that people are mammals, too.

Audioscript

Parrots are birds. They have wings, feathers, and a beak.
Sharks are fish. They have fins.
Kangaroos are mammals. They have fur.

Answers

1 c **2** b **3** a

Grammar Central

Fish have fins. ...

Ask the children to study the sentences and question. Point out the use of *have* for plural nouns and remind children that *fish* is both the singular and plural form. Explain that we use *don't* in the negative for *they* and *do* in the question. Say the sentences once for the children to repeat. Then have them practice in pairs.

For extra practice, try the **Grammar Booster** section in the Student Book (p. 116).

Answers p. 116

Activity 1: **1** have **2** don't **3** Do **4** do **5** don't

Activity 2: **1** have, don't have **2** don't have, have **3** have, don't have **4** don't have, have **5** have, don't have

Activity 3: **1** Do birds have scales? No, they don't. **2** Do mammals have fur? Yes, they do. **3** Do fish have feathers? No, they don't.

2 Write M (mammals), B (birds), or F (fish).

- Have a child read the example sentence. Give them some time to read the sentences on their own and write M, B, or F. Monitor and encourage them to refer to the pictures in Activity 1 and Lesson 1 as necessary.
- Ask the children to compare answers in pairs, then elicit answers.

Answers

1 B **2** M **3** B **4** F **5** B

3 Play a guessing game.

- Demonstrate the game by doing the example with a child. Point out the structures in Grammar Central to help them play the game.

- Give the children time to play the game in groups. Monitor and help.

Optional activity: Four questions

Brainstorm more animals, e.g. *dolphin, bear*. Divide the class into groups. Groups take turns to write an animal in a notebook secretly. The other teams each take turns asking questions to guess the animal. Encourage them to use *Can they . . . ?* questions too.

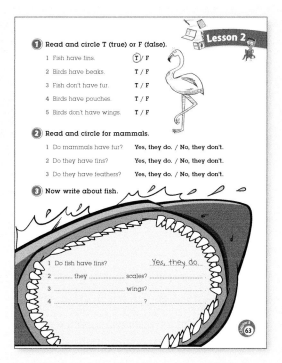

1 Read and circle T (true) or F (false).

Have the children read the sentences and, if necessary, explain that the animal in the picture is a flamingo (bird). Have them choose true or false. Elicit answers, including the correct version of the false statements.

Answers

1 T 2 T 3 T 4 F 5 F

2 Read and circle for mammals.

Ask the children to read the questions about mammals and circle the correct answers. Elicit answers and check with the class.

Answers

1 Yes, they do. 2 No, they don't. 3 No, they don't.

3 Now write about fish.

Have the children complete and write questions and answers about fish. Have them practice their questions and answers in pairs.

Answers

1 Yes, they do. 2 Do, have; Yes, they do. 3 Do they have; No, they don't. 4 Children's own answers.

Cooler: Favorite animal

Do a class survey to find the most popular animal. Elicit responses by asking, e.g. *Do you like sharks?* and count raised hands for *yes*. Ask the children to draw a small picture of their favorite animal and label its parts. They can also write a few sentences.

Competency Focus

Learn

By identifying animal features in a different context with new grammatical structures, the children demonstrate their understanding of previously acquired vocabulary from Lesson 1.

Digital Resources

Student eBook • Using *Pen*, circle the different body parts in each of the animal photos to elicit the words in SB Activity 2.

Teacher Resource Center • For extra grammar practice, print out Grammar Worksheet 8A.

Reading: Story Extract

Lesson objectives: offer and accept help; use the title and pictures to predict story content; read the extract from *The Kangaroo's Pouch* (middle)

Functional language: *Let me help you. Thank you. You're welcome.*

Secondary language: *boomerang, daytime, help, hunter, wombat*

Materials: Tracks 8.3 and 8.4; picture of a wombat (Warmer)

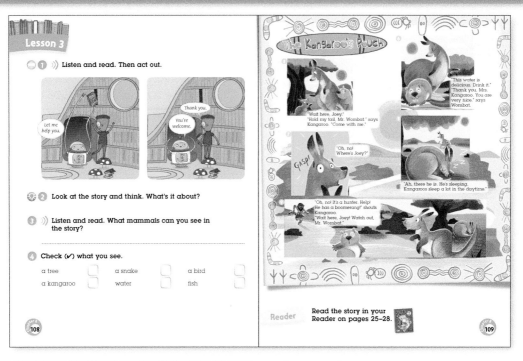

Warmer: Wombat

Write *wombat* on the board and have children say anything they know about this animal. Show them the picture you have or use the story extract. Elicit what body parts wombats have and what the children think about the animal. Ask questions, e.g. *Is it cute? Is it funny?*, etc.

Functional language

1))) 8.3 Listen and read. Then act out.

- Have the children look at the picture and say what Tom and Biblio are doing. (*tidying up*)
- Play Track 8.3 and ask them to listen and read.
- Play Track 8.3 again, pausing for the children to repeat.
- Divide the class into pairs. Have them take turns being Biblio and Tom and acting out the dialogue. They can use their books when acting Biblio's role.

Before reading

2 Look at the story and think. What's it about?

- Have the children look at the title and the pictures and identify the animals. Pre-teach *hunter* and *boomerang* using the last picture.
- Ask *What's the story about?* Elicit answers.

3))) 8.4 Listen and read. What mammals can you see in the story?

- Play Track 8.4 and have the children listen and read along. Then ask them to look at the pictures again to find the mammals. Remind them that people are mammals.
- Check understanding by pointing to the pictures and asking questions, e.g. *Where does Mrs. Kangaroo take Mr. Wombat?* (*to the river to drink water*) *What's Joey doing?* (*He's sleeping.*) *Why are they afraid of the hunter?* (*He wants to catch them.*)

Answers

kangaroos, wombat, man

4 Check (✔) what you see.

- Give the children time to read the words and refer to the pictures. Ask them to check which of the things they see in the pictures.

- Check answers. Invite the class to call out other things they see, e.g. *the sun*, *grass*.

Answers

a tree, a kangaroo, water

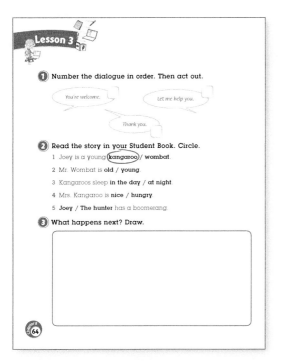

Lesson 3

1 Number the dialogue in order. Then act out.

You're welcome.   Let me help you.

Thank you.

2 Read the story in your Student Book. Circle.

1 Joey is a young kangaroo / wombat.

2 Mr. Wombat is old / young.

3 Kangaroos sleep in the day / at night.

4 Mrs. Kangaroo is nice / hungry.

5 Joey / The hunter has a boomerang.

3 What happens next? Draw.

64

1 Number the dialogue in order. Then act out.

Give the children time to order the dialogue. Check answers and have them act it out in pairs. Ask pairs to act out for the class.

Answers

3 You're welcome. **1** Let me help you. **2** Thank you.

2 Read the story in your Student Book. Circle.

Ask the children to read the sentences and circle the correct words. Have them check their answers in the story extract. Elicit answers and check with the class.

Answers

1 kangaroo **2** old **3** in the day **4** nice **5** The hunter

3 What happens next? Draw.

Elicit ideas on what happens next in the story. Then give the children time to draw their pictures. Have them show and explain their drawings in small groups.

Cooler: What happened before?

Explain that the extract is the middle part of the story. Have the children talk in small groups about what they think happened before. Encourage them to be imaginative. Elicit ideas.

Competency Focus

Collaborate and Communicate

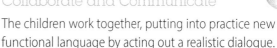

The children work together, putting into practice new functional language by acting out a realistic dialogue.

Think! Critical Thinking

By looking at the story artwork, the children use prediction skills to help them engage with the story.

Digital Resources

Student eBook • Focus on the characters. Elicit how they are feeling in each picture. (The children will need L1.) Have children act out a character for the class to guess. Choose a child to use *Pen* to circle the character in the correct picture.

Lesson objective: read and understand the Australian aboriginal myth *The Kangaroo's Pouch* in the Reader
Materials: Track 8.5; Reader

Warmer: It's wrong!

Write sentences from the story extract with a mistake, e.g. *Hold my ears, Mr. Wombat. / Oh, no! It's a firefighter.* Have the children work in pairs to correct the mistakes. Check and recap the story extract.

Story Summary

Mrs. Kangaroo and her baby, Joey, meet an old wombat. He is hungry and thirsty, so Mrs. Kangaroo gives him grass and water. A hunter tries to catch her but she escapes. The wombat is really a spirit, Byamee, and he gives her a fur pouch to keep Joey safe as a reward for helping him.

Value: Help others.

))) 8.5 While reading

- Ask the children to look at *The Kangaroo's Pouch* in their Reader. Have them point to the new character in the story (the spirit Byamee in picture 14).

- Play Track 8.5 and have the children listen and read along.

- Play the story again, pausing to check comprehension by asking *Why can't Mr. Wombat walk?* (*He's old.*) *Who's Mr. Wombat really?* (*the spirit Byamee*) *Why does he give her the bag/pouch?* (*to help her/because she's nice*) (They might need to use L1.)

After reading: Reflect

- Ask the children to look at pictures 9–11 again and say if they were worried about the kangaroos and the wombat. Do they think Mrs. Kangaroo was brave? What would they do in her situation? Elicit their ideas. (They may need L1 for this discussion.)

Optional activity: Favorite character

Have the children choose their favorite character. Ask them to draw a picture of them and write a line they say in the story. Then have children read out the line and say why they like the character.

Act the part

Encourage the children to copy the characters' gestures and actions when following the story. This will help them understand the storyline and engage with the story and characters.

Reading Strategy

Which Question?

The Which Question? strategy helps the children understand and tackle different types of questions: the "Look" questions that are found by spotting words in the text, the "Think" questions that require critical skills, and the "Up to you" questions that help the reader personalize the story.

For additional explanation and activities, see the Literacy Handbook on Teacher Resource Center.

Cooler: Bounce like a kangaroo

Divide the children into small groups. Ask each group a question about the story. If their answer is correct, have them bounce like a kangaroo for five seconds. Repeat with different groups and questions.

Digital Resources

Reader eBook • Display the Reader. Point to one picture at a time. Before moving on each time, elicit what is going to happen next.

- Children use *Highlighter* to identify the sound effects in the story. (*MUNCH! GASP! BOING! BOING! ZZZ*) As each one is highlighted, encourage the class to make the noise enthusiastically!

- Say names of body parts. Children use *Pen* to circle the body parts in the pictures, each time saying e.g. *This is the kangaroo's* (*tail.*)

Reading Comprehension and Critical Literacy

Lesson objectives: use *Mr.* and *Mrs.* appropriately; interpreting the theme of the story

Materials: Track 8.5; Reader; colored paper/card for thank you notes (optional)

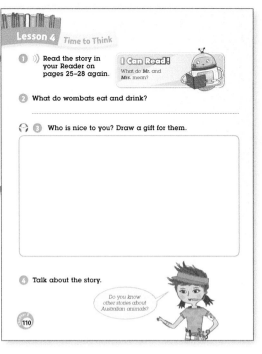

Note: Please ensure that your class has read the Reader story before you do this lesson.

Warmer: Things in the story

Ask the children to remember things that appear in the story, e.g. *sun, tree, grass, water, boomerang, bag/pouch.* List them on the board. Have the children order them in their notebook. Then have them check in their Reader.

1))) 8.5 Read the story in your Reader.

* Ask the children to read the story. (Alternatively, play Track 8.5 and have them read along.) Ask them to look for sound effects, e.g. *Munch! Gasp! Boing!* Practice the sounds.

I Can Read!

Ask the children to circle *Mr.* and *Mrs.* in the story. Elicit the meaning. If desired, teach *Miss* and *Ms.* Then, have the children say hello to friends using a title and their surnames accordingly. Invite children to demonstrate.

Answer

Mr. is a polite title for a man. *Mrs.* is a polite title for a married woman.

2 What do wombats eat and drink?

* Elicit the pictures where Mr. Wombat is eating and drinking. (*pictures 4 and 6*)

* Give them time to write their answer. Elicit answers and check with the class.

Answers

Wombats eat grass and drink water.

3 Who is nice to you? Draw a gift for them.

* Ask *Who is nice in the story?* (*Mrs. Kangaroo; then Wombat/Byamee*) Elicit how they are nice.

* Have the children think of someone who is nice to them. Elicit answers with reasons. Then elicit ideas for a present for this person. (They might need L1.)

* Give the children time to draw their present. Tell them to write who it is for. If they know their surname they can use their title, e.g. *For Ms. (name).* Ask children to show their drawing to the class.

4 Talk about the story.

* Ask the children if they liked the story and why/why not.

* Have a child read Libby's question. Have the children share other stories about Australian animals. (They might need to use L1.)

Optional activity: Thank you note

Have the children write a thank you note for the person who is nice to them. Write useful language on the board, e.g. *Dear …, Thank you for …* Distribute the colored paper/card. The children write their note. They can give it to the person after class.

Competency Focus

Me: Critical Literacy

The children use critical literacy skills to reflect on the story and relate it to their own experiences.

1 Find Joey. Then complete.

Give the children time to help Mrs. Kangaroo find Joey. Then ask them to complete the text with the words supplied.

Answers

1 nice **2** grass **3** hunter **4** catch **5** pouch

2 Complete with *Mr.* or *Mrs.*

The children practice the **I Can Read!** feature by writing *Mr.* and *Mrs.* under the pictures. Check answers.

Answers

Mr., Mrs., Mr.

3 Complete with *good* or *bad.*

Ask the children to think about the three characters from the story. Have them complete the descriptions. Elicit answers and check with the class. Ask why the characters are good or bad.

Answers

good, good, bad

Cooler: Who said it?

Read a sentence/phrase from the story and have the class say which character said it. Then prompt them to say what happens in the story after this line. Repeat with a few more lines.

Digital Resources

Reader eBook • Display the Reader on the board. To give feedback on the Warmer activity, have children find and circle the items they remembered using *Pen*.

• Have children use *Pen* to circle *Mr.* and *Mrs.* in the Reader story to help understand the I Can Read! feature.

Vocabulary, Song, and Phonics

Lesson objectives: identify geographical features; practice the *s* and *z* sounds

Key vocabulary: *caves, forest, jungle, ocean, river, sky*

Secondary language: *bats, dolphins, high, wide*

Materials: Tracks 8.6 and 8.7; pictures for Key vocabulary (Warmer) ; Phonics Worksheet 8 [TRC printout] (optional)

Warmer: Noisy places

Pre-teach the vocabulary using pictures. Agree a different sound effect for each word. Say the words to elicit the sound effects from the class.

1))) 8.6 Listen and match. Then sing.

- Ask the children to look at the picture and identify all the animals and their habitats.

- Play Track 8.6 and have the children listen and draw lines to match the words to the locations in the picture. Choose individual children to say a word and point to the picture.

- Play Track 8.6 again and have the class sing along.

- Divide the class into three groups. Allocate a verse to each group. Play the song again and have the class sing along and mime the animals in their verse.

Answers

Lines from the red words to the correct locations.

2 Play a guessing game.

- Choose two children to read the example. Point out that the language is from the song in Activity 1.

- Then divide your class into pairs. Have them take turns saying a sentence from the song for their friend to call out the animal. Monitor and help if necessary.

3))) 8.7 Listen and say the chant.

- Ask the children to identify the animals in the picture. Then have them notice the red letters in the chant.

- Play Track 8.7 and have the children listen to the chant.

- Play Track 8.7 again, pausing for them to repeat.

- Practice the chant a few times with the class. Then focus on the sounds *s* and *z*. Have the children put their hand gently over their throats as they say *sssss* and *zzzzz*. Make sure they notice the vibration when they say *zzzzz*.

Optional activity: Sam the snake and Zak the lizard

Write *reptiles* and *amphibians* on the board and explain what they are. Have children give examples for each category, e.g. *snakes*—reptiles and *frogs*—amphibians. Then have the children draw a snake (Sam) and a lizard (Zak). Monitor and help. Say the chant as a class and have the children hold up each drawing accordingly.

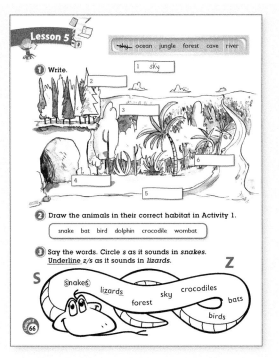

Play the game with words from the lesson
(see Games Bank, p. 222).

Competency Focus

Think! Critical Thinking

The children use critical thinking skills to identify the meaning of geographical features by processing the written and spoken forms, and matching them to the correct picture.

1 Write.

Ask the children to label the parts of the picture with the words. Elicit answers and check with the class.

Answers

1 sky **2** forest **3** jungle **4** cave **5** ocean **6** river

2 Draw the animals in their correct habitat in Activity 1.

Check with the class where each animal lives. Then give the children time to draw the animals in the picture in Activity 1.

Answers

Animals drawn as follows in the picture:

snake—jungle, bat—cave, bird—sky, dolphin—ocean, crocodile—river, wombat—forest

3 Say the words. Circle *s* as it sounds in *snakes*. Underline *z/s* as it sounds in *lizards.*

Have the class say the two sounds and words before they circle and underline the letters. Elicit answers and check with the class.

Answers

Circled **s** *in:* **s**nake**s**, fore**s**t, **s**ky, bat**s**
Underlined **z/s** *in:* li**z**ards, crocodile**s**, bird**s**

Digital Resources

Student eBook• Play ASL Vocabulary Video 8.4 to pre-teach key vocabulary. Play it again, pausing for the children to repeat the word and copy the sign.

• Play Music Video 8.2 (8.3). Encourage the children to dance and sing along. The lyrics appear on screen for support. Pause the video for the children to continue dancing and singing.

Teacher Resource Center • For phonics practice, print out Phonics Worksheet 8.

Grammar and Reading

Lesson objectives: ask and answer about animals and their habits

Key grammar: *What do they eat? They eat (grass).*
Where do they live? They live in (Australia). When do they sleep?
They sleep (in the day).

Secondary language: *Australia, crocodiles, information, meat, under*

Materials: Track 8.8; Grammar Worksheet 8B [TRC printout] (optional)

Warmer: Play "Whisper It!"

Play the game with words from the chapter so far, e.g. *wombat, forest, grass, meat, tree, kangaroo, pouch.* (see Games Bank p. 222).

1))) 8.8 **Listen and read.**

- Have the children look at the pictures. Ask *What animal are they learning about?* (*wombats*)

- Play Track 8.8 and ask them to listen and read along. Ask the questions that appear on the information screen and elicit the answers.

- Play Track 8.8 again, pausing for them to repeat. Pay attention to the intonation of questions.

2 **Write about crocodiles.**

- Ask the children to look at the picture of the crocodile. Ask *What's he doing?* (*He's swimming.*)

- Give them time to complete the questions and answers, referring to Grammar Central. Have them compare in pairs before you check as a class.

Answers

1 Where, They **2** do, eat **3** When, sleep

Optional activity: Ask about animals

Ask the children to write questions about different animals, e.g. kangaroos, bats, etc. Write the question prompts from Grammar Central on the board to help. Invite children to ask their question(s) for the class to answer.

Grammar Central

What do they eat? …

Have the children look at the questions and point out the word order. Say *What, Where,* and *When* for the children to repeat. Explain meaning if necessary. Divide the class into pairs and have them practice asking and answering the questions.

For extra practice, try the **Grammar Booster** section in the Student Book (p. 117–119).

Answers p. 117

Activity 1: **1** do **2** eat **3** Where **4** live **5** When **6** sleep

Activity 2: **1** Where, d **2** When, b **3** Where, a **4** What, c **5** What, e

p. 118

Activity 1: **1** have **2** Do **3** What **4** eat **5** don't **6** have

Activity 2: **1** Do dolphins have, No they don't. **2** Do they have, Yes, they do. **3** What do they, They eat **4** Where do they, They live

p. 119

Activity 1: **1** has, **2** eats, **3** lives, **4** run, **5** work, **6** finding, **7** catch, **8** bark, **9** take

Activity 2: **1** What does Blaine do? He's a police officer. **2** Where does Simba live? / He lives in a house with Blaine. **3** Does Simba eat meat? / Yes, he does. **4** Where do they work? / They work at the police station. **5** When do they work? / They work at night.

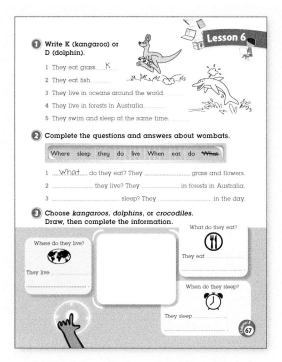

1 Write K (kangaroo) or D (dolphin).

Have the children read the sentences and write K for kangaroo or D for dolphin. Elicit answers and check with the class.

Answers

1 K **2** D **3** D **4** K **5** D

2 Complete the questions and answers about wombats.

Have the children complete the questions and answers with the words in the box. Have them practice asking and answering the questions in pairs.

Answers

1 What, eat **2** Where do, live **3** When do they, sleep

3 Choose *kangaroos*, *dolphins*, or *crocodiles*. Draw, then complete the information.

Have the children choose one of the animals. Then give them time to draw the animal and complete the information about it. Have them show and tell in pairs.

Answers

One of the following:

Kangaroos: They live in forests. They eat grass. They sleep in the day.

Dolphins: They live in the ocean. They eat fish. They sleep in the day and at night.

Crocodiles: They live in the river. They eat meat. They sleep in the day.

Cooler: Memory check

Write the questions from Activity 2 on the board. Put the children in pairs. Have them take turns asking a question from Activity 2 for their friend to answer without looking in their book.

Competency Focus

Learn

The children demonstrate their understanding of the new grammatical patterns by reading the text and completing the activity.

Digital Resources

Student eBook • Use *Timer* to give the class one minute to look at SB Activity 1. Then stop displaying the SB story extract. Elicit the text.

Teacher Resource Center • For extra grammar practice, print out Grammar Worksheet 8B.

CLIL: Science—Animals and their habitats

Lesson objective: find out about animal habitats
Materials: Track 8.9; CLIL Graphic Organizer 8 [TRC printout] (optional); pictures of animals using camouflage (Warmer)

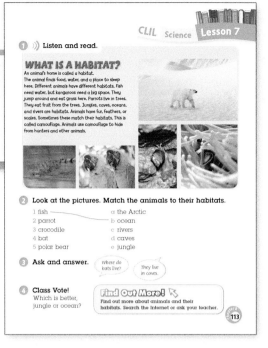

Warmer: Camouflage

Pre-teach *camouflage* and show the class the pictures you brought. Have them find the animals and say what they have camouflaged themselves to look like. Elicit other animals that use camouflage. (They might need to use L1.)

1))) 8.9 Listen and read.

- Have the children look at the photos and identify the animals. Have the class read the title and the first line. Elicit the meaning of *habitat*.

- Play Track 8.9 and have the children listen and read along.

- Play Track 8.9 again and ask children why animals use camouflage. (*to hide from hunters and other animals*)

2 Look at the pictures. Match the animals to their habitats.

- Do the example with the class. Then give them time to match the rest of the animals and habitats.

- Have them refer to the text to find the answers. Elicit answers and check with the class.

Answers

1 b **2** e **3** c **4** d **5** a

3 Ask and answer.

- Ask two children to read the example. Call on children to do one more example.

- Divide the class into pairs. Have them take turns asking and answering questions using the information in Activities 1 and 2.

4 Class Vote!

- Organize your class vote. Ask the children if they prefer the jungle or the ocean. Give them a minute to think. Then write *jungle* and *ocean* on the board. Have the children raise their hand for each answer. Count the votes and write the totals on the board. Elicit the result of the vote.

Find Out More!

Ask the children to choose two different animals. Have them find out more about the animals' habitats and find photos of the animals. Suggest appropriate resources, e.g. Internet, library books, etc., or provide the information yourself. The children will need to complete this research before doing the follow-up activity in the Activity Book. (It could be set as homework.)

Optional activity: Home sweet home

Write *Home sweet home* on the board and explain its meaning. Then ask the children to draw a wild animal in its habitat, e.g. a parrot in a tree, and title it *Home sweet home*.

Competency Focus

Act

The children carry out research to find out about animal habitats. This helps them to expand their learning and relate it to their world, both inside and outside the classroom.

1 Match and complete.

Have the children complete the sentences and match them to the pictures. Elicit answers and check with the class.

Answers

1 Bats a **2** Crocodiles d **3** live in the Arctic c
4 Fish live in b **5** live in jungles e

2 Use your Student Book research. Choose a habitat. Draw and write.

Ask the children what they know or have found out about animals and their habitats. Then give them time to draw and write about one of the animals.

Cooler: Class discussion

Discuss with the class why it is important to protect wild animals' habitats. Have the children work in groups to think of ways they can help protect these habitats. (You will need L1.)

Digital Resources

Student eBook • Display the SB page for an alternative "heads-up" introduction to the topic in Activity 1 point 1. Children use *Highlighter* to identify words for animal habitats in the text.

Digital Activity Book • Model an answer for AB Activity 2. Use *Pen* to write and draw.

Teacher Resource Center • Print out CLIL Graphic Organizer 8 for the children to use in collating their Find Out More! research.

CLIL eBook • The children can use the CLIL eBook to expand their knowledge of the lesson topic.

Project

Lesson objectives: review language from Chapter 8; complete a craft project—making a boomerang; act out the story from the Reader
Materials: Reader; scissors, glue, paintbrush, watercolors, coloring pens; Project Template 8 [TRC printouts]; picture of a didgeridoo (optional)

Warmer: Play "The Shark Game"

Have the children play the game with words from the lesson (see Games Bank p. 222).

Prepare

1 Make a boomerang.

- Have the children look at the completed boomerangs. Elicit if they have ever played with a boomerang. Ask *Where do boomerangs come from?* (*Australia*) *Why did people in Australia use them?* (*for hunting*) Ask *Which do you like best?* Tell them they are going to make their own boomerang.

- Hold up the materials to show the class. Point to the pictures and explain the stages. (You might need to use L1.)

- Demonstrate how to make a boomerang, stage by stage.

- Divide the class into pairs or groups if it is necessary to share materials. Give out the materials.

- As the children make their boomerangs, monitor and give help as necessary.

Alternative craft activity

A simpler option would be to cut out a single template for each child simply to color.

Showcase

2 Tell the story. Use your boomerang.

- Divide the class into groups and ask the children to look at the story again. Have them choose their role or allocate roles in each group.

- Give them time to practice acting out the story. Omit the narrator's part. Monitor and give help during rehearsal time.

- Have each group perform the story for the class with a boomerang.

Optional activity: Didgeridoo

Show the class the picture of a didgeridoo. Explain that it is a wind instrument that aboriginal people in Australia started using thousands of years ago. Have the children draw a didgeridoo in their notebook, label it, and decorate it.

1 Circle what's wrong. Talk to a friend.

Give the children time to circle the wrong facts in the picture. Then have them compare and talk about them in pairs. Check with the class.

Answers

Giraffes don't sleep in trees. Monkeys don't have wings. Parrots don't eat pizza. Polar bears don't live in jungles. Crocodiles don't eat bananas. Lizards don't have beaks. Kangaroos don't have scales.

Cooler: Play "Hot Potato"

Play the game with a boomerang, using words from the lesson (see Games Bank p. 222).

Competency Focus

Collaborate and Communicate

By acting out the story, the children consolidate their understanding in a fun and engaging way. They also demonstrate their ability to work with friends and use interpersonal skills.

Digital Resources

Student eBook • Show the Prepare photos, stage by stage, as you talk the class through the activity process.

Digital Activity Book • Use *Timer* for AB Activity 1. Give the children one minute to identify all the mistakes in the picture. Choose children to circle mistakes using *Pen*.

Teacher Resource Center • Print out Project Template 8 to use for the SB craft activity.

Language Review

Lesson objective: review language from Chapter 8
Materials: Tracks 8.10, AB 8.1 and AB 8.2

1))) **Listen and circle T (true) or F (false).**

1 They are good at swimming. (T) / F
2 They have fins. T / F
3 They are mammals. T / F
4 They have scales. T / F
5 They have fur. T / F
6 They have a beak. T / F

2 **Write questions about platypuses.**

1 What ____do they eat____? They eat small animals in the water.
2 Where _____? They live in rivers in Australia.
3 When _____? They sleep in the day.
4 _____ a pouch? No, they don't.

3 **Think about Chapter 8. Color the books.**

GREAT!
OK
I'M NOT SURE

Treasure Hunt!

Look back at
pages 4 and 5. Find:
a shark fin

115

Warmer: Play "The Shark Game"

Have the children play the game with habitats from Lesson 5 (see Games Bank p. 222).

1))) 8.10 Listen and circle T (true) or F (false).

- Ask the children to look at the picture. Give them time to read the sentences once. Then play Track 8.10 twice and have the children choose true or false.

- Have them compare in pairs before you check as a class. Call on children to read a sentence and say if it is true or false. Ask the class to correct the false sentences.

Audioscript

This funny animal is a platypus. Platypuses are good at swimming, but they don't have fins. Platypuses are mammals. They don't have scales; they have fur. They don't have a nose. They have a beak.

Answers

1 T **2** F **3** T **4** F **5** T **6** T

2 Write questions about platypuses.

- Have a child read the example question and answer. Give the children time to read the sentences and complete the questions.

- Have the children check in pairs, then check answers as a class.

Answers

1 do they eat **2** do they live **3** do they sleep **4** Do they have

3 Think about Chapter 8. Color the books.

- Have the children look back at Chapter 8. Elicit their favorite parts. The children then color the book which represents how they feel about their own progress (self-evaluation).

Treasure Hunt!

Ask the children to look at Student Book pp. 4–5 and find a shark fin. Have the children raise their hand when they find it.

Cooler: True or false?

Ask the children to make a true or false sentence about an animal. Invite children to say their sentence, e.g. *Kangaroos have scales.* Have the class call out *True!* or *False!* and correct the false sentences, e.g. *Kangaroos don't have scales. They have fur.*

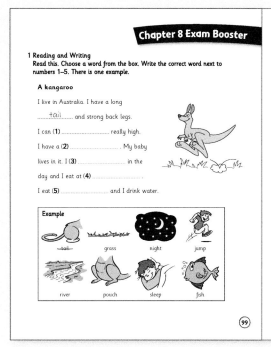

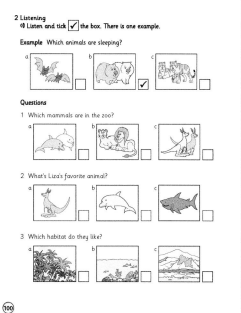

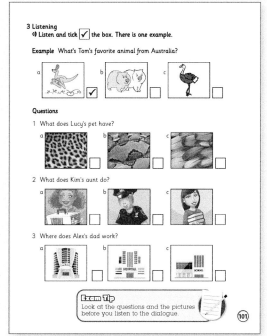

1 Reading and Writing. Read this. Choose a word from the box. Write the correct word next to numbers 1–5. There is one example.

Have the children complete the text using the words supplied. Check answers.

Answers

1 jump **2** pouch **3** sleep **4** night **5** grass

2))) AB 8.1   Listening. Listen and tick (✔) the box. There is one example.

Give the children time to read the questions. They then listen and check the correct picture in each section. Play Track AB 8.1 twice, then elicit answers and check with the class.

Answers (Audioscript on p. 224)

1 a **2** c **3** a

3   Listening.))) AB 8.2   Listen and tick (✔) the box. There is one example.

Give the children time to read the questions. They then listen and check the correct picture in each section. Play Track AB 8.2 twice, then elicit answers and check with the class.

Answers (Audioscript on p. 224)

1 b **2** a **3** c

Competency Focus

Me: Self-evaluation

The children reflect on the chapter and express their opinions about their own progress. This encourages them to evaluate and make decisions about how they learn and what they need to revisit.

Digital Resources

Teacher Resource Center • Print out Test Chapter 8 to use at the end of this lesson. The Test Generator also allows you to create customized tests.

Student's App • Encourage the children to play the games on their smartphone/tablet. Ask them to record their scores to compare in the next lesson. (*The Inks* Apps are free and available on the App Store and Google Play.)

Chapter 9

Town and Countryside
Overview

The children will:

- use critical thinking skills to identify free time activities.
- ask and answer questions about what they like to do in their free time.
- read, understand, and act out a story.
- talk about things in nature.
- ask and answer if they prefer the town/countryside and give reasons why.
- find out about famous paintings.
- make town and country hats.

Key Vocabulary

Free time activities: go horseback riding, go shopping, go to the movies, listen to music, meet my friends, play computer games, stay home
Nature: bees, butterflies, farms, fields, flowers, stars

Key Grammar

- What do you like to do (on weekends)?
- I like to (stay home).
- I don't like to (play tennis).
- Do you like (the town or the countryside)?
- I like (the countryside).
- Why? I like it because there are (flowers).

Reading Skills

Story: *The Town Mouse and the Country Mouse*
Genre: traditional fable

Literacy Development

- predict story content from title and pictures
- focus on the text in thought bubbles
- personalize the story by thinking about where they live

Functional Language

- Would you like to come to my house on Saturday?
- Yes, that sounds fun!
- OK, great. See you Saturday.

Phonics

The children practice pronunciation of *ou* sound as in c*ou*nt and *ow* as in fl*ow*er.

CLIL: Art—Famous artists

The children find out about famous paintings and the artists who painted them.

Competency Focus

The children will:

use critical thinking skills to identify free time activities. (Lesson 1)	apply new grammar to previously learned vocabulary. (Lesson 2)	work in pairs to act out a dialogue. (Lesson 3)	personalize their response to the story by thinking about the place where they live. (Lesson 4)	learn about an artist from their own country. (Lesson 7)
predict the content of a story. (Lesson 3)	ask and answer about preferences, giving reasons. (Lesson 6)	work in groups to act out the story. (Lesson 8)	evaluate their own progress in the chapter. (Review)	
identify things in nature. (Lesson 5)				

Digital Overview

Teacher Presentation

Student eBook and Digital Activity Book

- ASL Vocabulary Video 9.1: Free time activities
- ASL Vocabulary Video 9.3: Nature
- Oral Storytelling Video 9.2: *The Town Mouse and the Country Mouse*
- Interactive versions of AB activities
- Integrated audio and answer key for all activities

Teacher resources for planning, lesson delivery, and homework

Teacher Resource Center

- Class Planner Chapter 9
- Worksheets to print out (including notes and answers):
    - Grammar Worksheet 9A: What do you like to do …? I like to …
    - Grammar Worksheet 9B: Do you like …? I like …
    - Oral Storytelling Video Worksheet 9: *The Town Mouse and the Country Mouse*
    - Phonics Worksheet 9
    - CLIL Graphic Organizer 9
    - Test Chapter 9 and End-of-year Test
- Test Generator
- Speaking Assessment: Cambridge English Young Learners Exams
- Literacy Handbook

Watch the Oral Storytelling Video

Children's resources for consolidation and practice at home

Student eBook

- ASL Vocabulary Video 9.1: Free time activities
- ASL Vocabulary Video 9.3: Nature

Student eBook and Reader eBook

- Oral Storytelling Video 9.2: *The Town Mouse and the Country Mouse*

The Inks **Student's App**

Vocabulary games: Free time activities and nature

Town and Countryside

Lesson 1

Vocabulary

Lesson objective: identify free time activities

Key vocabulary: *go horseback riding, go shopping, go to the movies, listen to music, meet my friends, play computer games, stay home*

Materials: Track 9.1

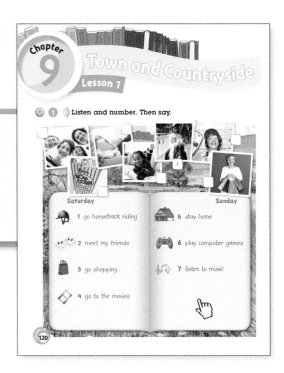

Chapter **9** Town and Countryside Lesson 1

1)) Listen and number. Then say.

Saturday   Sunday

1 go horseback riding   5 stay home

2 meet my friends   6 play computer games

3 go shopping   7 listen to music

4 go to the movies

120

Warmer: Saturday and Sunday

Write scrambled versions of *Saturday* and *Sunday* on the board. Have the children unscramble the letters. Then ask *What do you usually do on the weekend?* Elicit answers and have the children draw two of their activities.

1)) 9.1 Listen and number. Then say.

- Have the children open their books and look at the pictures. Elicit if they drew any of these pictures in the Warmer. Have the class call out things they do on the weekend, in English if possible.

- Give them time to study the activities for each day. Then play Track 9.1 and have them listen and point. They then match the phrases to the photos, writing the numbers.

- Play Track 9.1 again for them to check. Elicit answers and check with the class.

- Have the children practice saying the activities in pairs. One child says the number of a picture for their friend to say the activity. Monitor and help with pronunciation.

Audioscript

I love weekends. On Saturday morning, I go horseback riding. In the afternoon, I meet my friends. We sometimes go shopping or we go to the movies. On Sunday, I stay home.
I play computer games and listen to music.

Answers

2, 4, 5, 6, 1, 7, 3

Optional activity: Expanding vocabulary

Have the children think of one or two more activities they do on the weekend and add them to Activity 1. They can use their ideas from the Warmer. Monitor and help with language. (They might need to use L1.)

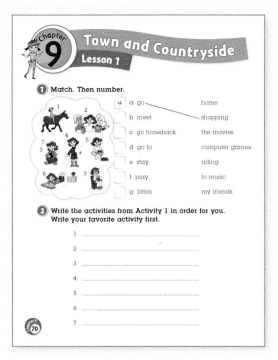

Chapter 9 — Town and Countryside
Lesson 1

1 Match. Then number.

- 4 | a go — home
- | b meet — shopping
- | c go horseback — the movies
- | d go to — computer games
- | e stay — riding
- | f play — to music
- | g listen — my friends

2 Write the activities from Activity 1 in order for you. Write your favorite activity first.

1 ....
2 ....
3 ....
4 ....
5 ....
6 ....
7 ....

70

Competency Focus

Think! Critical Thinking

The children use critical thinking skills to identify free time activities by using visual clues and processing the written and spoken forms.

1 Match. Then number.

Have the children match the words to make phrases. They then match the phrases with the pictures, writing the numbers.

Answers

a go shopping 4
b meet my friends 2
c go horseback riding 1
d go to the movies 7
e stay home 6
f play computer games 5
g listen to music 3

2 Write the activities from Activity 1 in order for you. Write your favorite activity first.

Ask the children to copy the activities from Activity 1 in order of preference. Do a class vote to find out the most popular activity.

Answers

Children's own answers.

Cooler: Play "Simon Says"

Play the game with words from the lesson (see Games Bank p. 222).

Digital Resources

Student eBook • Play ASL Vocabulary Video 9.1 to pre-teach key vocabulary as an alternative to the critical thinking approach.

• Play "Kim's Game" with the new vocabulary. Display the SB page and point to the labeled pictures in Activity 1. Divide the class into teams. Use *Timer* and give them one minute to memorize the pictures, then one minute to recall them in order (with SB page closed). Repeat several times.

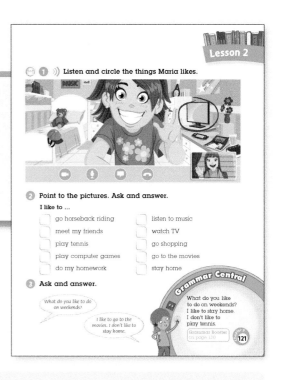

Grammar

Lesson objectives: ask and answer questions about what they like and don't like doing on weekends

Key grammar: *What do you like to do (on weekends)? I like to (stay home). I don't like to (play tennis).*

Materials: Track 9.2; Grammar Worksheet 9A [TRC printout] (optional)

Warmer: Draw a clue

Call on children to draw a clue for a free time activity from Lesson 1 on the board for the class to guess, e.g. a big screen—go to the movies. Have pairs ask and answer *Do you like to (go to the movies) on weekends?*

1))) 9.2 Listen and circle the things Maria likes.

- Ask the children to look at the picture and identify objects in Maria's bedroom, e.g. TV, flowers, etc. Point to Kelly on the bottom right corner and ask *What are they doing?* (*talking on the computer*)

- Play Track 9.2 and have them listen and circle the objects to show what Maria likes. Play Track 9.2 again for them to check. Elicit answers and check with the class.

Audioscript

Maria: Hi, Kelly. Can you see me?
Kelly: Hi, Maria. Yes, I can. Oh, you have a TV in your room! I like to watch TV on weekends. What do you like to do on weekends?
Maria: Well, I like to watch TV. I like to play computer games. I like to go horseback riding. I like to go to the movies. I like to play tennis.
Kelly: Me, too!
Maria: I don't like to do my homework.

Answers

Circled objects: TV, computer game, riding hat, film guide, tennis racket

Grammar Central

What do you like to do on weekends? …

Have the children read the patterns. Point out the word order in the question and the verb with *to* after *like/don't like*. Remind them to use *don't* in negative sentences and *do* in questions. Then divide your class into pairs and have them practice the question and answers.

For extra practice, try the **Grammar Booster** section in the Student Book (p. 130).

Answers p. 130

Activity 1: **1** do you, **2** play **3** play **4** like to do **5** like to go **6** don't like to go

Activity 2: **1** I like to meet my friends. **2** I don't like to stay home. **3** I like to go shopping. **4** I don't like to play computer games. **5** I like to listen to music. **6** I don't like to go horseback riding.

2 Check (✔) the things you like to do.

- Have the class read the activities together. Then they check the ones they like to do on weekends.

Answers

Children's own answers.

3 Ask and answer.

- Divide the class into pairs. Invite a pair to read out the example.

- Write on the board *What do you like to do on weekends? I like to …/ I don't like to …* Ask the children to talk about their weekends in pairs.

Optional activity: Mini-survey

Do a class survey. Have the children write a list of the activities from Lesson 1. Then have them ask the question (from Activity 3) around the class and check the activities. Find out the most popular activity.

Competency Focus

Learn

By identifying what people like to do in a different context with new grammatical structures, the children demonstrate their understanding of previously acquired vocabulary from Lesson 1.

1 Write for you.

Give the children time to write about what they like and don't like to do on Saturdays. Have them compare their answers in pairs.

Answers

Children's own answers.

2 Complete. Then ask and answer.

Have the children complete the questions. In different pairs, have them practice asking and answering the questions.

Answers

1 What **2** What, like **3** What do you like to do

Cooler: Play "Whisper It!"

Have the children play the game with free time activities from the lesson (see Games Bank p. 222).

Digital Resources

Student eBook• Choose children to use *Pen* to check something they like to do in SB Activity 2. Each time, the children raise their hand if they agree. Write a tally each time. Identify the most popular activity.

Student eBook, Digital Activity Book • TIP Use *Add personal note* to note weaknesses in the children's vocabulary, grammar, or pronunciation so you can revisit in later lessons.

Teacher Resource Center • For extra grammar practice, print out Grammar Worksheet 9A.

Reading: Story Extract

Lesson objectives: give and accept an invitation; use the title and pictures to predict story content; read the extract from *The Town Mouse and the Country Mouse* (middle)

Functional language: *Would you like to come to my house on Saturday? Yes, that sounds fun! OK, great. See you Saturday.*

Secondary language: *dirty, mall, noisy, town*

Materials: Tracks 9.3 and 9.4

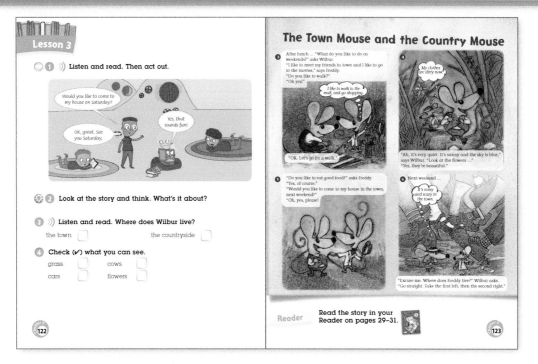

Warmer: Would you like to ...?

Ask around the class *Would you like to play tennis on Saturday?* The children who answer yes stand up. Repeat with a different activity. Call on children to suggest different activities for next Saturday. Do not insist on them using the structure at this point.

Functional language

1)》 **9.3 Listen and read. Then act out.**

- Have the children look at the picture. Ask *What's Ellie doing?* (*She's reading a book and she's talking to Tom.*)
- Play Track 9.3 and have the children listen and read along.
- Play Track 9.3 again, pausing for them to repeat.
- Divide the class into pairs and have them act out the dialogue.

Before reading

2 Look at the story and think. What's it about?

- Ask the children to look at the title and the pictures in the story extract. Pre-teach *country/countryside*. Ask *What's the story about?* (*two mice: one from the town and one from the countryside*)

3)》 **9.4 Listen and read. Where does Wilbur live?**

- Play Track 9.4 and have the children listen and read along. Then point and ask *What are their names?* (*Wilbur, Freddy*) *Where are they?* (*in the countryside, in the town*)
- Have the children read the question and check the correct answer. Elicit the answer.
- Play Track 9.4 again. Check comprehension by asking *Does Wilbur like the town? Does Freddy like the countryside?*

Answer

the countryside

4 Check (✔) what you can see.

- Choose a child to read the list of words. Have the children look at the pictures and check what they can see.
- Elicit answers and check with the class. Have the children say other things they can see, e.g. *shoes, boots, trousers, jacket, rug.*

Answer

grass, flowers

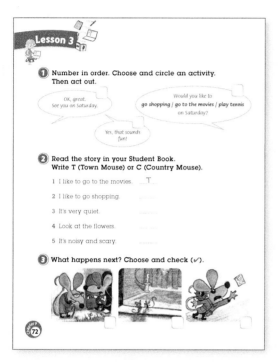

1 Number in order. Choose and circle an activity. Then act out.

Ask the children to number the dialogue in order and choose an activity from the options given. Then have them act it out in pairs. Ask pairs to act out for the class.

Answers

OK, great. See you on Saturday. 3
Would you like to (go shopping) on Saturday? 1
Yes, that sounds fun! 2

2 Read the story in your Student Book. Write T (Town Mouse) or C (Country Mouse).

Have the children read the sentences and write T or C depending on which character said or thought the line. Have them look at the story extract.

Answers

1 T 2 T 3 C 4 C 5 C

3 What happens next? Choose and check (✔).

Ask the children to think about what is going to happen next in the story. Have them check a picture. Elicit ideas.

Answers

Children's own answers.

Cooler: What happened before?

Explain that the extract is not the beginning of the story. Have the children imagine what happened before the story extract. (You might need to use L1.)

Competency Focus

Collaborate and Communicate

The children work together, putting into practice new functional language by acting out a realistic dialogue.

Think! Critical Thinking

By looking at the story artwork, the children use prediction skills to help them engage with the story.

Digital Resources

Student eBook, Digital Activity Book • TIP Choose an assistant! Ask a child to be responsible for choosing the relevant buttons (e.g. to go to the next activity or answer key).

Lesson objective: read and understand the traditional fable
The Town Mouse and the Country Mouse in the Reader
Materials: Track 9.5; Reader; Oral Storytelling Video Worksheet 9 [TRC printout] (optional)

Warmer: Story recap

Have the children say what happened in the story extract. Ask them to remember what each mouse likes to do, e.g. *Wilbur likes to walk in the countryside. Freddy likes to walk to the mall.* Have them say what will happen next.

Story Summary

Freddy, a town mouse, visits his cousin Wilbur in the country. Freddy does not like the simple ways of the country while Wilbur does not like the dangers of the town. Both mice are attacked by a cat and a maid in the town. In the end, Freddy stays in the town and Wilbur returns to the country, both preferring where they live.

Value: We are all different.

))) 9.5 While reading

- Have the children look at the pictures in *The Town Mouse and The Country Mouse* in their Reader. Have them identify Freddy's house and the other two characters. (*the maid, Tiggy*)

- Play Track 9.5 and have the children listen and read along.

- Check comprehension of the story by asking *What do they eat at Wilbur's/Freddy's house?* (*bread, cheese, water / cake, chocolate, fruit*) *Which house is bigger?* (*Freddy's*) *Who else is in Freddy's house?* (*a cat, a maid*) *What is Wilbur doing in the last picture?* (*putting on his jacket, leaving*) *Why?* (*He's scared of the cat/maid.*) (They might need to use L1.)

- Play Track 9.5 again, pausing for the children to repeat. You could divide your class into two groups: Freddy and Wilbur. Have them repeat only their character's lines.

After reading: Reflect

Have the children think about the message behind the story. Explain that the country is a beautiful place for Wilbur but not for Freddy, and vice versa for the town. Invite them to say which mouse they agree with and why.

Optional activity: Questions from the story

Have the children underline the questions Wilbur and Freddy ask each other in the story. Divide the class into pairs and have them take turns asking and answering Wilbur and Freddy's questions.

Story Time

Picture talk

The story pictures can be used in many ways to help children build the thinking skills of sequencing and storytelling. Have the children choose their favorite pictures in the story and say what is happening using simple language.

Reading Strategy

Audio-assisted Reading

Audio-assisted Reading is a strategy where the children read the story out loud as they hear the teacher read or the recording of the story. They can do this individually or as a group. It helps them improve their reading skills, pronunciation, and intonation.

For additional explanation and activities, see the Literacy Handbook on Teacher Resource Center.

Cooler: Food

Divide the class into pairs and have them make a list in their notebook of the food in the pictures. Monitor and help if necessary. Check vocabulary with the class. Then ask them to number the objects in order of preference (1 being their favorite). Have them compare with a friend.

Digital Resources

Reader eBook • Show Pictures 9–12. Use *Timer* and give the children one minute to study the pictures. Then close the story and elicit key details (e.g. food, color of clothes).

• Watch Oral Storytelling Video 9.2 together before you do the After reading: Reflect activity.

Teacher Resource Center • Print out Oral Storytelling Video Worksheet 9 to help you get the most out of the video.

Reading Comprehension and Critical Literacy

Lesson objectives: focus on thought bubbles; personalize the story by thinking about where they live

Materials: Track 9.5; Reader; Oral Storytelling Video Worksheet 9 [TRC printout] (optional)

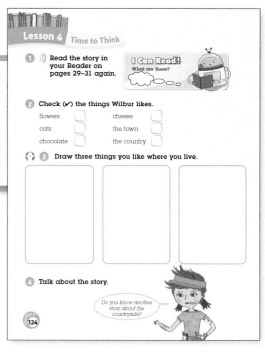

Note: Please ensure that your class has read the Reader story before you do this lesson.

Warmer: Photographic memory

Have the children look at the pictures of the story in their Reader for a minute. Then ask them to close their book and say words to describe things in the pictures. They can do this in pairs or small groups.

1))) 9.5 Read the story in your Reader.

- Have the children read the story. (Alternatively, play Track 9.5 and have them read along.) Ask what the relation is between the mice (*cousins*). Elicit their names and where they live. (*Freddy and Wilbur, the town and the countryside*)

I Can Read!

Ask the children to find thought bubbles in the story. Have them say what they are. Point to the thought bubble in picture 1 and ask *Does Freddy say "It's very small!"?* (*No. He's thinking it.*) Have the children read out other thought bubbles in the story.

Answer

Thought bubbles

2 Check (✔) the things Wilbur likes.

- Give the children time to study the words. Then have them look in their Reader and check the things Wilbur likes.

- Ask them to compare in pairs before you check as a class. Elicit why he does not like the cats (*He's a mouse.*) and the town. (*It's scary, big,* etc.)

Answers

by flowers, chocolate, cheese, the country

3 Draw three things you like where you live.

- As a class, brainstorm things children like about their home and where they live. Have them think about places in town, things they can do, places they can visit, etc.

- Then tell them to draw something they like in each box. Monitor and help.

- Ask them to show their finished drawings to a friend. Then call on children to show their picture and say a sentence, e.g. *I like the sports center.*

Answers

Children's own answers.

4 Talk about the story.

- Ask the children if they like the story and which mouse they prefer. Do a class vote, asking them to raise their hands for *yes* or *no.* Encourage them to give reasons why/why not. (They might need to use L1.)

- Have a child read Libby's question. Have the children share their stories about the countryside with the class.

Optional activity: Where I live

Ask the children to draw three things they do not like where they live, e.g. traffic, no park, etc. Monitor and help. Then invite individuals to present their drawings to the class.

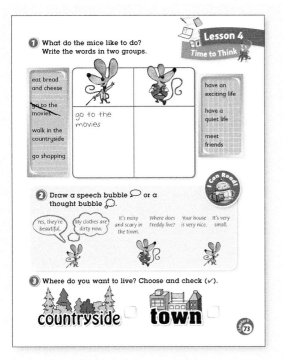

Cooler: Draw the Country Mouse

Ask the children to draw a picture of the Country Mouse sitting in his small house and relaxing after his trip. Have them draw a thought bubble with *Home sweet home!* or their own sentence.

Competency Focus

Me: Critical Literacy

The children use critical literacy skills to reflect on the story and personalize the topic by thinking about where they live.

---

1 What do the mice like to do? Write the words in two groups.

Have the children write the activities under the correct mouse. Check answers.

Answers

Freddy: go to the movies, go shopping, have an exciting life, meet friends

Wilbur: eat bread and cheese, walk in the countryside, have a quiet life

2 Draw a speech bubble or a thought bubble.

The children practice the **I Can Read!** feature by drawing a speech bubble or a thought bubble around each text.

Answers

Speech bubble: Yes, they're beautiful. Where does Freddy live? Your house is very nice.

Thought bubble: My clothes are dirty now. It's noisy and scary in the town. It's very small.

3 Where do you want to live? Choose and check (✔).

Have the children check the correct picture for themselves. Elicit answers from the class and invite individuals to explain why they prefer the country or town.

Answers

Children's own answers.

Digital Resources

Student eBook • To give feedback on SB Activity 3, have children draw one thing they like where they live using *Pen*. Each time, elicit whether the class agrees or not by a show of hands.

Student eBook, Digital Activity Book • If you haven't already, show Oral Storytelling Video 9.2.

Teacher Resource Center • If you haven't already, print out Oral Storytelling Video Worksheet 9 to do the support activities.

Vocabulary, Song, and Phonics

Lesson objectives: talk about things in nature; practice the sounds *ou* and *ow* with a chant

Key vocabulary: *bees, butterflies, farms, fields, flowers, stars*

Secondary language: *count, high up*

Materials: Tracks 9.6 and 9.7; pictures for Key vocabulary (Warmer) ; Phonics Worksheet 9 [TRC printout] (optional)

Warmer: Picture dictation

Write *The Country* as a heading on the board. Pre-teach the vocabulary using pictures. Say the words in random order for the children to draw.

1))) 9.6 Listen and number. Then sing.

- Ask the children to look at the pictures and identify the day and night scene. Give them time to study the red words, eliciting the ones they already know.

- Play Track 9.6 and have the children listen and match the words to the pictures. Choose individual children to say a word and the number of the picture.

- Play Track 9.6 again and have the class sing along miming the actions, e.g. listen to birds, look at flowers, walk across the fields, and count the stars.

Answers

flowers 3, butterflies 6, bees 2, fields 4, farms 5, stars 1

2 Talk to a friend.

- Choose two children to read the example question and answer. Elicit a few more example questions from the class (e.g. *Do you like to look at flowers/walk across the fields?*)

- Write question and answer prompts on the board (*Do you like to …? Yes, I do. / No, I don't.*) Then divide your class into pairs. Have them take turns asking and answering questions using language from the song. Monitor and help if necessary.

3))) 9.7 Listen and say the chant.

- Ask the children to describe the picture, e.g. *There are yellow and orange flowers*. Play Track 9.7 and have the children listen to the chant. Then play Track 9.7 again, pausing for them to repeat. Focus on the sounds in red, *ou* and *ow*. Then practice the chant a few times with the class.

Optional activity: New chants

Have the children say the chant again, replacing *flowers* with things they see in class, e.g. *chairs, desks, jackets, shoes*, etc.

Competency Focus

Think! Critical Thinking

By matching the words to the pictures, the children use critical thinking skills to identify things in nature and assimilate the written and spoken forms.

1 Unscramble the words and count. Then write sentences.

Ask the children to write the words and then count the objects in the picture to complete the sentences.

Answers

1 4, fields, four fields

2 4, butterflies, four butterflies

3 7, bees, seven bees

4 20, flowers, twenty flowers

5 2, farms, There are two farms.

6 13, stars, There are thirteen stars.

2 Say the words. Circle *ou* and *ow* as in *count* and *town*.

Have the children say the words before they circle the *ou* and *ow* letters. Elicit answers and check with the class.

Answers

Circled: **ou** *in* c**ou**nt, p**ou**ch, m**ou**se

Circled: **ow** *in* fl**ow**ers, h**ow**, t**ow**n

Cooler: Count the flowers

Have the children count the flowers in the picture in Student Book Activity 3. (*40*) Then ask them to count the yellow flowers (*15*), then the orange flowers (*25*).

Digital Resources

Student eBook • Play ASL Vocabulary Video 9.3 to pre-teach key vocabulary. Play it again, pausing to elicit the word when the picture and sign are shown.

Student's App • Encourage the children to play the games on their smartphone/tablet. They could arrange to do this with a friend as a fun way to review the chapter vocabulary together. (*The Inks* Apps are free and available on the App Store and Google Play.)

Teacher Resource Center • For phonics practice, print out Phonics Worksheet 9.

Grammar and Reading

Lesson objectives: ask and answer if they prefer the town/ countryside and give reasons why

Key grammar: *Do you like (the town or the countryside)? I like the (countryside). Why? I like it because there are (flowers).*

Secondary language: *country park, malls*

Materials: Track 9.8; Grammar Worksheet 9B [TRC printout] (optional); paper with *Town* and *Countryside* headings (Warmer)

Warmer: Town vs. countryside

Write *Town* and *Countryside* headings on two pieces of paper and stick them at opposite ends of the room. Have the children walk to the "place" they like most. They talk with others in the same group about why they do or do not like the town/countryside. Elicit ideas from the class.

1))) 9.8 Listen and read.

- Have the children look at the pictures. Ask *What's Tom reading about?* (*the Country Park*) Then ask them what happens in pictures 5 and 6. (*Biblio has an accident.*)

- Play Track 9.8 and have the children listen and read along.

- Play Track 9.8 again, pausing for them to repeat the phrases.

- Ask questions about what Ellie, Tom, and Libby prefer (town or countryside) and why. Who do they agree with most? Then ask why Biblio can see stars in picture 6. (*because he fell and hurt his head*)

2 Write about you.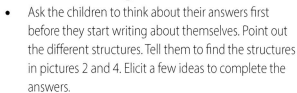

- Ask the children to think about their answers first before they start writing about themselves. Point out the different structures. Tell them to find the structures in pictures 2 and 4. Elicit a few ideas to complete the answers.

- Give them time to write their answers and compare in pairs. Then call on individual children to talk about their preference.

Answers

Children's own answers.

Grammar Central

Do you like the town or the countryside? …

Have the children look at the questions and answers. Point out that we use *because* to explain and give reasons. Tell the children that it is important to answer with full sentences. Divide the class into pairs and have them practice the short dialogue.

For extra practice, try the **Grammar Booster** section in the Student Book (p. 131–133).

Answers p. 131

Activity 1: **1** Do you like **2** or **3** Why? **4** because

Activity 2: **1** or **2** I like the **3** Why? **4** because **5** Why **6** like it

p. 132

Activity 1: **1** b **2** e **3** c **4** a **5** d

Activity 2: **1** b, What **2** a, to **3** c Why, **4** d, because **5** e, do

p. 133

Activity 1: **1** She's a teacher. **2** No, I don"t. **3** I like to go horseback riding. **4** I like the countryside. **5** Do you like to go **6** Why do you like **7** Do bats live **8** Why do you like

Optional activity: Punctuation and capitals

Write on the board *do you like the summer or the winter I like the winter why I like it because it snows and I can make a snowman*. Have the children copy and add punctuation and capital letters. Check answers.

Have the children mingle and ask as many friends as possible the questions from Activity Book Activity 2. Monitor and make sure they give reasons for their answer. Then have the children sit down and report in groups.

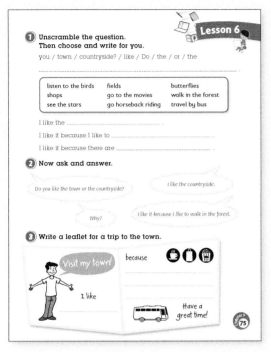

Competency Focus

Learn

The children demonstrate their understanding of the new grammatical patterns by reading the text and completing the activity about themselves.

1 Unscramble the question. Then choose and write for you.

Ask the children to write the questions. Check answers. Then give the children time to complete their own answers to the questions.

Answers

Do you like the town or the countryside?

Children's own answers.

2 Now ask and answer.

Invite two children to demonstrate the example. Then, in pairs, the children practice asking and answering the questions about the countryside.

3 Write a leaflet for a trip to the town.

Give the children time to complete the leaflet about their own town or an imaginary one. Allow them to work in pairs. Have them show and tell other children when they finish.

Answers

Children's own answers.

Digital Resources

Student eBook, Digital Activity Book • TIP With the answer key button, you can reveal the answers all at once or one by one, in order to customize feedback.

Teacher Resource Center • For extra grammar practice, print out Grammar Worksheet 9B.

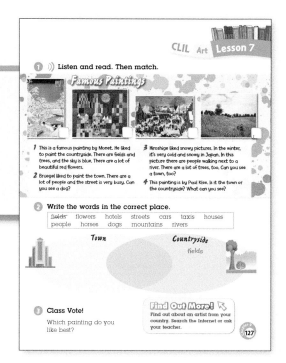

CLIL: Art—Famous artists

Lesson objective: find out about famous paintings and the artists who painted them

Materials: Track 9.9; CLIL Graphic Organizer 9 [TRC printout] (optional); pictures of different famous paintings (Warmer); different art materials (paints, crayons, pencils, etc.) (optional)

Warmer: Art

Ask *What do you do in art class? Do you like it? Why? Why not?* Then show them the pictures of the paintings. Have them say whether they like them or not and give reasons why. (They might need to use L1.)

1))) 9.9 Listen and read. Then match.

- Ask the children if they know any famous painters. Then have them open their books and look at the paintings. Ask *Do you think the paintings are of the town or the countryside?* Play Track 9.9 and have the children listen and read along. Ask them to notice the names of the artists and focus on the descriptions.

- Allow time to refer to the texts again and match them to the paintings, writing the numbers. Elicit answers and check with the class.

- Invite the children to talk about Paul Klee's painting and say whether it is the town or the countryside.

Answers

3, 4, 2, 1

2 Write the words in the correct place.

- Give the children time to study the words. Then ask them to write them in the correct category, town or countryside. Point out that the darker section in the middle is for things they can find in both places.

- Elicit answers and check with the class. Draw the ovals and invite children to write words on the board.

Answers (suggested)

Town—cars, taxis, hotels
Countryside—fields, flowers, mountains, rivers, horses
Both—streets, houses, people, dogs

3 Class Vote!

- Organize your class vote. Ask the children which painting in Activity 1 they like best. Give them a minute to think. Have them talk in pairs and give reasons if possible. (They might need to use L1.) Then write on the board *Monet, Bruegel, Hiroshige, Klee.* Have the children raise their hand for each answer. Count the votes and write the totals on the board. Elicit the result of the vote.

Find Out More!

Ask the children if they know of an artist from their country. Write names on the board. Ask the children to choose one and find out more about them. Suggest appropriate resources, e.g. Internet, library books, etc., or provide the information yourself. The children will need to complete this research before doing the follow-up activity in the Activity Book. (It could be set as homework.)

Optional activity: Art gallery

Have the children draw or paint a town or the countryside. Encourage them to use different art materials and different styles, and to sign their painting. Display their work and have the children admire the paintings and make comments, e.g. *It's beautiful! Look at the colors!*

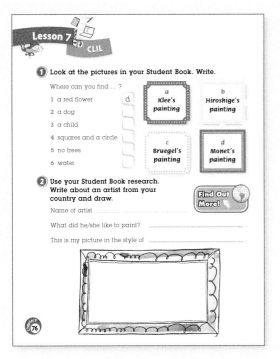

Competency Focus

Act

The children carry out research to find out about the artists from their country. This helps them to expand their learning and relate it to their world, both inside and outside the classroom.

1 Look at the pictures in your Student Book. Write.

Give the children time to look at the pictures and find the items listed in the paintings, writing the letters. Elicit answers and check with the class.

Answers

1 d **2** c **3** d **4** a **5** a **6** b

2 Use your Student Book research. Write about an artist from your country and draw.

Ask the children what they have found out about artists from their country. Then give them time to write about their chosen artist and draw a picture in his/her style.

Cooler: Play "Spelling Bee"

Have the children play the game with words from the lesson (see Games Bank p. 222).

Digital Resources

Student eBook • Show the pictures in SB Activity 1. Have the children predict the topic, then say what is special about each painting.

• TIP Remember—you can use *Add personal note* to log the results of the class vote. Involve the children in tallying the results and writing the scores on the board.

Teacher Resource Center • Print out CLIL Graphic Organizer 9 for the children to use in collating their Find Out More! research.

CLIL eBook • The children can use the CLIL eBook to expand their knowledge of the lesson topic.

Project

Lesson objectives: review language from Chapter 9; complete a craft project—making a town/country hat; act out the story from the Reader

Materials: Track 9.6 Reader; scissors, glue, paper, card, coloring pens, sticky tape; stapler (Alternative activity); two game pieces and a dice for each group; hat (Cooler)

Warmer: Hats

Write *Hats* on the board and ask *When do we use hats?* Elicit ideas from the class, e.g. *when it's cold, to go swimming,* etc. Ask *Who uses a hat at work?* (e.g. *a chef*)

Prepare

1 Make town and country hats.

- Have the children look at the hats. Ask *Which do you like more, the country hat or the town hat?* Tell them they are going to make their own hat.

- Hold up the materials to show the class. Point to the pictures and explain the stages. (You might need to use L1.)

- Demonstrate how to make a hat, stage by stage.

- Divide the class into pairs or groups if it is necessary to share materials. Give out the materials.

- As the children make their hats, monitor and give help as necessary.

Alternative craft activity

A simpler option would be to have the children staple the ends of card/paper together to make it fit on their head (without including a brim and top). Then have them decorate the band as their hat.

Showcase

2 Tell the story. Use your hats.

- Divide the class into pairs and have them choose a role, Wilbur or Freddy. Ask them to look at the story again. Ask them to focus on their lines.

- Give the children time to practice the story in pairs using their Reader. Walk around, monitor, and help with pronunciation.

- Call out pairs to the front of the class to perform a part of the story. Have them wear their hats. (They can borrow someone else's hat if theirs does not fit the role.)

Optional activity: Mini-dialogue

Write prompts on the board for short dialogues, e.g. *Two people meet in the street—take off their hats to say hello— ask how they are,* etc. Divide the class into different pairs. Have them wear their hats and act out the dialogue.

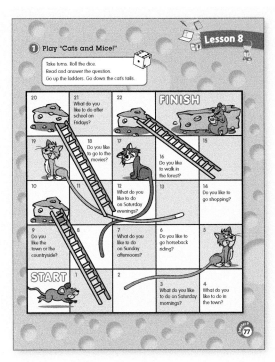

1 Play "Cats and Mice!"

Read the instructions with the class. Explain that when a player lands at the bottom of a ladder they go up to the square with the cheese. When they land on a cat, they go down to the tip of its tail. Have the children play the game in small groups. When they finish, invite children to answer a question from the game.

Cooler: Sing "I Love the Country"

))) 9.6

Play the song from Lesson 5 and have the children sing it wearing their hats. Use a hat yourself and demonstrate moves to the song, e.g. take off/put on the hat, hold it in the air, etc. Have the children copy the moves.

Competency Focus

Collaborate and Communicate

By acting out the story, the children consolidate their understanding in a fun and engaging way. They also demonstrate their ability to work with friends and use interpersonal skills.

Digital Resources

Student eBook • Show the Prepare photos, stage by stage, as you talk the class through the activity process.

Language Review

Lesson objective: review language from Chapter 9
Materials: Tracks 9.10, AB 9.1, AB 9.2 and AB 9.3

Warmer: Action circle

Have the children sit in a circle. Start a chant saying an activity from Activity 1, e.g. *I like to listen to music.* Say it with the class, starting quietly and building up the volume. Clap at the end. Continue with more activities.

---

1))) **9.10 Listen and check (✔) the things Billy likes to do on weekends. Then write about you.**

- Ask the children to look at the picture. Have them say what he is doing. (*listening to music*)

- Give the children time to study the activities. Then play Track 9.10 twice and have the children check the things Billy likes to do on weekends.

- Elicit answers and check with the class.

- Then tell the children to complete the two sentences about themselves. Monitor and help if necessary.

- Have the children say what they like/do not like to do in pairs.

Audioscript

Narrator: *Hi, Billy. What do you like to do on weekends?*
Billy: *I love weekends. On weekends, I like to play computer games and listen to music. I don't like to go shopping. I like to meet my friends and play tennis, but I don't like to go horseback riding. I don't like to go to the movies. I like to stay home and watch TV. Oh, and I don't like to do my homework!*

Answers

meet my friends, play tennis, play computer games, listen to music, watch TV, stay home; Children's own answers.

2 Write for you.

- Have the children read the prompts. Brainstorm a few ideas as a class.

- Have the children complete the sentences about themselves and compare in pairs.

- Ask children to share their opinions/preferences with the class.

Answers

Children's own answers.

3 Think about Chapter 9. Color the books.

Have the children look back at Chapter 9. Elicit their favorite parts. The children then color the book which represents how they feel about their own progress (self-evaluation).

Treasure Hunt!

Ask the children to look at Student Book pp. 4–5 and find flowers. Have the children raise their hand when they find them.

Cooler: Story Central favorites

Have the children look through the book and say which story/song/activity/game they liked most and why.

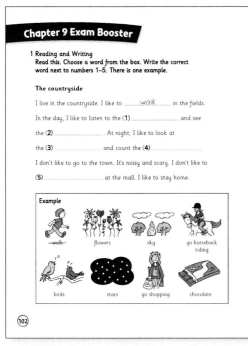

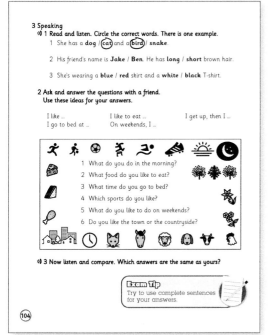

1 Reading and Writing. Read this. Choose a word from the box. Write the correct word next to numbers 1–5. There is one example.

Children complete the text using the words supplied.

Answers

1 birds **2** flowers **3** sky **4** stars **5** go shopping

2))) AB 9.1 Listening. Listen and color. There is one example.

Children listen and color the butterflies.

Answers (Audioscript on p. 224)

Butterflies colored: yellow on girl's hat, red on boy's hand, orange large on flower, purple small on flower, green in tree

3.1))) AB 9.2 Speaking. Read and listen. Circle the correct words. There is one example.

Children listen and circle the correct words.

Answers (Audioscript on p. 224)

1 cat, bird **2** Ben, short; **3** blue, white

3.2 Speaking. Ask and answer the questions with a friend. Use these ideas for your answers.

Have children ask and answer the questions.

3.3))) AB 9.3 Speaking. Now listen and compare. Which answers are the same as yours?

Ask children to listen and compare their answers.
(Audioscript on p. 224)

Competency Focus

Me: Self-evaluation

The children reflect on the chapter and express their opinions about their own progress.

Digital Resources

Teacher Resource Center • Print out Test Chapter 9 and End-of-year Test to use at the end of this lesson. The Test Generator also allows you to create customized tests.

• For the Cambridge English Young Learners Exam activities, there are speaking prompts available for this chapter.

Bingo

Draw a grid with nine squares on the board and have the children copy it into their notebooks. The children add a vocabulary item to each square. Call out items. The children cross them off if they have them. When all are crossed off, they shout *Bingo!*

I Spy

Divide the children into two teams. Have a child from the first team look around the class and secretly choose one object. They say *I spy with my little eye something beginning with (C)!* The other team guesses the object. Teams take turns.

Ready, Set, Draw!

Divide the children into teams. Secretly give a child from each team a word to draw. The first team to identify the word correctly wins a point.

Simon Says

Have the children stand. Say actions for them to mime. They can only mime when you say *Simon says (swim)*. If you say just *Swim*, they stand still. If a child does the wrong mime, they sit down. The last child standing is the winner.

Spelling Bee

Divide the class into two teams. Say a word. The children from each team take turns writing it on the board. Each correctly spelled word wins a point.

The Chain Game

Have the class stand. Start off a chain, e.g. *I went to the store and I bought apples.* Each child repeats the chain so far and adds an item, e.g. *I went to the store and I bought apples and oranges.* If a child makes a mistake or can't think of an item, they sit down. The last child standing wins.

The Shark Game

Draw on the board six steps leading down to water. On the top step, draw a stick person. In the water, draw a shark. Think of a word and draw a line to represent each letter. The children take turns calling out a letter. If it's correct, write the letter on the corresponding line. If it's wrong, erase the stick person and move him down one step, closer to the shark. If the children guess the word correctly, the class wins a point.

)) AB 1.1

N: *Example*
G1: *Look at the picture. Can you see my mom?*
G2: *Yes. She has short hair.*
G1: *That's right. Color her hair black.*
G2: *OK. Your mom has black hair.*
N: *One*
G2: *Who's the boy? Is he your brother?*
G1: *Yes. He's my brother. He has blond hair.*
G2: *Blond hair? OK. I have a yellow crayon.*
N: *Two*
G1: *Now, can you see my dad?*
G2: *Is your dad behind your brother?*
G1: *Yes, that's my dad. He has a gray mustache.*
G2: *OK. I can color his mustache gray.*
N: *Three*
G2: *Does your dad have gray hair?*
G1: *No, he doesn't. My dad has brown hair.*
G2: *So he has brown hair.*
G1: *Yes, that's right.*
N: *Four*
G2: *What about your sister? Is her hair long?*
G1: *That's right. My sister has long straight hair.*
G2: *What color is it?*
G1: *It's blond.*
G2: *Your sister has blond hair. I can color her hair yellow.*
N: *Five*
G2: *And your hair is curly.*
G1: *Yes, my hair is black and curly!*
G2: *OK. I can color it black. It's beautiful!*
G1: *Thanks!*

)) AB 2.1

N: *Example*
W: *What's your name, please?*
G: *Sue.*
W: *Is that S-u-e?*
G: *Yes, Sue.*
W: *How old are you, Sue?*
G: *I'm eight.*
N: *One*
W: *Whose pen is this, Sue?*
G: *Um, it isn't my pen. It's his pen.*
W: *Who is he?*
G: *He's Dan. D-a-n. He's new.*
W: *Hello, Dan.*
B: *Um … hello.*
N: *Two*
W: *How old are you Dan?*
B: *I'm seven today.*
W: *Oh, happy birthday, Dan.*
B: *Thank you.*

N: *Three*
W: *And what's your family name?*
B: *It's Wilson. W-i-l-s-o-n.*
W: *Dan Wilson! Welcome to our school.*
B: *Thank you.*
N: *Four*
G: *Where do you live, Dan?*
B: *I live on Old Street.*
W: *Old street?*
B: *Yes. O-l-d -- Old Street. It's next to the park.*
N: *Five*
G: *I live on Old street, too! What's your street number?*
B: *It's 150.*
G: *Hey! You live across the street from me.*
B: *Great! Come to my birthday party after school!*

)) AB 2.2

N: *Example*
M: *Whose photo is this?*
G: *It's my photo. That's my family.*
M: *What's your family name, Annie?*
G: *It's Lopez. That's L-o-p-e-z.*
M: *How many brothers do you have?*
G: *I have two brothers.*
N: *One*
M: *So this is the Lopez family.*
G: *Yes, That's my grandma. She has big glasses.*
M: *What's her name?*
G: *Pat.*
M: *P-a-t?*
G: *Yes, Pat.*
N: *Two*
M: *And is this your grandpa?*
G: *Yes. That's Grandpa Tony. He has glasses and a moustache.*
M: *T-o-n-i?*
G: *No. T-o- n-y.*
N: *Three*
M: *How old is your grandpa?*
G: *He's 65.*
M: *65?*
G: *Yes!*
N: *Four*
M: *Do your grandparents live with you?*
G: *No, they don't. They live in Newtown.*
M: *Newtown? Is that N-e-w-t-o-w-n?*
G: *Yes, that's right.*
N: *Five*
G: *They live on High Street, in apartment number 11.*
M: *Number seven? Seven is my favorite number!*
G: *No, number 11! They have a really big apartment.*

)) AB 3.1

N: *Example. What's the weather like?*
W: *What's the weather like today?*
B: *It's raining.*
W: *Is it windy?*
B: *No, it's cloudy and it's raining. It isn't windy.*
N: *One*
B: *This is my brother, Joey.*
W: *Which one? Is he wearing jeans?*
B: *No, he's wearing pants.*
W: *Oh, yes, he's wearing pants and a shirt.*
N: *Two*
B: *Can you open the window?*
G: *No, I can't. Ask Jenny.*
B: *Who's Jenny?*
G: *She's very tall. She has short hair. She's wearing a dress.*
B: *OK. A tall girl. She's wearing a dress … I can see her.*
N: *Three*
B: *Is it cold today?*
W: *No, it isn't. It's hot and sunny.*
B: *Great. I like sunny weather. I'm wearing my shorts today.*

)) AB 3.2

G: *What's the girl wearing?*
B: *She's wearing shorts and a white t-shirt.*
G: *I like her t-shirt! What are you wearing?*
B: *I'm wearing red pants and a yellow hat.*
G: *Yellow and red, cool!*

)) AB 3.3

N: *One*
B: *How many pets are there?*
G: *There are two pets, a cat and a dog.*
B: *Do you have any pets?*
G: *Yes! I have a lizard and a hamster.*
N: *Two*
G: *What toys are these?*
B: *There's a teddy bear and a ball.*
G: *What's your favorite toy?*
B: *It's a car.*
G: *Do you have a ball?*
B: *Yes, I do.*
N: *Three*
G: *How many animals are there?*
B: *There are two animals.*
G: *What's your favorite animal?*
B: *It's a lion. I like elephants, too.*
N: *Four*
B: *What's the dad wearing?*
G: *He's wearing a sweater.*
B: *How many people are in your family?*
G: *There's my mom, dad, brother, and little sister.*
I love my family!

)) AB 4.1

N: *Example*
W: *Is this your family?*
B: *No, it's my friend's family.*
W: *What's their last name?*
B: *Clark.*
W: *Is that C-l-a-r-k?*
B: *Yes, that's right.*
W: *They have a big house.*
B: *Yes, it has four bedrooms.*
W: *Four bedrooms! That's big!*
N: *One*
W: *How many pets do they have?*
B: *They have five cats, two turtles, a dog, and a snake.*
W: *So they have nine pets?*
B: *Yes, nine pets!*
N: *Two*
B: *And there's one brother. Look. He's sitting down.*
W: *Oh, yes. What's his name?*
B: *His name is Eric.*
W: *How do you spell that?*
B: *E-r-i-c.*
W: *Great, thanks.*
N: *Three*
W: *How old is Eric? Seven or eight?*
B: *He's seven.*
W: *Seven. OK.*
N: *Four*
W: *The dog is jumping. What's his name?*
B: *His name is Rex.*
W: *Is that R-e-x?*
B: *Yes.*
N: *Five*
W: *Do you have a big family, David?*
B: *No, I don't. I have one sister.*

)) AB 5.1

N: *Example*
M: *Look at the picture. Can you see Ann?*
G: *Yes. She has short hair. She's running.*
M: *Oh, yes. Ann is running fast!*
N: *One*
M: *Who's that boy? He's jumping.*
G: *Oh, that's Alex. He's jumping up to catch the ball. Alex is good at jumping.*
N: *Two*
G: *And look at Kim.*
M: *Which one is Kim?*
G: *That girl. Look. She's scoring a point.*
M: *Oh, yes, she's scoring. Great job, Kim!*
N: *Three*
G: *Oh, there's Grace.*
M: *Is Grace playing basketball?*
G: *No. She's sitting down.*
M: *I see her. She's sitting and watching.*
N: *Four*
M: *What's Ben doing?*
G: *He's here. He's bouncing a ball.*
M: *Is Ben playing?*
G: *No, he's watching and bouncing a ball.*

N: *Five*
G: *Tony is watching, too. He's shouting.*
M: *What's he shouting?*
G: *Um … Tony is shouting, "Come on, Kim!"*

)) AB 5.2

N: *Example*
W: *What are these children doing?*
G: *They're having lunch. They're my friends. That's Alex.*
W: *Which one?*
G: *He's the boy on the left. He isn't eating. He's drinking.*
W: *Does Alex have short blond hair?*
G: *Yes, he does.*
N: *One*
G: *This girl is Sally.*
W: *What does Sally look like?*
G: *She has dark hair.*
W: *Is she eating an apple?*
G: *Yes, she is.*
N: *Two*
G: *Can you see Ben?*
W: *Where is he sitting?*
G: *He's sitting next to Sally.*
W: *Does Ben have straight hair or curly hair?*
G: *He has straight hair. He has a sandwich, too.*
N: *Three*
G: *Peter has curly hair.*
W: *What's he eating?*
G: *He's eating salad and fries. Peter loves fries.*
W: *Do you like fries?*
G: *Mm … Yes, I do!*
N: *Four*
W: *So, who's this girl?*
G: *The girl next to Alex?*
W: *No. The girl sitting across from Peter.*
G: *Oh, that's Ann.*
W: *Oh, yes, that's Ann. She has long hair. I see she has a sandwich, too.*
N: *Five*
W: *So, I guess this girl is Katy.*
G: *Yes. Katy has blond hair. She's sitting next to Ann. They're best friends.*
W: *They aren't talking.*
G: *Ha, ha! No, they aren't. They're eating. They're hungry!*

)) AB 6.1

N: *Example*
W: *The bus is at three o'clock. What time is it?*
B: *It's a quarter after nine.*
W: *Are you sure? I think it's a quarter to three.*
B: *Ha, ha! Oh, yes!*
N: *One*
B: *I don't take a shower in the morning.*
W: *You don't?*

B: *No. I get up late and get dressed.*
W: *Do you have breakfast, Sam?*
B: *No, I don't.*
N: *Two*
W: *Emily, do you watch TV before bed?*
G: *No, I don't. I go to bed at 8:30 and I read my book.*
W: *That's good.*
G: *And then I go to sleep at 9 o'clock.*
N: *Three*
B: *I'm tired.*
W: *Why? Do you go to bed late, Mark?*
B: *No, I get up early.*
W: *Do you get up before seven o'clock?*
B: *Yes, I do! I get up at five thirty.*
W: *Wow! That's early!*

)) AB 6.2

B: *Let's look at this picture.*
G: *OK.*
B: *What are they doing?*
G: *The boy is eating breakfast. The woman is reading and drinking.*
B: *Where are they?*
G: *Um … they're in the kitchen.*
B: *Tell me about the food.*
G: *There's bread on the table. The boy's drinking apple juice. Oh, no! I mean orange juice.*
B: *Ha, ha! What do you do in the mornings?*
G: *I get up …*

)) AB 6.3

B: *Let's look at this picture.*
G: *OK.*
B: *What are they doing?*
G: *The boy is eating breakfast. The woman is reading and drinking.*
B: *Where are they?*
G: *Um … they're in the kitchen.*
B: *Tell me about the food.*
G: *There's bread on the table. He's drinking apple juice. Oh, no! I mean orange juice.*
B: *Ha, ha! What do you do in the mornings?*
G: *I get up at 8:30 … No! I mean 8:00. I get up at 8 o'clock.*
B: *Do you eat breakfast?*
G: *Yes, I do. Then I wash my face and brush my teeth.*
B: *Do you make your bed?*
G: *Um … no, I don't. Do you?*
B: *Um … no!*

)) AB 7.1

N: *Example*
W: *Is this your school?*
B: *Yes, it is.*
W: *How many children are there?*
B: *There are 100.*
W: *100 children in the school?*

B: Yes.
B: I can see my W, Miss Evans.
W: How do you spell that?
B: E-v-a-n-s.
W: Oh, OK!
N: One
W: Is that your friend?
B: Yes. His name is Kenny.
W: Is that K-e-n-n-y?
B: Yes. That's right.
N: Two
B: I can see some children.
W: What class are you in?
B: Class four.
W: Are these children from class four, too?
B: Yes.
N: Three
W: Is this man a W?
B: No, he doesn't teach. He's a cleaner. His name is Jack.
W: How do you spell that?
B: J-a-c-k.
W: Oh, Jack! Thanks.
N: Four
W: And who is this girl?
B: Ha, ha! She's the chef. She cooks our lunch.
W: Really! She's so young!
B: Yes, she's twenty-one.
W: Twenty-one! Are you sure?
B: Yes.
N: Five
B: Her name's Amelia.
W: How do you spell that?
B: A-m-e-l-i-a.
W: That's a nice name.

)) AB 8.1

N: Example
B: I can see two tigers, but I can't see any wombats.
M: The wombats are sleeping.
B: Oh, yes! They sleep in the day.
N: One
G: Are there any kangaroos in the zoo?
M: No, there aren't any kangaroos or lions. There are some dolphins.
G: Oh, good! I like dolphins. They're my favorite fish.

M: They aren't fish. They're mammals.
G: Oh—I didn't know that.
N: Two
B: What about you, Liza? What's your favorite animal?
F: I like ocean animals.
B: Do you like dolphins?
F: Yes, but my favorite animal is a shark.
B: But they're scary!
N: Three
M: That looks cold.
B: Yes, I don't like cold weather. I'd like to go to the jungle.
M: Yes, me too. There are lots of interesting animals in the jungle.

)) AB 8.2

N: Example
G: What's your favorite animal from Australia, Tom?
B: Um …
G: Is it a bird?
B: No, it isn't a bird. It's a mammal.
G: Is it a wombat? I love wombats.
B: No, it isn't. My favorite animal is a kangaroo.
N: One
M: Do you have a pet, Lucy?
G: Yes, I do.
M: Is it a bird?
G: No it isn't. It doesn't have feathers. It has scales.
M: Is it a lizard?
G: No. It's a turtle.
N: Two.
W: What does your aunt do, Kim?
G: Oh, she has a great job.
W: Is she a M?
G: No, she isn't. She doesn't work with Gren. She takes care of animals.
W: Oh! Is she a vet?
G: Yes, she is.
N: Three
M: What does your dad do, Alex?
B: He's a cleaner.
M: Does he work in a hotel?
B: No, he doesn't.
M: Where does he work?
B: He works in this school.

M: Oh, dear. Let's clean up!

)) AB 9.1

N: Example
M: Do you like to go horseback riding?
G: Yes, I do. This forest looks nice.
M: Yes, can you see the butterflies?
G: Yes. There's a butterfly on the horse.
M: Yes. There's a beautiful pink butterfly on the horse.
G: Oh, yes. Pink is my favorite color.
N: One
G: There's another butterfly on the girl's hat.
M: Yes. Can you color it yellow?
G: OK … Now there's a yellow butterfly on the girl's hat.
M: Great.
N: Two
M: Look at the boy.
G: There's a butterfly on his hand.
M: That's right. Can you color it red?
G: Sure. He has a red butterfly on his hand.
N: Three
G: There are two butterflies on the flowers.
M: Yes, the big butterfly on the flower is orange.
G: OK. I can color the big butterfly orange.
N: Four
G: And what color is the small butterfly on the flower?
M: Can you color it purple?
G: Yes, OK. This small butterfly on the flower is purple—and it is beautiful.
N: Five
M: Can you see one more butterfly?
G: No, I can't.
M: It's on the tree. Can you color it green?
G: Oh, yes, I can see a butterfly on the tree. OK. It's a green butterfly.

)) AB 9.2

N: One
B: Do you have any pets?
G: Yes, I do. I have a cat and a bird. Do you have any pets?

N: Two
G: Tell me about a friend. What does he or she look like?
B: OK, my friend's name is Ben. He has short brown hair. He's tall. I like Ben.
N: Three
B: What are you wearing today?
G: I'm wearing a blue skirt and a white T-shirt. It's my favorite T-shirt.

)) AB 9.3

N: One
G: What do you do in the morning?
B: I get up, then I eat breakfast. Um … next, I brush my teeth and I wash my face.
G: That's good! I don't like to brush my teeth.
N: Two
B: And what food do you like to eat?
G: I like to eat like yogurt, eggs, and toast. Now I'm hungry!
B: Mm, I love yogurt!
N: Three
G: What time do you go to bed?
B: I go to bed at um … 9 o'clock, or 9:30. I read a book in bed.
G: I go to bed at 9:30, too!
N: Four
B: Which sports do you like?
G: I like gymnastics. I do gymnastics after school. I don't like basketball.
B: I don't like basketball, either. Swimming is my favorite sport.
N: Five
B: What do you like to do on the weekends?
G: I like to go to the movies. I don't like to stay home. What about you?
B: Same! I go to the movies with my family.
N: Six
G: Do you like the town or the countryside?
B: Um … I like the countryside. I like to go horseback riding. I don't like the town.
G: Horseback riding, wow! Now that sounds fun.